A Decade of Tanzania

Politics, Economy and Society 2005–2017

By

Kurt Hirschler
Rolf Hofmeier

BRILL

LEIDEN | BOSTON

The Library of Congress Cataloging-in-Publication Data is available online at http://catalog.loc.gov

Typeface for the Latin, Greek, and Cyrillic scripts: "Brill". See and download: brill.com/brill-typeface.

ISBN 978-90-04-40786-2 (paperback)
ISBN 978-90-04-40787-9 (e-book)

Copyright 2019 by Koninklijke Brill NV, Leiden, The Netherlands.
Koninklijke Brill NV incorporates the imprints Brill, Brill Hes & De Graaf, Brill Nijhoff, Brill Rodopi, Brill Sense, Hotei Publishing, mentis Verlag, Verlag Ferdinand Schöningh and Wilhelm Fink Verlag.
All rights reserved. No part of this publication may be reproduced, translated, stored in a retrieval system, or transmitted in any form or by any means, electronic, mechanical, photocopying, recording or otherwise, without prior written permission from the publisher.
Authorization to photocopy items for internal or personal use is granted by Koninklijke Brill NV provided that the appropriate fees are paid directly to The Copyright Clearance Center, 222 Rosewood Drive, Suite 910, Danvers, MA 01923, USA. Fees are subject to change.

This book is printed on acid-free paper and produced in a sustainable manner.

Printed by Printforce, the Netherlands

Contents

Tanzania 2005–2017: From Liberal to Autocratic Democracy and in Search of a Development Strategy   1

Tanzania in 2005   9

Tanzania in 2006   27

Tanzania in 2007   45

Tanzania in 2008   64

Tanzania in 2009   82

Tanzania in 2010   102

Tanzania in 2011   122

Tanzania in 2012   142

Tanzania in 2013   164

Tanzania in 2014   185

Tanzania in 2015   205

Tanzania in 2016   225

Tanzania in 2017   243

Tanzania 2005–2017: From Liberal to Autocratic Democracy and in Search of a Development Strategy

This volume contains the original country chapters on Tanzania in the *Africa Yearbook. Politics, Economy and Society South of the Sahara* for the (long) decade covering the years 2005 to 2017. While no contents editing was done on these chapters, this brief introduction is intended to set the covered period into a longer historical perspective of the country and to provide some key political and socioeconomic background factors that are helpful for a better understanding of the developments that are presented in a year-to-year format.

Tanzania is widely recognized as a rather exceptional case of an African country that has seen political continuity and stability for more than five decades and has not experienced any major conflicts as has been the case elsewhere on the continent. The current government (in 2019) of President John Pombe Magufuli is often in the media dubbed as Tanzania's fifth phase government, thereby indicating that the country has only had five presidents in a time span of 57 years, and all under the rule of the same dominant political party CCM (Revolutionary Party).

The *first* and by far longest *governmental phase (1961–1985)* was outstandingly dominated by President *Julius Kambarage Nyerere*, the charismatic founding father of the nation upon the achievement of Tanganyika's independence in 1961. A key event was the creation of the United Republic of Tanzania in 1964 by joining Tanganyika (present Tanzania mainland) and the newly independent (former Sultanate) island state Zanzibar. Ever since until today the Union has remained a rather delicate construction, with Zanzibar strongly defending its semi-autonomous status. In the country chapters separate sections are, therefore, devoted to political developments in Zanzibar, apart from the main Tanzanian narrative. Only in 1977 the state parties from both sides of the Union were merged into the present CCM, but the Zanzibari wing still maintains a degree of autonomy. Nyerere's reign was crucial for a successful nation-building process that led to the emergence of a relatively strong sense of national identity (Zanzibari separatism notwithstanding) which sets Tanzania significantly apart from many other African countries and has undoubtedly remained a major legacy for all subsequent periods and governments. One strategy to stifle the potential emergence of diverging political interest groups was the introduction of a one-party political system (with limited internal democratic elements) in 1965. Nyerere was a convinced advocate of a home-grown, genuinely African set of socialist economic and social policies (known under the Swahili term 'Ujamaa'). The socialist era (from 1967 onwards) introduced fundamental economic changes, but achieved no convincing results and led to a nationwide socioeconomic crisis in the early 1980s. Under these circumstances, Nyerere decided in 1985 to retire and not run again as president in the next elections.

The *second phase government (1985–1995)* under President *Ali Hassan Mwinyi* (hailing from Zanzibar, so far the only one) was characterized by the introduction of significant economic and political reforms that were deemed unavoidable to bring the country back on a forward-looking course. In the economic field, a gradual liberalization of reducing the all-prevailing state control and a mechanism to privatize most of the hundreds of parastatal enterprises and public bodies were introduced. This enabled a rapprochement with the key financial institutions (IMF and World Bank) and most bilateral donor countries which in turn led to a renewed increase of substantial aid inflows. Also the era of the one-party state at last came to an end with constitutional amendments in 1992 that ushered in a return to a multi-party system.

The *third phase government (1995–2005)* under President *Benjamin William Mkapa* pursued enhanced efforts of consolidating both the economic and political liberalization. The 1995 national elections marked an important turning point as the first truly competitive political contest among a large number of newly founded parties, but with a strong showing and confirmation of the CCM as the dominant political force. The existence of other political parties was a new phenomenon that only gradually had an impact that was felt throughout the entire national territory. The transformation from the former state-led economic system to a liberal market economy was by and large completed in these years.

The subsequent *fourth and fifth presidencies* of *Jakaya Mrisho Kikwete (2005–2015)* and *John Pombe Magufuli (since November 2015)* are covered in detail in the following country chapters as they appeared in the respective volumes of the *Africa Yearbook*. While the Kikwete years generally proved to be a continuation of the policies pursued by his two predecessors, Magufuli rather unexpectedly introduced a drastically different leadership style and significantly changed the prevailing liberal political climate into one of outright confrontation between an increasingly autocratic presidential rule and weakened opposition forces.

The key developments of the (long) decade of Tanzania covered in this volume and their underlying structural determinants can be most conveniently grouped in four subject areas: domestic politics, economy, societal change and international relations. These factors are to be briefly outlined in the following paragraphs.

During Kikwete's presidency the *domestic political situation* experienced a significantly growing dissatisfaction of large segments of the population with the performance of the government due to generally felt economic and social hardships and a concomitantly noticeable decline of CCM's popularity and supremacy. The widely perceived impression of systemic corruption problems without any noticeable actions by the authorities to combat this vice also contributed to a general loss of confidence and to a growing chorus of critical voices and enhanced civil society activities. The two leading opposition parties made substantial gains in terms of parliamentary seats in the 2010 and 2015 elections, but were still unable to gather enough votes for winning the presidency. Although maintaining its long held control of all public affairs and its all-encompassing presence throughout the entire national territory, CCM proved to be a conglomerate of different factions representing separate ideological and personalized interest groups. In a complex and competitive internal contest for the selection of CCM's presidential candidate in the 2015 elections, Magufuli (not considered as favorite, but a well-known reputable minister) emerged as winner to the surprise of most observers. Initially highly popular with his declared focus on fighting corruption and insisting on strict frugality of all state institutions, Magufuli soon showed traits of an autocratic personalized leadership style that antagonized any diverging opinions and intimidated political opponents. The space for open political deliberations was severely curtailed, and also all party organs of the CCM were more tightly controlled. Rather abruptly, the election of a new president had thus decisively changed the political climate of the country from a fairly liberal to an increasingly autocratic environment. The strained political situation in Zanzibar and the delicate relationship between the islands and the mainland remained unresolved, although superficially calm, in the aftermath of disputed elections in 2015 and of a successful boycott of repeat elections by strong popular opposition forces.

The *economic situation* is characterized by two seemingly contradictory facts: the persistence of severe poverty affecting large parts of the population, but at the same time an impressive macroeconomic growth performance. Tanzania has a population of almost 60 million people (2019) and is the fourth-largest country in Sub-Saharan Africa. The average annual per capita income has remained quite low at around $ 1,000 (in nominal terms) and $ 2,500 (in purchasing power terms). Extreme poverty has only been reduced rather slowly over the years, and about one third of the population still lives below the internationally-accepted poverty line of $ 1.90 per day. At the same time, the GDP growth rate has been consistent between about 6% and 7% for well over a decade since the early 2000s, and Tanzania continues to be among the group of fastest-growing countries in Africa. This macroeconomic growth is mainly fueled by mining activities (e.g. gold) and different service sectors (including tourism), while manufacturing is only growing slowly and agricultural output has remained disappointingly low. Tanzania has for many decades (with intermittent ups and downs) been a major recipient of multilateral and bilateral aid flows from the traditional Western aid donors and was often characterized as a preferred 'donor darling'. For some years now it has also attracted substantial foreign direct investments from private investors (mainly in mining). However, during the last decade China has become an ever more important partner in respect to trade, investments and developments projects. Subsequent governments have formulated a plethora of development plans, culminating in the still valid 'Tanzania Development Vision 2025' that aims to transform Tanzania into a low middle-income country by 2025. During Kikwete's presidency the focus was strongly on attracting foreign investors, supporting local entrepreneurs and creating an enabling environment for a liberal market economy, but this has markedly shifted under Magufuli in the direction of more state-led initiatives and doubts and uncertainty about the intended role of the private sector. Magufuli's declared goals are centered on the expansion of modern infrastructure as a prerequisite for a more rapid industrialization. Several utterances smack of a new type of 'economic nationalism', sometimes with reminiscence to the long-past socialist era under Nyerere. It is clear that different competing interest groups are still grappling to identify the most adequate development strategy that Tanzania is to pursue in the next few years.

As everywhere in Africa, Tanzania has undoubtedly experienced fundamental *societal change* over the more than five decades since independence, and this has definitely accelerated during the most recent decade that is under review here. Urbanization is advancing at an ever growing pace, with urban live styles significantly altering long-established traditional behavioral patterns. Large population segments are nevertheless still remaining in the rural areas and are subjected to a life of (sometimes) extreme poverty. Despite an amazingly fast utilization of modern electronic communication devices everywhere in the vast territory, a rapidly further accelerating cleavage between rural and major urban areas is very noticeable, with clear repercussions on changes of political attitudes and behavior. Many different religious beliefs have followers in Tanzania who by and large traditionally live in relative harmony, but there are recurring flare-ups of religiously-motivated clashes, particularly with Islamic fundamentalists. Despite the existence of about 120 different ethnic groups, Tanzania is fortunate for its historically evolved nation-building process and general absence of negative forms of tribalism that are so often prevalent in Africa. The quality and coverage of social services (health and education facilities, water, electricity) has despite some recent expansion generally remained poor, particularly in most rural areas, thus contributing to a loss of support for the government. With an annual growth rate of still around 3%, Tanzania's population is on average quite young and thereby faced by a tremendous problem of only an utterly insufficient creation of new job opportunities. The growing numbers of idle and frustrated youth constitute a factor for potential unrest.

Past Tanzanian governments have left a legacy of active involvement in the field of *international relations*. This was particularly true under Nyerere who during his reign was known and widely admired as an advocate of the solidarity of non-aligned countries and as an active supporter of freedom and anti-Apartheid movements in Southern Africa. Kikwete was fond to represent Tanzania in many international bodies and to visit many foreign countries in the interest of fostering better bilateral relations. This even earned him recurring domestic criticism of spending too much time abroad and of neglecting other tasks. All this changed quickly and drastically under Magufuli who has openly expressed his disinterest in foreign policy issues and stressed the need to concentrate fully on the domestic development agenda. Magufuli himself has so far not traveled outside of East Africa and sent other government representatives to international conferences wherever necessary. Apart from pursuing Tanzania's national interests in the context of the East African Community, the country has meanwhile taken up a conspicuously low profile in international affairs.

Tanzania in 2005

National elections in December confirmed the overwhelming dominance of the former state party CCM ('Chama cha Mapinduzi'/Party of the Revolution), and also the country's reputation as a pillar of political stability in Africa. CCM candidate Jakaya Kikwete became the new president. Separate, and controversial, October elections in semi-autonomous Zanzibar resulted in the continuation of the political confrontation on the islands, but not the feared major explosion of violence. Macroeconomic performance continued to be quite satisfactory, while the country remained a preferred beneficiary of substantial international aid.

Domestic Politics

Throughout the year, political life was preoccupied with *preparations and the campaigning for the general elections*, scheduled for 30 October. Presidential, parliamentary and local council elections for the institutions of the union were to be conducted by the National Electoral Commission (NEC), while elections for Zanzibar institutions fell under a separate body, the Zanzibar Electoral Commission (ZEC). After two terms in office, *President Benjamin Mkapa* was constitutionally barred from seeking a new mandate. The selection of his successor thus became the single most important issue.

Pre-election activities began with *amendments to the electoral laws*, passed in January in parliament with ease by the large CCM majority. The formation of a coalition government was ruled out in respect of the union. The attorney-general argued that any party unable to win a majority of votes should not have the chance to come to power through the back door. Also, the inclusion of an opposition member on the NEC was not foreseen, although this was already the case for ZEC. The frequently raised request that independent candidates be allowed to participate was once again rejected. Hotly discussed was the confirmation of the legality of 'takrima' (Swahili for hospitality), which had been declared a traditional value before the 2000 elections. However, NGOs, academics and opposition parties criticised the practice of handing out small presents to voters during election campaigns as just a veiled form of corruption.

The establishment of a *permanent voters' register* was the most important innovation. Government spent about $ 30 m and donor countries $ 9 m on this exercise. The registration process was accompanied by numerous irregularities and violent squabbles. About 2,000 people were, upon verification, identified as having registered twice, while many thousands were assumed not to have registered at all, mainly because of transport problems or the restricted opening hours of the registration centres.

Following the Kenyan example of 2002, some *feeble attempts* were made by the *opposition parties* to *form an alliance* to challenge the ruling party with a single strong presidential candidate. However, these efforts failed owing to the personal ambitions of the leading politicians in the opposition camp. Ironically, the result was an even greater split within the opposition. Whereas in both previous elections Mkapa had to face three competitors, the votes were now split among *nine opposition contestants*. Running for a third time were Ibrahim Lipumba, chairman of the primarily Zanzibar-based Civic United Front (CUF), who had been the strongest opposition candidate in 2000, and Augustine Mrema from the Tanzania Labour Party (TLP), who had finished second in 1995. John Cheyo from the United Democratic Party (UDP), who had also run twice but never gained much support, withdrew his candidacy. 'Chama cha Demokrasia na Maendeleo' (CHADEMA/Party of Democracy and Development) for the first time fielded a candidate, its chairman Freeman Mbowe. Sengondo Mvungi of the National Convention for Construction and Reform – Change (NCCR-Mageuzi) was supported by four smaller parties (FORD, NRA, UMD, UPDP). Another five very small parties, not represented in parliament, put forward their own candidates, among them the first female presidential candidate in Tanzania's history. Only four of the 18 fully registered parties ('Sauti ya Umma'/ Voice of the Community was only registered in February) did not nominate presidential candidates.

The *nomination process for CCM's presidential candidate* attracted major attention. Whereas only a small group of persons had made these decisions in the opposition camp, the *CCM process followed strict rules* and involved a considerable number of party members and organs. Fierce infighting had begun long before the official process started in March. Members of the National Executive Committee (CCM-NEC) felt obliged to appeal to the party membership to beware of some prominent figures touring the country and attempting to buy votes in order to obtain the necessary 2,000 signatures from supporters in at least ten different regions, two of which had to be on Zanzibar. By 15 April, 11 candidates had successfully submitted their applications. Among them were several political heavyweights, such as CCM vice-chairman and former Prime Minister John Malecela, representing the traditionalist wing of the party; former OAU Secretary-General Salim Ahmed Salim; Prime Minister Frederick Sumaye; several ministers and Foreign Minister Jakaya Kikwete. Other contenders were less well known.

The 36-member *CCM Central Committee* (CC) selected five of the candidates on 2 May after an ethics committee had met the day before and made recommendations to the CC. The successful contestants were Sumaye, Salim, Kikwete, Planning and Privatisation Minister Abdallah Kigoda and Communications and Transport Minister Mark Mwandosya. Subsequently, *CCM-NEC* eliminated two more, Kigoda and Sumaye, who were both considered Mkapa's favourites. The final step on 4 May was the official nomination by a *special party congress* of 1,800 delegates. As was widely expected, Kikwete easily obtained a clear majority (64%), followed by Salim (29%) and Mwandosya (7%). All the unsuccessful candidates accepted the verdict of the party organs and promised to support Kikwete loyally, except Malecela, who filed an appeal claiming foul play. However, the special committee that heard his case upheld the CC's decision.

Kikwete's nomination was no surprise. In 1995, when Mkapa was chosen, Kikwete had already been the favourite of the party membership. It was only ex-President Julius Nyerere's intervention that stopped Kikwete from becoming the presidential candidate. Then, aged 45, Kikwete was the candidate of the youth and – thanks to his pleasant public appearance – of women, an image that he has been able to preserve. He was, however, also acceptable to older party members since he had served the party for many years. Unlike many other current top politicians, Kikwete was a *well-connected CCM cadre*. He had joined the army after leaving university in 1975, risen through the party ranks, had been an MP since 1988 and had served in various posts as deputy minister or minister. As foreign minister for the past ten years, he had been able to keep out of internal power struggles and scandals.

The economic reforms of the Mkapa government had left many Tanzanians in doubt about the social consequences of these policies, so an open confrontation between a reformist and a conservative party wing had been expected to dominate the nomination process. Even a possible party split had not been completely ruled out as a result of the selection of one or the other side's candidate. This would have posed a far greater threat to the CCM than all the efforts of the opposition. However, the CC left no doubt that it wished for a *reformist candidate*. All five selected contenders favoured continuation of the reforms. The early rejection of Malecela's candidacy – as the most prominent representative of the conservative wing – precluded heightened conflict between the ideological wings.

Since Mkapa was a Christian from the mainland, demands had been heard that his successor should be a Muslim from Zanzibar. An unwritten law was cited that the presidency should alternate between a Christian and a Muslim and between a mainlander and a Zanzibari. In the absence of a strong candidate from Zanzibar

(Salim, from Pemba, was regarded with suspicion by many inhabitants of the main island, Unguja, and was also perceived as an outsider to Tanzanian politics owing to his long absence at the OAU), the selection of the 'moderate Muslim' Kikwete, who kept good relations with the Christian churches and had adopted a modern lifestyle, was acceptable to almost everybody in the party. With the nomination of Vice-President *Ali Mohamed Shein* as his running mate, a *Zanzibari* was indeed included in the team that aspired to the top leadership of the country. Thus, Kikwete appeared a good candidate to bridge the major divides in the party as well as in the country.

CCM was the only party able to nominate *candidates for the parliamentary seats* in all 232 constituencies (182 on the mainland, 50 on Zanzibar). The local constituency nominations were heavily contested. Because of CCM's clear dominance in most constituencies, party nomination almost guaranteed that the nominee would win a lucrative parliamentary seat. Nominations took place through competitive primaries at the constituency level. All candidates, however, had to be vetted by CCM-NEC, which rejected 16 primary winners because of doubts about the correctness of the electoral process at the lower level. Seven sitting parliamentarians refrained from a re-nomination, including Prime Minister Sumaye after his failure to win the presidential nomination. About 50 MPs failed in their re-nomination bids. The most prominent 'victim' in the local nomination process was Energy Minister Daniel Yona. CUF managed to nominate candidates in 212 constituencies, CHADEMA in 167, TLP in 111, and NCCR-Mageuzi in 69. Each of the 18 fully registered parties nominated at least a handful of candidates.

The *electoral campaigns*, which started officially on 21 August, proceeded largely peacefully, barring some minor incidents. CCM clearly dominated the field and took advantage of its close relationship with the state organs and its incumbency in office. In addition, it had far superior material resources as a result of the state subsidies all parties received in accordance with their share of votes in the presidential election. However, despite these obvious advantages, *CCM's major strength* derived from its *good organisational presence* throughout the country, which none of the opposition parties had succeeded in matching since the introduction of the multiparty system in 1992. Also, the opposition parties in their *election manifestos* were unable to portray a genuine political alternative to CCM. In their campaigns, opposition parties mainly criticised the shortcomings of the economic reforms, especially their failure to reduce poverty, the rising gap between rich and poor, the problem of corruption and the growing influence of foreign companies in the economy. However, these populist criticisms did not offer a consistent and convincing alternative to the government's economic and social policies. All parties bar TLP signed a *code of conduct* that obliged signatories to treat each other respectfully during the campaign.

The elections had long been scheduled for 30 October. However, only three days before that date, CHADEMA's vice-presidential candidate died. In accordance with electoral regulations, the *elections were postponed* to 14 December. The extension of the campaign period posed particular problems for the opposition parties, which had exhausted their meagre financial resources. For the union government, the postponement was less inconvenient, and the Zanzibar elections proceeded as scheduled (see below).

CCM obtained *overwhelming victories* in all three (presidential, parliamentary and local) elections. Kikwete won the presidential election with 80.3% of the vote, topping even Mkapa, who got 61.8% and 71.1% in 1995 and 2000 respectively. As in 2000, CUF's Lipumba was in second place, but with only 11.7%. Mbowe of CHADEMA finished third with 5.9%. In 2000, CHADEMA had not put up a candidate and had supported Lipumba. Mrema of TLP, who had been Mkapa's strongest challenger in 1995 with almost 28% of the votes, now received only 0.75%. All other candidates won below 1%. Turnout was given as 72.4% of the 15.6 m registered voters, 12% lower than in 2000.

The *results of the parliamentary elections* presented a similar picture. CCM won 206 of the 232 constituencies, a slight increase on the 202 seats five years earlier. CHADEMA was the only opposition party able to increase its seats, from four to five. It was able to retain the two seats of Moshi Urban and Karatu. The loss of Hai (Kilimanjaro region) and Kigoma Urban constituencies (both to CCM) were offset by victories in Kigoma North, Tarime (Mara region) and Mpanda Kati (Rukwa region), all previously held by CCM. TLP, which had held four seats and UDP (three), won only one seat each. TLP lost all its seats in Kilimanjaro, Mara and Kagera regions to CCM, but gained one from CCM in Biharamulo (Kagera region). UDP Chairman Cheyo was able to retain his seat in his home constituency of Bariadi East (Shinyanga region). NCCR-Mageuzi lost the single seat it had won in 2000. As before, CUF remained the strongest opposition party although it lost its two mainland constituencies to CCM, winning 18 seats on Zanzibar's Pemba Island, where CCM failed completely, and one in Zanzibar's Stone Town. The number of seats held by the opposition on the mainland had dropped steadily from 22 (1995), 14 (2000) to only seven, while CUF kept its stronghold on Pemba and had a strong minority position in Unguja.

Observers from EAC, SADC and AU as well as local NGOs expressed full satisfaction with the conduct of the elections – despite minor problems. A number of defeated contestants fruitlessly challenged the results, among them TLP's presidential candidate Mrema. The overwhelming majority of CCM parliamentarians was further increased through the *'special seats' for women*. In order to increase the representation of women in parliament, 75 additional seats (30% of directly elected MPs) were allocated to parties that had won seats in the house according to their relative strength. Thus, CCM got 58 of these seats, CUF 11 and CHADEMA six additional seats. Another five MPs (three from CCM, two from CUF) delegated from the Zanzibar house of representatives complemented the parliament, plus the attorney-general in an ex officio capacity.

At the first meeting of the new parliament on 28 December, Samuel Sitta was elected unopposed as *speaker*, after having been pre-selected by CCM-CC and CCM's parliamentary faction. He had previously held ministerial positions and was the director of the Tanzania Investment Centre. He had supported Kikwete's ambitions and was expected to establish a close link between parliament and the president. Anna Makinda was elected as the first female deputy speaker. Pius Msekwa, who had been speaker for eleven years, tried to be nominated again, but given the discontent over his handling of the role that had repeatedly been expressed by CCM MPs, he was not able to muster much support.

In exercising the president's privilege to appoint *ten additional members* of parliament, Kikwete on 29 December nominated three female and three male parliamentarians, among them Zakia Meghji (who subsequently became minister of finance) and the veteran CCM politician and chief strategist, Kingunge Ngombale-Mwiru, who had been special advisor to former presidents Nyerere and Mkapa. Four seats for nominated MPs remained to be filled.

The close cooperation among opposition forces in parliament advocated by CHADEMA and UDP failed to materialise owing to the unwillingness of the strongest group, CUF. This was the only opposition party to have won more than the necessary 30 seats to form a parliamentary faction, and decided to pursue its own political agenda and formed a *shadow cabinet* without including members of the other three opposition parties. CHADEMA and UDP were critical of the fact that opposition in the national parliament was now mainly voiced by MPs from Pemba.

Elections for local councillors (for town and district councils) also took place on 14 December. Councillors were elected in 2,552 wards. Although councils have increasingly become decision-making bodies at the local level under the policy of decentralisation and local government reform, not much public attention was given to these elections. Isolated published results indicated a clear sweep for

CCM, surprisingly even in major urban centres like Dar es Salaam, which normally tend to be opposition strongholds.

The formation of the *new government* started with Kikwete's inauguration as president on 21 December, followed on 29 December by Kikwete's nomination of *Edward Lowassa*, the current minister of water and livestock development, as *prime minister*, thereby ending feverish public speculation. His selection was overwhelmingly confirmed by parliament, in which only two members voted against Lowassa. He had been most often mentioned as the favourite and he had long kept close contact with Kikwete, although they had been competitors in 1995 for the CCM presidential nomination. Like Kikwete, Lowassa had the image of a young and reform-oriented politician. The new cabinet was not announced before the end of the year.

The political situation in *Zanzibar*, a semi-autonomous part of Tanzania since 1964, had all along been very different. Since the introduction of the multiparty system, the electorate had been almost equally split into two camps, vehemently and sometimes violently confronting each other. The smaller island of Pemba was an absolute stronghold of CUF, whereas the main island of Unguja was predominantly CCM, but with a considerable CUF minority. None of the other 16 parties played a relevant role. Zanzibar has a political culture distinct from the mainland, and this distinction is also reflected in the political parties. The Zanzibar wings of both dominant parties enjoy considerable autonomy and follow different rules and agendas from their parent bodies at the union level.

The implementation of the *reconciliation agreement* (*'Muafaka'*) *of 2001* was seen as a precondition for maintaining the fragile peace between the two parties. In accordance with 'Muafaka', *CUF representatives* were admitted as members of ZEC, which had previously been accused by CUF of clearly favouring the ruling party. CUF, however, criticised the fact that their members constituted only a minority in ZEC and were overruled by the CCM majority. ZEC is completely independent from NEC and responsible for all electoral affairs relating to government institutions in Zanzibar, whereas NEC was charged with all elections for union institutions – even in Zanzibar. A *permanent voters' register* was also established. CUF in particular complained of numerous irregularities. Some of their supporters had allegedly been denied registration in their home constituencies. CUF also protested against the registration of army and police personnel that were newly stationed on the islands, particularly in Pemba. According to Zanzibar's electoral laws, a Zanzibari voter must have resided on the islands for three consecutive years, and anyone from the mainland for ten consecutive years. Even CUF's presidential candidate Hamad was initially denied registration in April, on the grounds that he had been out of Zanzibar several times. Only after public demonstrations in Dar es Salaam did ZEC agree to register him. Hamad claimed that 32,400 Zanzibaris had been denied registration. He called upon them to follow his example and file appeals. CCM complained that their voters had been denied registration in Pemba, where they had been allegedly intimidated by CUF paramilitary forces. Various NGOs, foreign envoys and representatives of international organisations criticised the election preparations. Based on the 2002 census, ZEC redrew the constituency boundaries. The number in Pemba was reduced from 21 to 18, whereas the Unguja constituencies were increased from 29 to 32. In the prevailing tense circumstances, this adjustment appeared to CUF as obvious manipulation in CCM's favour.

The *CCM nomination process* for the Zanzibar presidency saw the appearance of an unexpected rival to *President Amani Karume*, who stood for re-election. Mohammed Gharib Bilal, Zanzibar's chief minister (1995–2000) under former President Salmin Amour, challenged Karume, despite a tradition of not standing against an incumbent. It was only during the CCM congress in early May that Bilal was forced to withdraw. He justified his initial move on the basis of the discontent among party members and the electorate over government policies, clearly indicating continuing rivalry between a moderate party wing supporting Karume and a group of Amour supporters who advocated a more autonomous Zanzibari stance vis-à-vis the union. Karume was perceived as a much weaker president and dependent on the mainland CCM. As in 2000, Karume's nomination was secured by the national CCM leadership rather than by its Zanzibar branch. Bilal's withdrawal did not, however, precipitate a split in the party.

CUF's secretary-general, *Seif Shariff Hamad*, a former CCM Zanzibar chief minister, was nominated unopposed. After two unsuccessful attempts at winning the presidency, Hamad's dominant role had in recent years been subject to criticism, particularly his conciliatory course towards CCM. He was, however, seen as a possible door-opener to bring CUF into a coalition government with CCM, a possibility that had been discussed since the 'Muafaka' agreement. Four other aspirants from small parties remained insignificant during the campaign.

The *elections* were held on *30 October* as scheduled. Tension was very high for several preceding weeks and on election day, with a heavy police presence at some polling stations. An outbreak of violence was feared based on the experience of the 2000 elections. In the event, election day passed without major. However, election day passed without major incidences. But ZEC declared Karume the winner, *opposition supporters clashed with CCM militia and the police.* CUF declared the elections flawed and claimed victory for Hamad. The leadership, however, appealed to supporters to refrain from violence. Instead, a strategy similar to the 'orange revolution' in Ukraine was advocated, but never carried out. After a few days, the situation again calmed down. As soon as the official results were announced, CUF declared it would not recognise Karume's government and threatened to boycott the house of representatives. It quickly softened this stance and then decided to participate in house business. Opposition spokesmen alleged that the ruling party had sent groups of supporters from one polling station to the next to vote. However, national and international *election observers*

(AU, SADC) declared the elections generally *free and fair*, despite minor irregularities such as double voting and the lack of transparency of the voters' rolls. The results were seen as a realistic reflection of the voters' will. Also, the running of the elections by ZEC had much improved compared to previous elections. Only in one Unguja constituency were the polls annulled by ZEC because of irregularities, and the vote was repeated on 14 December. Other observers (US-based National Democratic Institute, Commonwealth observer group, Electoral Institute of Southern Africa) were more critical, reporting numerous irregularities, biased media coverage, overreaction by police forces and a continuing close alliance between senior members of the police and army and the former state party.

The official results gave *Karume 53.2%* of the votes (2000, 67%), *Hamad 46.1%* (2000, 33%) and the four other candidates a combined total of 0.7%. In the contest for the 50-member house of representatives, CUF won all 18 constituencies on Pemba and one on Unguja (in Zanzibar town). CCM obtained 30 of the 32 constituencies on Unguja. Zanzibar was thus completely divided between one island clearly dominated by CUF and one dominated by CCM. However, even in Unguja about 30% of the voters opted for CUF. Voter turnout was 80% of the 510,000 registered voters. In addition to the 50 directly elected seats, parliament was supplemented by 15 women from the party lists for 'special seats' (CCM, nine; CUF, six) and five persons appointed by the president. As on the mainland, the election of 139 local councillors attracted little attention.

Karume was sworn in on 3 November. He confirmed *Chief Minister Shamsi Vuai Nahodha* in his position. An only slightly changed cabinet was immediately announced and consisted of 13 ministers, including three women. This quick move was somewhat surprising, given that ever since the 2001 'Muafaka' a coalition 'government of national unity' had frequently been discussed as a possible means of preventing a renewed outbreak of political turmoil and violence following another CUF electoral defeat. In his first address to the union parliament, President Kikwete promised to find a lasting solution to the political divisions and rivalry on the two islands. For this he received praise even from CUF.

Although the *tensions between the rival parties* did not result in fatalities similar to those in 2000, at least four people (two civilians and two soldiers) were killed and nearly 200 people were injured in election-related violence. At least another 20 people were wounded in unrest during the December elections, which sent hundreds of villagers fleeing their homes on Tumbatu island. Already on 6 March, CCM and CUF supporters had clashed during electoral rallies, with 14 people wounded, several cars destroyed and three CUF offices set alight. In early April, about 400 people tried to occupy a registration centre but were beaten back by the police. A few days later, the house of a CUF leader was set on fire. Later that month, a CCM office was bombed and the dead body of a CCM official was found. Further clashes occurred in September and October, when about 70 people were injured in various incidents.

On the *mainland also political tensions led to some violent disturbances*. In June, a CCM office in Bagamoyo was set on fire and Kikwete's house was invaded. During that incident, some of his family members were injured. In Marangu (Kilimanjaro region), several persons were severely injured in a clash between supporters of TLP and CCM in July. Clashes and riots occurred in several other locations throughout the country.

The limited international support for Tanzania's *large refugee population* remained a problem. About 400,000 refugees, mainly from Burundi (240,000) and DR Congo (150,000), continued to live in camps in western Tanzania. In March, the World Food Programme announced that its latest appeal had not been as successful as required. Instead of the $ 34 m needed, only $ 23 m had been raised. As a result, the food supply to refugees was drastically reduced, which led to increased theft of food from the villages surrounding the camps. As in previous years, prevailing attitudes favoured restricting the refugees. Refugees in the camps were still denied farmland, thus contributing to the food shortage.

Foreign Affairs

As in previous years, Tanzania maintained *good and cordial relations* with all *neighbouring states*, as well as with *donor countries*. The election to the presidency of Kikwete, who had been the foreign minister for ten years, guaranteed a continuation of this situation. One focus was the integration process of the EAC. The slow implementation of the new *customs union protocol*, in force since 1 January, was a source of political contention. Tanzania was accused by Kenyan business circles and politicians of obstructing exports to Tanzania and was urged to eliminate trade barriers immediately. Tanzanian business leaders, on the other hand, tried to revive a debate about rejoining COMESA, membership in which had been terminated by government in 2000.

Tanzania continued to be an important player in the settlement of the conflict in *Burundi* and was fully supportive of the new Bujumbura government installed in August. It was hoped that most of the Burundian refugees would be able to go home. However, a mediation attempt in mid-May in Dodoma to bring the last remaining rebel group FNL ('Forces Nationales de Libération') into the peace process failed owing to FNL intransigence.

President *Mkapa* had a busy travel schedule visiting many countries, particularly in Africa, as a farewell gesture before the end of his term. In Zimbabwe, to the surprise of many observers, he enthusiastically supported the internationally criticised policies of President Robert Mugabe, who was also official guest of honour at the Zanzibar revolution day celebrations on 12 January.

A potential source of conflict with *donor countries* was avoided by the relatively peaceful elections in Zanzibar. Since 1995, the political turmoil on the islands had always caused some contention. An official EU statement about the elections expressed satisfaction with their general conduct, but also expressed concern about the continued political confrontations on Zanzibar. Reports about plans for an arms factory in Mwanza with the assistance of a

Belgian company led to a temporary diplomatic row with *Belgium*, since Brussels feared the repercussions for the regional conflict situation.

Tanzania was a low-profile member of the UN Security Council for the first year of its two-year membership. Mkapa was one of the few African members of the Commission for Africa, initiated by British Prime Minister Blair, which submitted its report in mid-March.

A demonstration by young Muslims protesting against the presence of US soldiers in Muslim countries and the presumed denigration of the Koran in Guantanamo went ahead peacefully. A delegation of the demonstrators was received by representatives of the US embassy and the incident did not affect the generally good relations between Tanzania and the US.

Socioeconomic Developments

Macroeconomic performance continued to be quite *satisfactory* and to confirm Tanzania's image as one of the more successful reform countries in Africa, even though it remained very poor in absolute terms ($ 300 per capita in 2004) and despite a rapidly growing gap between the beneficiaries and relative losers of the strictly market-oriented policies. Preliminary data for 2005 indicated a good *GDP growth rate of 6.8%* in continuation of the trend since 2001, a stable low inflation rate of 4.2%, a narrowed but still considerable trade deficit (exports $ 1,595 m, imports $ 2,378 m) and an acceptable current account deficit of about 4.3% of GDP. Foreign reserves of $ 2 bn were sufficient for eight months import coverage. The exchange rate of the shilling, with some fluctuations, remained virtually stable over the year and did not even experience a temporary drop as a result of anxiety over the elections. Rather, the high level of aid inflows kept the shilling at an artificially elevated level.

Towards the end of the year, a lack of rain in parts of the country led to warnings about impending *partial food shortages* and problems for regular power and water supplies as a result of low water levels in dams and rivers.

The policy of *strict fiscal discipline* was continued with notable success. For the fiscal year 2004–05, the revenue collection target was slightly surpassed (mainly on account of income tax and VAT), while total expenditures remained somewhat below target. All revenue collected during the year reached an average of TSh 145 bn per month, a fourfold increase on the situation ten years earlier, and the tax ratio had been raised to 13.8% of GDP. The overall budget deficit, nevertheless, was of the order of 3.8% of GDP (11.8% without accounting for external grants). Surprisingly, the new *2005–06 budget* introduced in parliament on 8 June did not contain any measures to please the populace ahead of the elections and was generally short on significant new tax initiatives. Emphasis was laid on further increasing the efficiency of the Tanzania Revenue Authority (TRA), with a target for the tax ratio of 14.3% of GDP. Despite this ambition, external aid resources were still expected to meet 41% of all envisaged expenditures, largely in the form of budget support. The IMF expressed its appreciation for the intended slowing of the rate of expenditure increases, fearing a lack of implementation and financial control capacity. A share amounting to 4.5% of all external budget support finance was to be passed on to Zanzibar, where the government introduced its own separate budget on 16 June.

Tanzania was among the countries included in the new *debt relief initiative* of the G8 in July for 100% multilateral debt stock cancellation. On 22 December, the IMF formally decided to cancel outstanding debt of $ 336 m, while the ADB and World Bank still had to follow suit. Total external debt at the end of 2005 was about $ 7.7 bn, almost 70% of it multilateral. In February and July, the IMF carried out two fully satisfactory reviews on the progress of the current PRGF (expiring in August 2006) and released two further tranches of $ 4.2 m each. On 8 September, the World Bank approved a new PRSC of $ 150 m for direct budget support. Tanzania also qualified for funding from the new US Millenium Challenge Account.

In June, the government launched its new *National Strategy for Growth and Poverty Reduction* (Swahili acronym: MKUKUTA), in preparation since 2004 as a second-generation PRSP. The new, more comprehensive orientation was focused on three main pillars: growth and reduction of income poverty, improvement of quality of life and of social development and good governance. Over half the expenditures in the new budget were earmarked for these three cluster areas. More attention was to be given to the stimulation of domestic savings and the promotion of private investment. Mkapa advocated the idea of a so-called Mini-Tiger Plan 2020, attempting to emulate Asian experiences, to serve as the implementation vehicle for MKUKUTA and to create a conducive legal and regulatory framework. The treasury in May published the draft of a *Joint Assistance Strategy* (JAS), intended to provide a basis for more harmonised and better coordinated ways of dealing with the multitude of external donors and envisaging a rapidly increasing role for financial budget support, rather than traditional project or programme aid.

Mkapa repeatedly stressed the need for the continuation of the *economic reform policies* and defended the positive effects of privatisation and of attracting foreign investors against recurring public criticism about the lack of visible effects, and advocated a policy of stricter indigenisation. Even in the budget speech, some hints were made about a possible rethinking of the approach hitherto pursued. This led to some anxiety in the private business community, worried about the potential fall-out from antagonistic election-related campaigns. In 2004, Tanzania had again attracted much higher foreign direct investments of $ 470 m than Kenya and Uganda, most of them in the still-growing *mining sector*, where the country was ranked eighth worldwide as investment destination. Many critics, however, suspected that the contracts were far too generous to the multinational companies and that Tanzania did not benefit enough. A worldwide study by the World Bank of the business climate showed that procedures and bureaucracy in Tanzania were particularly cumbersome, but that some improvement was noticeable.

The *privatisation policy* continued to be very contentious. Particular attention was drawn to the sudden cancellation on 13 May of the management contract with a British-led consortium to operate the water supply for Dar es Salaam. The consortium was accused of poor performance and failure to fulfil promised tasks, and the ensuing dispute was eventually submitted to an international arbitration panel. The case, however, also raised questions about government's ability to conclude unambiguous contracts for such complex subjects. Other remaining major privatisation items also proved difficult. The Parastatal Sector Reform Commission (PSRC) was not yet able to bring the long-delayed tender process for the Tanzania Railways Corporation (TRC) to an end. In September, PSRC announced the sale of 49% of the shares of the National Microfinance Bank (NMB) to a consortium led by the Dutch Rabobank, but soon a controversy erupted about the financing and distribution of shares among the envisaged local partners. Of the shares, 30% were to remain with government while 21% were expected to be sold to the general public. Mixed results from the South African management of the power utility TANESCO left the extension of the contract somewhat in doubt. In the telecom sector, an earlier deal was partly undone in July when the management of the land-line operator Tanzania Telecommunications Co. (TTCL) was returned to government, leaving only the mobile operations with Celtel International.

State-employed doctors in major hospitals demanded better pay and went on *strike* in June and again, on a larger scale, in November. The government reacted harshly by sacking them and offering re-employment for the majority only after formal apologies. Students at various universities and colleges also initiated several strikes to demand better conditions and payment of their loans. In October, government clashed with a local NGO, Hakielimu, and threatened its deregistration after the publication of a very critical report about the primary education programme.

Tanzania in 2006

The year marked the beginning of a new political era under the *newly elected president, Jakaya Mrisho Kikwete*, but under the continued undisputed leadership of the ruling party 'Chama cha Mapinduzi' (CCM, Party of the Revolution). Although this implied some change in leadership style, the general orientation of gradual reform policies remained practically unchanged. Neither the domestic political arena nor the foreign policy field presented any outstanding challenges. Despite the partial effects of drought and recurrent power shortages, economic performance remained satisfactory.

Domestic Politics

After his overwhelming election victory in December 2005, the *new president, Kikwete*, was expected to lead the country for the next ten years (two constitutional terms). Although fundamental changes were not expected, the 'fourth phase government' (in continuation of the Nyerere, Mwinyi and Mkapa governments) was likely to focus on different issues than its predecessors. Kikwete stated that he wanted to be judged according to the success of his government in tackling the country's many problems and set himself a three-year timetable. Inaugurating the Union parliament on 30 December 2005, Kikwete named *solving the Zanzibar crisis* and *fighting corruption* as his government's overarching priorities.

The first major challenges for the new government were the consolidation of its power and the healing of wounds within the *ruling CCM* after the severe infighting that had marked the nomination process for its presidential candidate. Although 12 cabinet members from the previous administration were re-appointed, *the new cabinet* reflected an even more reformist composition than that of Benjamin Mkapa. Kikwete was clearly able to impose his will on the party. Being a real CCM insider with a strong power base, he could expect support for most of his political projects and reforms. To avoid a serious split in the party, however, he had to reconcile those less reform-oriented CCM factions that had been defeated during the nomination process. These considerations may have affected some of the reform projects, especially the anti-corruption drive.

Like his predecessor, Kikwete had featured this prominently in his election campaign. Despite some success in reducing small-scale corruption, Mkapa's record in fighting corruption among high-profile politicians had not been very convincing. Kikwete initiated a second phase of the *national anti-corruption strategy and action plan* specifically focused on fighting corruption at local government level. It remained, however, unclear to what extent these plans and public statements were put into practice. Tanzania hosted two important international conferences on corruption issues: the second global conference of Parliamentarians against Corruption in Arusha from 19–23 September, with 300 delegates from 50 countries, and the pan-African journalists' conference in mid-September in Dar es Salaam.

Having appointed his close friend and long-time political ally Edward Lowassa as new prime minister on 29 December 2005, Kikwete announced the *composition of the new cabinet* on 4 January. Contrary to promises to reduce governmental expenses, the president *increased the number of ministries* from 19 to 22 and the number of ministers from 45 to 60 (including 31 assistant ministers). He justified this step on the basis of the need to adjust governmental design to better suit the requirements of the country. The move was, however, contested by the opposition, which questioned whether a poor country could afford such a costly extension of ministries.

A newly created *ministry of public safety and security* was given responsibility for the police, which had been under the ministry of home affairs. A widely perceived increase in crime and common discontent with widespread corruption among the police as well as with the involvement of officers in crime was apparently the motivation for this step. Both issues had been major themes in Kikwete's election campaign. In March, a number of high-ranking police officers were replaced and the structure of police organisation in Dar es Salaam was changed. In August, to reduce armed robbery, the authorities of several towns called upon the population to register small arms.

Improvement of the poor infrastructure was to be much more vigorously tackled through the creation of a new *ministry of infrastructure development* under the well-respected former finance minister, Basil Mramba. The former ministry of livestock and water development was split into two separate ministries. Also new were the ministry for East African cooperation and the ministry of planning, economy and empowerment. The inclusion of aspects of empowerment reflected a desired new emphasis on empowering people to start their own businesses instead of waiting for service-delivery by government or aid agencies.

The cabinet reflected a good blend of new and experienced ministers and a good balance between change and continuity. Several former deputy ministers were promoted and the number of *female ministers* was increased from three to six. Two key ministries were now headed by women: Asha-Rose Migiro was appointed minister of foreign affairs and Zakia Meghji minister of finance.

The new president started energetically to give effect to his *campaign slogan* 'new zeal, new vigour, new speed', but made it clear that this was not to be understood as complete change of his predecessor's policies but in terms of speeding up the ongoing reform process and of ensuring that all government institutions were committed to hard work. Shortly after his inauguration, Kikwete visited every ministry to make clear his expectations of them. A week-long retreat for ministers, deputy ministers and permanent secretaries in Arusha in mid-March served to inculcate Kikwete's agenda into all members of his government team and to strengthen cohesion among them. The primary aim of this approach was to commit top-ranking government leaders to work unselfishly for the interests of the country and its people. Both Kikwete and Lowassa were keen to demonstrate that the new government was actively tackling the most urgent problems. This also involved *various symbolic actions*. Cabinet representatives were repeatedly sent to the regions to demonstrate the government's concern and presence. Juma Akukweti, state minister in the prime minister's office, became a prominent victim of this activism. On 16 December, he was involved in a plane crash en route to Mbeya to inspect the extent of damage caused by a fire that had destroyed a major market. Three members of the delegation were killed instantly, while Akukweti died on 4 January 2007 in a South African hospital. Kikwete's new approach was also aimed at *improving the performance of civil servants*. The finance minister was given powers to punish wasteful civil servants. On 1 July, a presidential commission to investigate the need to increase civil service salaries began its work.

A number of projects decided in principle but never implemented under Mkapa were now put into practice. The *eviction of street vendors* ('machinga') from Dar es Salaam's city centre had been decided years before, but the changes came only after Lowassa instructed city authorities to take action. An estimated 40,000 'machinga' were evicted and kiosks and other property destroyed after a deadline set by Lowassa expired at the end of September. Despite government promises to provide the 'machinga' with small loans and to construct three new business complexes in the city (one in each district), the eviction was generally viewed with mixed feelings and also provoked criticism. Although both government and city council claimed to have plans for the further development of the 'machinga' sector, it remained unclear whether these plans could work out in practice and whether they would meet the needs of the 'machinga' and further their empowerment.

After only ten months, much of which had been used for reorganisation and to establish new working structures, a surprise *cabinet reshuffle* was announced on 15 October. Although no official explanation was given, this was most likely mainly prompted by public discontent with the long-standing electricity crisis. Ibrahim Msabaha, the minister of energy and minerals, was accused misleading the public by promising that the power crisis would be resolved by October, when in fact the problems had become even worse. Altogether *ten ministers and eight deputy ministers were transferred* to new portfolios, including key personalities like Mramba, who was transferred to the ministry of industry and trade. Given that Kikwete was seemingly dissatisfied with the performance of some ministers, it remained unclear why the cabinet was reshuffled without any of its members being sacked. This was particularly true of the transfer of the much criticised energy minister to another portfolio (East African cooperation). Observers more sympathetic to the new administration, however, described the reshuffle as a 'wake-up call', indicating the president's determination to react in cases of unsatisfactory performance. Whether the shuffle was an appropriate step or merely a publicity stunt to demonstrate governmental action, and the extent to which it had been constrained by CCM strongmen, were all subjects of public discussion.

The 7th *CCM national congress* held in Dodoma on 24–25 June (one year earlier than the regular five-year cycle) elected *Kikwete* as the new *party chairman* and successor to Mkapa, who relinquished the position before the end of his tenure. During its meeting on 29–30 April, the CCM national executive committee had unanimously nominated Kikwete as the sole candidate. The *CCM's secretary-general*, Philip Mangula, was replaced by Dar es Salaam's regional commissioner, *Yussuf Makamba*, who had strongly backed Kikwete's presidential candidacy. Other party posts as well as numerous district commissionerships were also filled with Kikwete supporters. The two important *CCM vicechairman* positions remained, however, in the hands of old-guard politicians who could potentially create problems for the new leadership. *John Malecela*, vice-chairman for the mainland, had been the most prominent representative of the anti-reformist faction in CCM's internal contest for nomination as presidential candidate in 2005. Zanzibar President *Amani Karume* remained the other CCM vice-chairman.

The new *parliament* was just as heavily dominated by CCM as the previous one (with 276 of 322 MPs). Opposing views were mostly expected to come from within CCM's ranks. The new speaker, Samuel Sitta, encouraged more open debate with the apparent tacit approval of the president, who had been instrumental in the selection of Sitta. The creation of a ministry of parliamentary affairs also indicated that Kikwete was seeking to cooperate more closely with parliament and thus to increase its political importance.

As a result of their poor electoral performance, all *opposition parties* remained weak. The *Civic United Front* (*CUF*), by far the strongest with 30 of the 43 opposition MPs, decided in January to form a shadow cabinet without including other opposition parties. This move was heavily criticised by these parties – especially since almost all CUF MPs came from Pemba Island (Zanzibar) and could hardly speak for the mainland opposition. Subsequently, CUF invited members from the other parties to join the shadow cabinet. Wilbroad Slaa, from the second largest opposition faction, *'Chama cha Demokrasia na Maendeleo'* (*CHADEMA* – Party for Democracy and Development) with 11 MPs, became deputy opposition leader.

On 6 May, the high court – in response to a petition by Christopher Mtikila, chairman of the small Democratic Party (DP) – ruled that *independent candidates* were allowed to run in presidential and parliamentary elections. This had for years been demanded by opposition parties, but had been persistently rejected by the government. Another high court ruling on 25 April declared illegal the use of *'takrima'* (traditional hospitality) during election campaigns. This practice of distributing free gifts to the electorate had been hotly disputed during the 2005 election campaign, since opposition parties and NGOs perceived it as a veiled form of corruption favouring the ruling party with its much better financial resources.

Expectations were high that Kikwete's government would start new efforts to find a lasting *solution to the political impasse in Zanzibar*. In his first address to the Union parliament, Kikwete promised to put this issue on top of his agenda. He expressed deep concern about the crisis on the islands and the deepening *political schism between Pemba* (dominated by CUF) and *Unguja* (held by CCM). CUF formed a 16-member shadow cabinet in the Zanzibar parliament on 15 January and criticised Zanzibar's President Karume for appointing just one of ten additional MPs from Pemba. CUF continued to refuse to recognise Karume's presidency because of alleged irregularities in the 2005 Zanzibar election, but nevertheless took part in all parliamentary proceedings. When visiting the islands for the first time as president in early April, Kikwete appealed in several public addresses for reconciliation and political tolerance. A positive indication of possible new moves was the government's decision to assign *responsibility for Union matters* to Vice-President Mohamed Ali Shein from Pemba. With Shein in this position and Hussein Mwinyi as new minister of Union affairs, two high-profile politicians were put in charge of the sensitive issue.

Whereas during Mkapa's presidency talks to resolve the crisis took place only between CCM and CUF, his successor involved the two governments. *Union Premier Lowassa and Zanzibar Chief Minister Shamsi Vuai Nahodha* met in May and November to identify the key issues to be tackled in reforming the complicated asymmetrical design of the Union. Other ministries and governmental agencies were also involved in this process, which reflected the insight that many of the islands' political problems derived not only from the competition between CCM and CUF, but also from the structure of the union and the unwillingness of Zanzibar's CCM leadership to subscribe to reforms. In late March, the Zanzibar government refused to ratify the *human rights and good governance commission that* had been established by the Union parliament in 2001. Zanzibar's attorney-general demanded amendments to the constituting act to enable Zanzibar to establish a separate commission, but this was rejected by the Union ministry of justice and constitutional affairs. Besides political talks, Kikwete proposed stronger efforts to boost Zanzibar's economy as possible steps to reduce tensions on the islands and in particular suggested greater diversion of national resources to Zanzibar as one measure.

It was, however, not clear to what extent CUF's concerns were also considered in the talks. CUF Secretary-General Seif Sharif Hamad in late October demanded a re-run of the 2005 Zanzibar elections and the formation of a government of national unity to organise and oversee new elections impartially. On 27 December, CCM Zanzibar's Publicity Secretary Vuai Ali Vuai stated that talks on the political impasse did not include the option of a coalition government. Zanzibar's President Karume even declared such a government unconstitutional. On 11 and 12 November, CUF staged demonstrations in Dar es Salaam and Zanzibar to protest Karume's statements that there was no political crisis on Zanzibar and to underscore the demands for new elections. These demonstrations were supported by the opposition Tanzania Labour Party (TLP) and National Convention for Constitutional Reform (NCCR).

CUF obviously viewed CCM Zanzibar and the Zanzibar government as its main adversaries, but closely cooperated with the new president on Union matters. The CUF's leadership praised Kikwete for his attempts to find lasting solutions, which were, however, dependent on CCM-Zanzibar's willingness to cooperate. The longer the talks continued without visible result, the stronger was the danger of radicalisation within CUF and the feared split within the party.

On 23 April, ten Zanzibaris submitted a petition in the Zanzibar high court challenging the *legality* of the *Zanzibar-mainland union*. Since this appeal appeared to be a relatively hopeless venture from the beginning and was eventually dismissed on 2 October, its probable intent was to bring the Zanzibar issue to international attention rather than to find a legal solution to a political problem. This view was supported by the fact that a number of high-profile witnesses, including UN Secretary-General Kofi Annan, were called before the court. Although the claimants lost the case, a new problem emerged from the proceedings: the original Union treaty, signed by both parties in 1964, was found to have been lost.

In August, Zanzibari members of the Union parliament pleaded for *separate representation of Zanzibar in the envisaged East African federation* and demanded at least associate membership for the islands. On 21 November, Lowassa made it clear that it was impossible for Zanzibar to join as a separate entity and that it should channel its interests in the EAC through the Union government.

The new government – contrary to prevailing sentiments towards the end of the 10-year Mkapa period – was initially supported by a *wave of public sympathy*. Expectations were high that the new administration would seriously tackle the country's various problems, especially corruption, the Zanzibar issue and poverty reduction. Public trust in the new administration was considerable throughout the year, but on the evidence of opinion polls dwindled significantly. Massive problems with the electricity supply, continued high crime rates, especially in Dar es Salaam, and a temporarily perceived economic crisis, mainly in response to the drought, contributed to a growing impression that the government's initial measures may have been merely cosmetic. Kikwete's frequent absences from the country and the fact that he and Lowassa were often accompanied by their families on state visits abroad fuelled critical views of the government's ability to find appropriate solutions for the country's problems.

Although the *refugee* population in Tanzania's western regions had been drastically reduced in recent years, it remained a concern. By year's end, about 290,000 refugees, more than 150,000 from Burundi and almost 130,000 from DR Congo, were still registered by UNHCR. In view of the improved situation in Burundi, Kikwete called on UNHCR and Burundian authorities to speed-up voluntary repatriation. While the government refrained from expelling Burundian refugees, several thousand alleged Rwandans, most of whom had lived for many years in Tanzania, were deported to Rwanda, causing annoyance on the Rwandan side. Both countries formed a team to resolve the issue. Tanzanian authorities also deported more than 1,000 Burundians, many of whom had stayed in Tanzania for more than 20 years. In talks with Kikwete at the AU summit in Gambia in July, UN Secretary-General Kofi Annan commended Tanzania for its immense contribution to hosting refugees from the Great Lakes region for extended periods.

The government further enhanced efforts to reduce the number of *illegal immigrants* and non-Tanzanians working in Tanzania. The major concern was the criticism that many foreigners came to work in Tanzania while citizens remained unemployed. Foreigners applying for work permits were screened more carefully and companies were told to look for Tanzanian workers first.

In July, the film *'Darwin's Nightmare'*, awarded the prize for best European documentary in 2005, caused massive public outrage. Although mainly aimed at criticising Western companies and globalisation for unscrupulously exploiting Africa's wealth and causing negative social effects in Africa, the film was perceived as damaging Tanzania's good reputation in the world. The film claimed that the planes used to transport fish from Lake Victoria to Europe brought weapons on their way to Mwanza, which were used to fuel the wars in the Great Lakes region. However, no clear evidence was provided to support these allegations. A local journalist who had contributed to the film later stated that most of the 'documentary scenes' had been arranged by the film's Austrian director. Also, accusations that Tanzanian authorities had threatened and even arrested journalists over the film proved to be false. Kikwete, as well as parliament and several ministers, strongly condemned the film. Several Tanzanian institutions, including the president, used this episode to accuse the Western media of painting a biased picture of Africa.

In February, the worldwide discussions about the caricatures of Prophet Mohammed published in a Danish newspaper prompted protests by some *Muslim groups*. Tanzania's highest-ranking sheikh,

Mufti Shabani Simba, demanded that the Danish government withdraw the newspaper's licence and apologise to all Muslims in the world. On 16 February, thousands of Muslims took part in a peaceful demonstration demanding that Danish and Norwegian residents leave Tanzania, but the excitement soon died down and had no lasting repercussions.

The killing of a Dar es Salaam *'daladala' (commuter bus) driver* on 4 November by *Tabora Regional Commissioner* Ditopile Mzuzuri attracted much public attention. After a road accident between the 'daladala' and the regional commissioner's car and a subsequent argument, Ditopile shot the driver in front of his passengers. Two days later, he was arrested and charged with murder. The trial was expected to be watched closely, since Ditopile, a prominent politician, was one of Kikwete's strong supporters and long-time allies.

Foreign Affairs

As in previous years, relations with foreign countries were generally unproblematic. Having been foreign minister for ten years, Kikwete had excellent international contacts and undertook an intensive travel schedule. He justified this on the basis of the need to introduce the new government to many international partners. Usually accompanied by highranking delegations, the visits were also vindicated as providing an opportunity to promote new investment in Tanzania. Despite these explanations, Kikwete's frequent absences and the costs of these journeys prompted charges that he may have forgotten he was no longer foreign minister.

Pleased by the good and peaceful conduct of the 2005 elections, particularly in Zanzibar, and by expectations that the new government would follow the reformist course of its predecessor, *donor countries and international institutions* remained generally sympathetic and praised Tanzania as a deserving recipient of substantial aid.

Relations with the *East African neighbours* remained generally harmonious. The creation of a separate ministry of East African cooperation indicated the importance given to all aspects of the EAC. This was also underlined by the fact that Kikwete began his round of state visits by travelling to Kenya, Uganda and Rwanda. On 5 April, Juma Mwapachu, former Tanzanian ambassador to France, was sworn in as new EAC secretary-general at its seventh summit in Arusha. On 13 October, the process was started to gather the views of the population on the envisaged creation by 2013 of an East African federation with common political institutions. A 16-member committee was given the task of visiting the entire country to solicit the opinions of the Tanzanian population. The accession of Rwanda and Burundi to the EAC on 30 November was generally welcomed in Tanzania, despite some fears that this move might result in the 'importation' of the political problems of the two neighbours. Some quarrels over EAC customs union regulations continued and fears of Kenyan economic domination led several observers to doubt the genuineness of Tanzania's commitment to the goal of full EAC integration.

On 19 September, the signing of a ceasefire between the Burundian government and the Palipehutu-FNL, the last remaining Burundian rebel group, highlighted a series of *peace talks* hosted by Tanzania. The Palestinian ambassador requested the Tanzanian government to take a lead in peace negotiations between Israel and the Palestinians. The request was supported by the deputy head of the Israeli mission in East and Central Africa. A few Tanzanian soldiers joined the new UN mission in Lebanon. The Sudanese government and the UN requested Tanzania to support the AU peace mission in Darfur. Kikwete stated that the government would be willing to send soldiers to Darfur only when the Sudanese government and the rebels had signed a peace agreement and when the military equipment for the mission had been provided by the AU.

Cooperation with *China* received new impetus, building on earlier close relations in the 1960s and 1970s. A number of projects, such as the revitalisation of the TAZARA railway to Zambia, the construction of a new 60,000-seat national stadium in Dar es Salaam, primary schools and a loan to improve the power supply system were initiated. Chinese premier Wen Jiabao visited Tanzania in June and Kikwete spent a week in China and participated in the large Sino-African summit in Beijing in November.

In the second year of Tanzania's two-year membership of the *UN Security Council* (the second time after a lapse of 30 years), the country held the rotating presidency in January and used the opportunity to give particular attention to the problems of the African Great Lakes region.

Socioeconomic Developments

Despite an intermittent public perception of an impending economic crisis (resulting from the combined effects of drought, persistent power cuts, falling exchange rate and increased inflation), the overall *macroeconomic performance* continued to be quite satisfactory. The estimated *GDP growth rate* of 5.9% was below the original target of 7%, but still above the African average and reasonable under the circumstances. The average inflation rate for the year was 6.3%, with unusually high monthly fluctuations mainly as a result of changing food prices. The trade deficit widened considerably, with a 35% jump in imports to $ 4,070 m (largely due to high oil and food imports) and only a modest increase in exports to $ 1,898 m (further growth in mineral and manufactured exports, but a slump in traditional agricultural export crops). The structural current account deficit was, therefore, expected to reach a new record of about $ 1,600 m (13.6% of GDP), while foreign reserves grew by about 10% to $ 2,259 m by the end of December (6.5 months import coverage). The Tanzania shilling (TSh) fell sharply against the US dollar to a low in August (without attempts at intervention by the Bank of Tanzania), but afterwards recovered somewhat due to seasonal foreign-exchange inflows (harvest receipts, aid transfers). At year's end, the shilling had lost 8.3% against the US dollar. The external debt was substantially reduced from $ 8.1 bn (end of 2005) to $ 4.7 bn as a result of MDRI write-offs. Despite the generally good performance, Tanzania remained one of the poorest countries with a 2004 per capita GDP of $ 288 ($ 674 in PPP terms) and ranked 162 on UNDP's HDI.

On 15 June, Finance Minister Zakia Meghji introduced the 2006–07 *budget* in parliament after providing a review of the generally successful fiscal performance in the *2005–06 financial year*. Overall domestic revenue collection of TSh 2,060 bn had been practically on target owing to various measures to increase the efficiency of tax collection, thus meeting the targeted tax ratio of 14.3% of GDP (only 13.6%, however, on the basis of revised GDP data). External aid resources accounted for 43% of total expenditures. Not all originally estimated aid funds were, however, actually secured, thus causing a higher-than-expected overall budget deficit of 4.9% of GDP.

In the *2006–07 budget*, the domestic revenue target was set at TSh 2,451 bn (an increase of 19.1%), assuming the attainment of a tax ratio of 14.5% of GDP, a GDP growth rate of 7.3% in 2007 and inflation not exceeding 4% by June 2007. Total expenditures were budgeted at TSh 4,850 bn (64% recurrent, 36% development expenditures), of which 46% were expected to come from external concessionary loans and grants (including debt relief). Although efforts to reduce dependency on aid funds had been stated repeatedly, this was clearly not reflected in the budget figures. To accommodate a large rise of civil service salaries, the budgeted public wage bill was increased by 46%.

Harmonious cooperation with and support from many *bilateral and multilateral donors* continued to be of crucial importance to all governmental development endeavours. The substantial new debt relief that had been promised in 2005 under the MDRI became reality with the formalisation of ADB's debt cancellation in April and the World Bank's announcement on 1 July of the cancellation of $ 3.9 bn in outstanding debt. These steps reduced the remaining debt to $ 4.7 bn. On 9 May, the World Bank approved a fourth PRSC of $ 200 m for general budget support and later started preparing for a similarly sized fifth PRSC (expected to be an annual exercise). A new source of funding was expected to become available with Tanzania's selection as a recipient under the US Millennium Challenge Account. The existing IMF support through a three-year PRGF expired as scheduled in December (last review and disbursement in February 2007) and was not renewed. This indicated Tanzania's vastly improved status as a successful reform economy no longer in need of this instrument. Instead, negotiations began with the IMF to conclude a Policy Support Instrument (PSI), a new form of economic policy advice and monitoring without any provision of financial funds. The PSI was expected to focus on strengthening the private and financial sectors and on fiscal efficiency.

The government's *national strategy for growth and reduction of poverty* (Swahili acronym: MKUKUTA), launched in 2005 as a second-generation PRSP, continued to be the basis for all domestic and externally supported development activities. It's three main clusters focused on economic growth and reduction of income poverty, social services and improvement of quality of life and strengthening good governance. The Tanzanian PRS process was generally acknowledged to be on track, yet needing regular review and more effective prioritisation of investments and mobilisation of domestic resources. The *Joint Assistance Strategy* (JAS) for harmonised cooperation between the government and all donors (produced as a draft in 2005) became effective in July.

The general thrust of *economic policy* under Kikwete was the continuation of the reform policies pursued by his predecessor Mkapa, with some proclaimed emphasis on fighting corruption, furthering local empowerment and environmental protection and enhancing governmental efficiency. In contrast with Kikwete's 'new zeal, new vigour, new speed' campaign slogan, actual performance was largely characterised by a rather cautious approach to real changes.

No new anti-corruption law was passed by November, as had been promised, thus triggering a reduction in Danish budgetary support. In April, an executive secretary of the national empowerment council (established in November 2005) was appointed and various statements stressed the importance of empowering local entrepreneurs through the formalisation of unregistered assets in the informal sector, also as a way to create more employment opportunities. This was formulated in a new *property and business formalisation programme* (Swahili acronym: MKURABITA). A new package of investment incentives (known as the 'Blue Book') apparently had a positive effect on the general business environment. In the World Bank's latest "Doing Business Report", Tanzania was praised as one of the top reforming countries, although in absolute terms it was still classified in a low rank (142 of 175).

There was continued prevarication about ending the *privatisation of parastatal enterprises*. On budget day, it was announced that the remaining 36 public corporations would be restructured and the Parastatal Sector Reform Commission (PSRC) be dissolved by December 2007, but doubts about meeting this deadline remained. Still no final agreement was reached to privatise the Tanzania Railways Corporation (TRC) and the National Insurance Corporation (NIC). In October, the PSRC announced the offering of a further 21% stake in the National Microfinance Bank (NMB) on the Dar es Salaam stock exchange in March 2007, and the Zanzibar government announced in December its intention to offer a 60% stake in the People's Bank of Zanzibar (PBZ) to a strategic investor. In view of the disappointing performance of Air Tanzania since the 2003 purchase of a 49% stake by South African Airways, it was agreed to reverse this deal and to restructure the airline for a new revitalisation.

There were also mixed signals about the *management* of existing *parastatals*. While the contract with a South African firm to manage the Tanzania Electric Supply Company (TANESCO) was terminated in December and responsibility was handed back into local hands, the management of the Tanzania Telecommunications Company (TTCL) was unexpectedly awarded to a Canadian firm. TANESCO had for years been severely criticised for bad service, exorbitant electricity tariffs and insufficient investment, and the foreign management had been unable to significantly improve the situation. In 2006, however, the *crisis* took on a new political dimension because of severe *power cuts* (resulting from prolonged drought conditions and low water levels in dams) and the inept handling of the situation by the political authorities, who gave misleading reassurances. Severe power rationing measures were applied early in the year, but contrary to official predictions had to be later reintroduced until the end of the year. This had a negative effect not only on private urban consumers, but also on all industrial activities due to production losses and significantly increased power costs resulting from reliance on generators.

Foreign direct investments have remained relatively constant in recent years ($ 473 m in 2005), considerably higher than in Kenya and Uganda, and went overwhelmingly into the *mining sector*. Gold was by far the most important export ($ 615 m in 2005) and Tanzania was the fourth-largest gold producer in Africa. In response to public allegations that many past contracts had been far too favourable to international mining firms, the new government promised to systematically review all existing mining contracts, but it turned out that the government did not possess much leverage.

The prolonged drought in parts of the country had severe negative effects on the *agricultural sector*. Most traditional export crops (except tea) experienced poor harvests, while many farmers shifted to the production of food crops in response to a significant rise in local food prices. In February, with 3.7 m people estimated to be at risk of food shortages, the government appealed for international food aid, but overall the country was able to avert a major famine. The national strategic grain reserve was run down to an extreme low of 3,165 tonnes in April, but had already been replenished (partly through imports) to 110,203 tonnes in December.

Some private sector business interests continued to lobby for a reconsideration of Tanzania's withdrawal from *COMESA* (in 2000), but opinions were divided and no immediate change of position was in sight. There was also some growing concern about potential problems arising from Tanzania's overlapping membership in the *EAC customs union* and in *SADC* (aiming to create a customs union in 2008), which also had repercussions for the ongoing negotiations with the EU about concluding economic partnership agreements by the end of 2007. In the *NEPAD* context, the first self-assessment stage of the *APRM* process was launched, and was entrusted to independent persons free from direct government control.

Tanzania in 2007

With no major challenges from the notoriously weak opposition forces, the second year of the *presidency* of *Jakaya Mrisho Kikwete* confirmed the continued undisputed dominance of the *ruling party*, 'Chama cha Mapinduzi' (CCM, Party of the Revolution). The term 'fourth phase government' denoted uninterrupted CCM rule with only four presidents over the 45 years since independence. The government continued to pursue its strategy of *cautious socioeconomic reforms*. The economy performed relatively well and there were no significant problems in foreign relations.

Domestic Politics

The situation was characterised by *increasing public frustration* over the performance of Kikwete's government, which had been elected in December 2005 with overwhelming popular support. It had generally been expected that the new government would fulfil its electoral promises and tackle the country's many problems, especially the endemic corruption and poverty and the persistent political impasse in Zanzibar. As was already apparent in 2006, enthusiasm for the government continued to dwindle and reached even lower levels during 2007. An opinion poll by a university programme, Research and Education for Democracy in Tanzania (REDET), conducted in October revealed that Kikwete still enjoyed relatively high, although decreased support, whereas there was great discontent with the performance of his administration.

After only one year in office, Foreign Minister *Asha-Rose Migiro* was surprisingly appointed *UN deputy secretary general* on 5 January. This appointment was greatly welcomed throughout the country, as she was already the third Tanzanian woman to be appointed to a high-ranking international position. On 11 January, the deputy minister of energy and minerals, *Bernard Membe*, was appointed to take over from Migiro. Membe had been working in the ministry of foreign affairs when Kikwete was foreign minister. Kikwete promoted the deputy minister of planning, economy and empowerment, Batilda Salha Burian, as minister of state in the prime minister's office (parliament), taking over from the late Juma Akukweti, who died of the injuries he sustained in a plane crash on 4 January. Further accidents involving members of the cabinet and the parliament were blamed on the poor condition of the transportation infrastructure.

Kikwete repeatedly declared he was determined to resolve the persistent *political impasse in Zanzibar*. Efforts to reach a new agreement continued behind closed doors throughout the year. Only periodically was the public informed about the ongoing negotiations. A new round of talks between the secretaries general of CCM and the strongest opposition party, *Civic United Front (CUF)* began on 17 January. Surprisingly, the talks no longer involved the two governments, as was the case in 2006. Apparently returning to the strategy of his predecessor Benjamin Mkapa, Kikwete focused on direct negotiations between the two rival parties. This may have been an indication that CCM Zanzibar was perceived to be the main obstacle to a lasting solution, and CCM's island-wing was no longer directly included in the talks. In mid-August, CUF Chairman Ibrahim Lipumba was quoted in the media as complaining that 18 months of negotiations had led down a blind alley. He accused CCM hardliners of obstructing any changes or amicable solutions and called for international pressure on the ruling party. Kikwete reacted promptly, stating that the joint negotiation committee had held 12 meetings since January. He explained that agreements had been reached on three of the five items on the agenda. Talks continued on 31 August after a two-month standstill. In late November, CUF Secretary General Seif Shariff Hamad called for patience and understanding among Zanzibaris, predicting that negotiations with CCM would soon be concluded. He hailed Kikwete for demonstrating unswerving commitment to resolving the long-running political crisis and promised that the results of the talks would be made public in January 2008. Despite this rather optimistic statement, it was widely believed that the CCM-CUF negotiations would achieve no substantial solution before the next elections in 2010. The *Zanzibar Electoral Commission* (ZEC) released its *report on the conduct of the 2005 island elections* in early November, stating that security forces had interfered with ZEC's operations during the polls, particularly during the registration process. It recommended that local government leaders, commonly known as 'shehas', should be vested with less power during election processes.

Dissatisfaction with the perceived inertia of government in mounting an effective campaign against *corruption* was one factor contributing to public discontent. After several months of delay, the new *Prevention and Combating of Corruption Bill* for mainland Tanzania was passed by parliament in April. The bill envisaged a revamped Prevention of Corruption Bureau (PCB), which was renamed *Prevention and Combat of Corruption Bureau* (PCCB) and provided with extended investigative powers. The establishment of a seven-member prevention and combat of corruption board was suggested in the bill to advise the bureau and to review its work. Civil society organisations, experts, development partners and MPs welcomed the bill as a good instrument in the country's anti-corruption strategy. After a heated parliamentary debate, the bill passed without the establishment of the controversial board, which was perceived as being a government tool to control PCCB's work. Doubts remained that even the new PCCB would be more a government body than a truly independent public one.

The *fight against corruption and misuse of public funds* was a major theme throughout the year. *Bank of Tanzania (BoT) Governor Daudi Ballali* had come under pressure after Finance Minister Zakia Meghji had announced in December 2006 that the government was investigating alleged financial irregularities at the central bank. In late June, allegations against Ballali emerged, including the disappearance of millions of dollars from BoT's external debt service account and inflated construction costs for its new twin tower building in Dar es Salaam. The matter was taken up by the local media, the donor community (including the IMF), civil society organisations and opposition political parties and there were calls for an immediate probe and the resignation of the BoT governor. The government eventually gave in to this multi-pronged pressure and ordered an audit to be undertaken by Ernst & Young from September to December. By year's end, rumours were circulating that Ballali had tendered his resignation from office.

Another alleged case of grand corruption came to the public's attention. In June 2006, the government had signed a contract with the US-based *Richmond Development Company* to supply power generators in an effort to solve the severe power crisis. Although the government had already made a multimillion dollar deposit, the generators were never delivered. In May, the PCB director declared that investigations into the case had revealed no indications of corruption or favouritism in the deal. The case, popularly referred to as the "Richmond-Saga", resurfaced in mid-November in parliament when legislators demanded the establishment of a parliamentary select committee to investigate the circumstances of the controversial deal. Eventually, such a committee was formed under the chairmanship of CCM legislator Harrison Mwakyembe, and was given four weeks to complete its investigations.

Opposition parties focused much of their activity on issues of corruption and misuse of funds. A working group of four opposition parties, CHADEMA (Party for Democracy and Development), CUF, NCCR-Mageuzi (National Convention for Construction and Reform-Change) and TLP (Tanzania Labour Party) under the leadership of CHADEMA legislator Wilbrod Slaa publicised two so-called *'lists of shame'*, in which numerous prominent politicians, civil servants and institutions were accused of corruption. *Government and CCM officials reacted nervously and harshly* to members of the opposition who raised corruption allegations. *Energy and Minerals*

Minister Nazir Karamagi and the permanent secretary in the ministry of finance, whose names were found on the lists of shame, announced their intention to file legal suits against Slaa and other opposition leaders. In August, another CHADEMA MP, *Zitto Kabwe*, was even suspended from parliament for four months after he accused Karamagi of lying about a controversial mining contract that the minister had signed in a London hotel concerning *Buzwagi gold mine*. Kabwe had tabled a private member's motion demanding the establishment of a parliamentary committee to probe the contract between Karamagi and Barrick Gold Tanzania. After his suspension, Kabwe began touring the country and putting his case to the public, in which initiative he was supported by other members of the opposition parties. Kingunge Ngombale-Mwiru, minister of political affairs and civil society relations, then threatened to arrest Kabwe and other opposition leaders and accused them of abusing freedom of expression. CCM Secretary General Yusuf Makamba threatened to inform the public of the "misdeeds" of opposition leaders if they didn't stop their allegations against CCM. Despite these strong-arm reactions from CCM leaders, Kikwete (who is also CCM chairman) included Kabwe on a special 11-member committee formed in mid-November to *review existing mining contracts*. Kabwe's appointment to this committee indicated the president was well aware that any further moves against Kabwe could backfire for both CCM and government.

The highly controversial purchase of an expensive *radar system* in 2001 was back in the headlines following investigations by the British serious fraud office, which revealed that a Tanzanian middleman had received a $ 12 m commission in a Swiss bank account. This amount, constituting 30% of the purchase price, had been secretly paid by the UK's biggest arms supplier, BAE Systems. The radar system had been widely criticised as unnecessary and overpriced. Whereas the involvement of high-profile politicians was hotly discussed in Britain, PCB investigations centred on the role of the accused Tanzanian middleman. Demands by opposition parties to investigate the role of former President Mkapa were firmly rejected by the government and by CCM. It was obvious that the authorities were reluctant to dig too deeply into the issue and they left most of the work to their British counterparts. Tanzanian officials tried to present Tanzania as a victim misused by a rich country. Kikwete stated he would lodge claims against the British government if it was proved that the purchase price had been grossly inflated.

The common notion that high-profile politicians were not only using the taxpayers' money for their own benefit but were also treated preferentially was again fuelled by the case of *former Tabora regional commissioner, Ditopile Mzuzuri*, who had killed a commuter bus driver in Dar es Salaam in late 2006. Ditopile's case was watched closely by the media, since he had been a long-time ally of Kikwete. Originally charged with murder, Ditopile's sentence was reduced to manslaughter and he was released on bail in early March. After Ditopile's accelerated release, about 300 *remand prisoners* from two Dar es Salaam prisons *protested* against what they called preferential treatment of a prominent politician and referred to the poor conditions under which they were kept. Only one day later, about 150 inmates in Arusha region joined the protests, which quickly spread to prisons in Dodoma, Mwanza and Rukwa. The week-long protests ended on 19 March after delegations from the government, including Justice Minister Mary Nagu, met with the protesters. This was the first such strike in Tanzania.

Numerous protests and strikes indicated the discontent of wide sectors of society with their socioeconomic conditions, as well as a growing readiness to stand up for their interests. The Trade Union Congress of Tanzania (TUCTA) supported the strikes and finally pressured government to increase the official minimum wage – a rare success for this generally ineffective body. *Students* at various universities and colleges boycotted classes in January, April, June and October to *protest against reduced government loans.*

The government had also to deal with *increasingly self-confident civil society organisations*. In late January, *HakiElimu*, the NGO for the right to education, appealed against a government interdict of September 2005 which prohibited the organisation from publishing educational research materials. The government criticised posters issued by HakiElimu that highlighted existing problems especially in the primary and secondary education development programmes. Kikwete justified the ban on the grounds that HakiElimu highlighted only the shortcomings but not the achievements. When several other NGOs rallied behind HakiElimu, Prime Minister Edward Lowassa finally lifted the ban.

Elections for party leadership positions dominated the activities of CCM. All party members were called upon to elect their leaders from grassroots up to the national level. Because of CCM's political dominance, elections to the party's organs were of extraordinary significance for the entire country. On all levels, they were accompanied by allegations of vote-buying. Numerous party functionaries and even MPs were excluded from the process, sacked or arrested by the PCCB. Given that the next CCM elections were to be held only in 2012, whereas the next general elections were scheduled for 2010, it could not be ruled out that unwarranted corruption allegations were being used to sideline competitors. The lengthy process started with the election of CCM cell leaders in late February, followed by leadership elections at the district level in late April and at regional level in mid-October. The *eighth national congress of CCM*, held on 3–4 November in Dodoma, had to elect the National Executive Committee (NEC), the NEC secretariat, the central committee, the party chairperson and the two vice-chairpersons. About 1,900 delegates voted 85 out of 263 aspirants on to the NEC, which in turn elected 14 members to the central committee from a list of 30 that was submitted by the party chairman, Kikwete. The chairman himself and two vice-chairmen had been nominated by the outgoing central committee before the congress began and were subsequently confirmed by the full congress. The most remarkable change in the leadership was the replacement of the vice-chairman for the mainland, John Malecela, by the former long-serving parliamentary speaker, Pius Msekwa. Both were over 70 and were veteran CCM politicians of long standing. Replacing Malecela, a formerly highly influential representative of the conservative wing of the party and opponent of Kikwete, with the equally veteran but more liberal Msekwa was widely seen as an attempt to reconcile the modernising wing of the party with the traditionalist wing. Secretary General Yusuf Makamba, a strong Kikwete supporter, was also re-elected. As in previous party elections, a number of high-ranking members failed to be elected, among them several cabinet ministers. The CCM national congress was again a confident demonstration of the party's powerful position in Tanzania. Despite the appearance of intense infighting and numerous allegations of corruption and vote-buying, no deep rifts opened up between the factions and threatened to split the party. All the losing candidates accepted the outcome of the elections.

Although the space for *opposition activities* inside and outside parliament was relatively free, state authorities and CCM gave the opposition a hard time. In a number of cases, the accusation of "*abusive language*" was used to put pressure on members of opposition parties. CHADEMA MP Kabwe had been temporarily suspended from parliament on this basis, while the party chairmen of TLP and the Democratic Party (DP), Augustine Mrema and Christopher Mtikila respectively, were charged in court of this offence. In October, TLP lost its sole seat in parliament when a high court ruled that during the 2005 election campaign the legislator had defamed his CCM competitor and had thereby greatly influenced the result. The opposition camp remained generally weak and had to accept further *defections to CCM*, including several prominent politicians. Owing to the activities of their MPs, CHADEMA managed to become the strongest of the weak opposition parties on the mainland. On 10 May, four of the five *major opposition parties* (CHADEMA, CUF, NCCR-Mageuzi, TLP) signed an agreement to form a *coalition*. The alliance demanded the reform of the National Electoral Commission (NEC) as well as of Tanzania's constitution and declared it would boycott upcoming by-elections and the general election in 2010 unless their demands were met. This was the second attempt to form such a coalition since 2000, when the opposition parties had agreed to nominate a single joint presidential candidate. Based on the experience of 2000, when the coalition had quickly fragmented, it remained doubtful whether the main leaders of these four parties would really be willing to set aside their personal ambitions in the interests of a joint undertaking. On 21 December, *five smaller political parties* signed a similar political partnership agreement in the name of *Patriotic Front Parties* (PFP). None of those parties had, however, played a significant role in Tanzania's political arena. Owing to the prominence of its chairman, Reverend Christopher Mtikila, DP was the only one of the five that could claim some significance. The registrar of political parties, John Tendwa, announced in January that a *law allowing political parties to merge* was imminent, and he welcomed the idea of party amalgamation as a step towards strengthening the fragmented opposition.

On 18 March *by-elections* were held in Tunduru to fill the parliamentary seat that fell vacant upon the death of Minister Akukweti. Two NGOs urged government to comply with a high court judgment of May 2006 allowing *independent candidates* to stand for elections. Lewis Makame, chairman of the NEC, ruled, however, that no independent candidates would be allowed to contest the by-election since the electoral laws had not yet been amended in accordance with the court's verdict. DP chairman Mtikila filed a constitutional petition in the Dar es Salaam high court seeking an order barring the holding of the elections. The petition further demanded the *updating of the permanent voters' register* in order to include voters who had been under age during the last registration exercise in 2004 but were now eligible to vote. The court rejected the petition just two days before the election, stating that postponing the ballot would cause great harm to Tunduru's population and the nation at large. The CCM candidate won the by-election against four opposition contestants. The poll was conducted peacefully but marred by irregularities. The coalition of four opposition parties went to court in October demanding that the NEC update the permanent voters' register before *local government by-elections* were held in 16 wards later that month. After the court dismissed the application, the elections took place as scheduled. CCM emerged as winner in most of the rural constituencies, whereas the opposition parties were able to win in the urban areas. In mid-November, the NEC announced it would start updating the permanent national voters' register in January 2008. In the context of the appointment of Augustine Ramadhani as new chief justice in July, promises were made to significantly improve and speed up all judicial processes as an element of better public governance.

A special committee tasked with *collecting public views* on the intended fast-tracking of the EAC into a political *East African Federation* by 2013, commenced its work on 8 January. The committee, chaired by the distinguished economist Samuel Wangwe, was also charged with sensitising, informing and educating people on the intended federation. Strong opposition came from Zanzibar. Zanzibar, constantly seeking to extend its autonomy in the Tanzanian union, strongly feared being completely submerged in an East African federation. Many Zanzibari leaders preferred the idea of joining the envisaged federation as an independent state rather than as part of Tanzania. On 13 July, the Wangwe committee presented its findings. Some 65,000 Tanzanians from all 26 regions had been interviewed, 79.9% of whom had rejected the fast-track approach. On 20 August, the idea of fast-tracking the federation was abandoned by the presidents of the five EAC member states. The whole exercise had, nevertheless, contributed to open debate and a better understanding in Tanzania of the EAC.

Tanzanian authorities were determined to accelerate the *repatriation of refugees* to their home countries, although their numbers had already significantly decreased in recent years. Kikwete even raised the issue of repatriation of *Burundian refugees* in an address to the UN General Assembly at the end of September. More than

10,000 refugees without official status were deported to Burundi, prompting the Burundi government to protest against this action. UNHCR continued its repatriation programme. The number of camps was reduced from 11 to five and the refugee population within registered camps was reduced from 287,000 in December 2006 to about 200,000 by the end of the year. The total estimate of refugees from Burundi and the DR Congo was still 322,000 and 100,000 respectively. Rwandan officials protested at the *expulsion of about 60,000 Kinyarwanda-speaking* people from northwestern Tanzania to Rwanda since mid-2006. Tanzanian authorities insisted these were illegal immigrants who had refused to obtain residence permits or to become naturalised Tanzanians. Some of the expelled Rwandans claimed their property was illegally confiscated by Tanzanian residents and officials. Both countries formed a joint technical team to resolve the issue. The government insisted that it would close all refugee camps by the end of the 2007–08 fiscal year (the fiscal year ends on 30 June).

Foreign Affairs

Tanzania's good reputation and high international profile were reflected in the intensive travel schedule of Kikwete and members of his cabinet, as well as numerous international visits, conferences and workshops in Tanzania. In October, Kikwete was officially received by *Pope Benedict XVI*. The *frequent foreign trips* by government delegations were repeatedly criticised, even by CCM MPs. Government officials, however, justified these trips by noting they would bring more foreign investors to Tanzania. It was indeed notable that Kikwete used international relations as an instrument of investment policies.

Tanzania's two-year term as a non-permanent member of the *UN Security Council* ended on 31 December 2006. In August, Tanzania was selected as one of eight countries to test the *Delivering as One* pilot initiative of the UN family, intended to enhance cooperation among various UN agencies. Although Tanzania was generally praised as a political and economic success by *Western donors*, and relations remained excellent during the year, the government faced criticism over its handling of various corruption allegations. In several instances, Western envoys to Tanzania called on state authorities to respond to the allegations of grand *corruption and embezzlement* made by members of the opposition and in the media, particularly those against BoT. Foreign Minister Membe openly criticised the foreign diplomats and referred to the on-going investigations by the anti-corruption authority, while Kikwete repeatedly *complained that Western media* conveyed a much too negative image of Africa.

The government continued to play an active role in efforts to mediate violent conflicts on the continent. Chairing the SADC troika charged with solving *Zimbabwe*'s politico-economic crisis, Tanzania was deeply involved in numerous meetings and negotiations on this issue. Tanzania's director of intelligence held closed-door meetings with top Zimbabwean security officials in an attempt to revive an initiative led by former President Mkapa in response to a request by Mugabe to help establish dialogue between Zimbabwe and Britain. Kikwete strongly rejected European and US appeals to African leaders to take tougher steps against Mugabe and reacted outspokenly to Britain's threat to boycott the December EU-AU summit in Lisbon if Mugabe attended. In cooperation with South Africa, Tanzania continued its efforts to broker a lasting peace deal between the *Burundi* government and the one remaining rebel group, FNL ('Forces Nationales pour la Libération'). As the only African member of the international contact group on *Somalia*, Tanzania took part in several meetings of the group, one of which was held in Dar es Salaam on 9 February. A few days earlier, Tanzania had offered to train Somali government troops in the context of the AU mission to Somalia, but did not deploy any peacekeepers. Tanzania contributed 80 military police to the *UN interim force in Lebanon*. In August, all players involved in the peace process for Sudan's embattled *Darfur province* gathered for a crucial meeting in Dar es Salaam.

Apart from Zimbabwe, Tanzania sympathised with another state ostracised by Western countries. Concluding a ten-day tour to Egypt and *Iran* in late November, Vice President Ali Mohamed Shein indicated that Tanzania supported Iran's right to use nuclear power for peaceful purposes, as long as the technology was not used for the manufacture of weapons. Shein signed agreements with Iran on cooperation in agriculture, industry, science and technology and health training as well as on investments in joint ventures in the mining sector.

Regarding *regional cooperation*, Tanzania continued its long-standing double-track approach of maintaining close links with both the Eastern and Southern African sub-regions, most clearly exemplified in the parallel membership in EAC and SADC, despite growing pressures to choose between them in view of the formal requirements of the different economic integration schemes (see below). However, the government remained attached to the long tradition of Tanzania being a bridge between the two sub-regions. Even in respect of *military cooperation was* this the case. While participating fully in EAC military programmes, it played an active part in setting up the SADC brigade as the sub-regional component of the intended African Standby Force. The accession of *Burundi* and *Rwanda* as full members of the EAC on 1 July had particular significance for Tanzania, since both landlocked countries depended heavily on transit routes through Tanzania and were now expected to become even more closely integrated in the future.

Socioeconomic Developments

Compared to the previous year's slightly gloomy outlook, the *overall economic performance* and the prospects for the immediate future were generally considered to be highly satisfactory, at least on the basis of macroeconomic indicators. With favourable climatic conditions and an end to serious power shortages, most economic sectors showed a strong recovery. The estimated *GDP growth rate* (BoT figures) of 7.3% was slightly above the 7% target and well above the African average of 6.2%, with the final 2006 figure revised upwards to 6.7%. The average *inflation* rate for the year was contained with difficulty at 7%, considerably above the BoT target of 4.5%, with considerable monthly fluctuations, primarily due to changing food prices. The (preliminary) *trade deficit* widened further to an estimated $ 3,346 m, the result of a 26% surge in imports ($ 5,341 m), while exports only increased by 15% to $ 1,996 m. Thus only one-third of import costs were covered by export earnings. Oil products alone accounted for 30% of imports, and all capital goods for another 36%. Only 15.3% of all exports were traditional agricultural goods, while 43% were mineral products (mostly gold) and a respectable 15.5% manufactured goods. The structural *current account deficit* surged again to a new record (9.2% of GDP according to IMF, but probably higher), while foreign reserves grew by 33% to $ 3 bn by the end of December (6.8 months import coverage). The Tanzania Shilling (TSh) remained broadly stable against the US dollar until August and thereafter appreciated somewhat, but depreciated slightly against the euro over the year. Following the substantial debt cancellation obtained in 2006, the outstanding *external debt* was further reduced from $ 4.4 bn to $ 4.1 bn over the year due to further bilateral write-offs (particularly Japan in March), while multilateral debt had again increased slightly (accounting for 57% of the total). Eighty percent of debt was incurred by the central government and only 15.7% by the private sector. As a result of the write-offs, the debt service burden was very substantially reduced compared to the situation a few years earlier.

Despite all the recent macroeconomic achievements and positive acclamations from the international donor community, Tanzania remained one of the poorest countries in Africa and the world. In UNDP's latest *Human Development Index*, Tanzania was ranked slightly higher, in *position 159* (out of 177), near the top of the low human development category. The 2005 GDP per capita was only $ 316 and in PPP terms ($ 744) only three other countries had a lower average income.

On 14 June, Finance Minister Meghji introduced the *2007–08 budget* in parliament, providing an optimistic outlook for the government's budgetary operations based upon successful fiscal performance in the previous financial year. Only very minor changes to fiscal policies were felt to be necessary and were announced in the budget speech. The expenditure priorities were explained to be fully in line with CCM's 2005 election manifesto and the government's national strategy for growth and reduction of poverty (Swahili acronym: MKUKUTA), which had also been launched in 2005 as Tanzania's own second-generation PRSP.

In the 2006–07 *financial year*, the Tanzania revenue authority had once again greatly expanded its collection efforts, raising a total domestic revenue of TSh 2,739 bn (29% more than in 2005–06 and 11% above the budget provision). The national tax ratio had thus been substantially improved to 15.7% of GDP (above the target of 14.5%). Disbursed external grants of TSh 952 bn channelled through the budget, on the other hand, remained one-third lower than expected because of various delays in allocation. Total expenditures of TSh 4,475 bn were 6.5% below the budgeted figure, with recurrent expenditures practically on target, but investment expenditures were only 77% of the expected level. This situation demonstrated the continued problems government departments had in actually implementing intended programmes on time. Had there not been a need for emergency expenditures (drought and power problems), the under-performance of the government's spending capacity would have been even more visible. The overall budget deficit was estimated to be around 5% of GDP.

The *2007–08 budget* foresaw another hike (by 28%) of domestic revenue to TSh 3,502 bn and TSh 2,550 bn in foreign grants and loans (42% of expected total resources). Budgeted expenditures were set at TSh 6,067 bn, almost two-thirds being needed to meet recurrent expenditures. Of all development expenditures, 66% (TSh 2,201 bn) were expected to come from external sources. The target national tax ratio was given as 18.1% of GDP. Roughly one-third of foreign funds were expected in the form of general budget support and another 11% for sector basket funds, this apportionment being seen as proof of significantly increased trust by international donor institutions in the government's financial management. In conformity with MKUKUTA, over half of intended expenditures were to go to five priority areas (education, roads, health, agriculture, water). In October, the ministry of planning, economy and empowerment presented a comprehensive MKUKUTA implementation report for 2006–07. By the end of December, actual domestic revenue was slightly above target, whereas recurrent expenditures were 25% lower and investment expenditures 15% higher than budgeted. These were positive indications that the fiscal situation remained satisfactory.

Separate accounts for *Zanzibar* also showed improved performance by the *island economy*, with expected GDP growth of 6.6%, above the confirmed 2006 growth rate of 6.1%. Tourism, trade, agriculture and manufacturing did relatively well, coupled with further infrastructure improvements. Zanzibar's *external debt* of $ 106 m at year's end (71% with multilateral creditors), more than two-thirds of which was guaranteed by the Union government, continued as a check on more rapid economic growth. A new Zanzibar strategy for growth and poverty reduction (Swahili acronym: MKUZA) set ambitious goals for the 2007–10 period. Considerable efforts were also made to improve the government's fiscal performance.

In mid-February, the IMF completed the sixth and final review of the three-year PRGF that lapsed in December 2006, releasing a last tranche of $ 4.2 m and bringing total disbursements to a very modest $ 29.4 m (compared with the overall volume of aid flows). Since Tanzania no longer needed the IMF's financial assistance, a new three-year *Policy Support Instrument* (*PSI*) was arranged that expressed IMF's endorsement of the government's reform policies (focusing on improvement in the investment environment and the financial sector, raising domestic revenue and efficiency of public spending). In June and October, IMF missions visited Tanzania to review the PSI and expressed general satisfaction with the government's economic and financial policies. This testimonial by the IMF was invaluable in securing continued external support from a multitude of *bilateral and multilateral donors* and specifically in obtaining an increasing share of these funds in the form of budget support to complement the government's finance system (in contrast to the more usual donor-controlled specific projects). One sign of strong donor confidence was the US decision in October to award a $ 698 m package over five years under the *Millennium Challenge Corporation*.

Efforts to improve the business environment and to encourage more *private investment* were underscored by Kikwete during a second local investor round table in February in Dar es Salaam and during the sixth international investors' roundtable in mid-March in Arusha. On both occasions, promises were made to drastically reduce the bureaucratic hurdles and high fees that were deterring most investors. The latest *foreign direct investment* figures for 2006 showed a decline to $ 377 m, but were still the highest in the EAC. Almost all these investments were in large-scale mining ventures and raised questions about their limited spread effect on the national economy. The national investment ratio has gradually risen in recent years and was estimated to have reached 24% of GDP in 2007. A survey among members of the Confederation of Tanzania Industries (CTI) concluded that 60% considered the year to have been good or extremely good, while only 20% regarded 2007 as bad for their activities.

Kikwete's brainchild, the *Presidential Empowerment Fund*, popularly known as JK's billions, started its first phase in January with TSh 1 bn for each of the 21 mainland regions. The fund is managed by two banks with branch networks throughout the country. By May, over 20,000 small entrepreneurs had already benefited from this new scheme, intended to assist small economic ventures. The concepts of savings and credit cooperative societies and of providing micro-credits were also vigorously promoted throughout the year in an attempt to foster development. The national *minimum wage* was raised from November to TSh 150,000 (about $ 120) per month, despite warnings from CTI and the Tanzanian Chamber of Commerce, Industry and Agriculture (TCCIA) about serious job losses.

The cumbersome *privatisation* process for the last remaining parastatal corporations took one major step forward in October with a new beginning for the Tanzania Railways Corporation (TRC) under a 25-year lease with RITES of India. The intended sale of the National Insurance Corporation (NIC) was, however, still not concluded after years of negotiations, thus raising further doubts about government's commitment to privatisation to foreign buyers. While the 2006 electricity crisis had been largely overcome, there was considerable political hesitancy to approve the substantial tariff hikes demanded by the Tanzania Electric Supply Company (TANESCO) in its efforts to remain financially viable. TANESCO, in the largest ever corporate loan in East Africa, raised $ 240 m from a syndicate of local banks for its investment programme. No immediate remedies were at hand for solving the persistent port congestion problems, largely caused by the surge in imports.

In contrast to the drought in 2006, climatic conditions for *agriculture* were generally favourable and enabled good harvests for most crops. Some areas faced exceptionally heavy rains. By year's end the outlook for coffee and tea was very promising, but somewhat less so for cotton. Falling food prices had the effect of containing the inflation rate and in December the national strategic grain reserve reached a new record high of 142,000 tonnes. The *tourism* sector also performed fairly satisfactorily, with about 750,000 visitors and estimated revenue of $ 950 m.

Early in the year, Tanzania was the tenth country to start the elaborate self-assessment process under NEPAD's *APRM*, which was expected to culminate in a final external assessment in 2008. For this purpose, a national governing council and a secretariat were installed with an overwhelming majority of representatives being from NGOs or independent persons, without any attempt to keep the process under close government control.

Some sections of the business community with an interest in pursuing promising market opportunities continued to lobby for Tanzania to rejoin *COMESA*, but again the government took no decision. On 27 November, Tanzania joined its four EAC partner states in signing an interim *Economic Partnership Agreement (EPA)* with the EU, despite having initially participated in the EPA negotiations as part of the SADC group. However, no agreement was reached on a final EPA.

Tanzania in 2008

Most political attention was focused on various high-level cases of alleged corruption, leading to the unprecedented resignation of the prime minister and of several ministers. No solution was found to the long-simmering political confrontation in Zanzibar, and new strains emerged in the union between Tanzania's mainland and Zanzibar. Despite signs of the government's growing unpopularity, the control of *President Jakaya Kikwete* and his long-ruling 'Chama cha Mapinduzi' (CCM, Party of the Revolution) was never seriously in dispute. As AU chairman for most of the year, Kikwete assumed an active role in pan-African affairs. Macroeconomic performance continued to be fairly satisfactory, although the population enjoyed little direct improvement in its living standards.

Domestic Politics

Continuing efforts to fight *endemic corruption* were a major political issue throughout the year. In early February, the country was shocked by the surprising resignation of Prime Minister Edward Lowassa and two ministers in connection with serious corruption allegations arising from the scandal popularly known as the *'Richmond-Saga'*. Richmond, a reputedly US-based power supply company, had in 2006 been contracted during an energy crisis to deliver power generators, but failed to fulfil the contract. On 6 February, the report of a parliamentary commission, established in November 2007 and chaired by MP Harrison Mwakyembe, was presented to parliament. It stated that Richmond was registered neither in the US nor in Tanzania and appeared to have been a mere dummy company and that the whole bidding process had been marred by corruption and gross irregularities. Lowassa was openly accused of having personally selected Richmond among eight other bidders, and thus being responsible for what was called a "shameful act". He was called on to face the consequences. The report also accused East African Cooperation Minister Ibrahim Msabaha, who had been energy and minerals minister when the Richmond deal was made, and his successor, Nazir Karamagi, of having been directly involved in the dubious affair. Edward Hosea, director of the Prevention and Combat of Corruption Bureau (PCCB), was accused of covering up the deal by publishing a whitewash report on the issue. Mwakyembe's report also demanded the sacking of Attorney-General Johnson Mwanjika for failing to properly advise government on the various irregularities. The following day, Lowassa and the two ministers announced their resignations, but insisted on their innocence. Kikwete accepted the resignations and, as required by the constitution, *dissolved the cabinet*.

Since the prime minister's resignation was an unprecedented occurrence, Tanzania experienced its *severest government crisis* since the early 1980s. Public opinion, however, was positively disposed towards the resignations as a long awaited step forward in the effort to fight grand corruption instead of chasing only small fish. Kikwete was widely lauded for not having protected the prime minister, one of his closest political allies for many years. Not only were the resignations unprecedented, but also the frankness of the report and the fact that high-ranking persons had been named. This new approach was generally welcomed and favourably compared with the way in which allegations of grand corruption had been dealt with under Kikwete's predecessor Benjamin Mkapa. Suggestions of reintroducing some form of 'leadership code' (reminiscent of the Nyerere-era) and of more clearly separating the political and business arenas were, however, not followed up.

Some critics doubted whether Lowassa's resignation was indeed a victory for the rule of law over the personal interests of high-ranking politicians. Since Kikwete's and Lowassa's presidential campaigns in 2005 had reportedly been extremely costly, it was argued the Richmond deal may have been finalised to obtain funds to enable not only Lowassa but even the president himself to repay the financiers who had underwritten the campaigns. In this reading, Lowassa's resignation was the result of an agreement between both leaders and their friends to sacrifice one of them to allow the other to remain in office. This interpretation was fuelled by allegations made by another member of the Mwakyembe commission that Lowassa and Rostam Aziz were proprietors of the Richmond Company. Aziz, a businessman and influential MP, former CCM treasurer and close friend of Kikwete and Lowassa, had been the manager and a financier of Kikwete's presidential campaign. Whereas the general public understood Lowassa's resignation as a sign of Kikwete's commitment and strength, some analysts viewed it as a clear indication of the *weakened position of the president*, who was facing strong opposition from factions within CCM.

On 8 February, Kikwete nominated the little-known Minister of State for Regional Administration and Local Government *Mizengo Peter Pinda* as *new prime minister*. This surprising choice was widely welcomed in the media and 98.9% of parliamentarians voted Pinda into office. Pinda had been a long-serving civil servant and was known more as a quiet, hard-working technocrat than as a glamorous politician. On 13 February, the new cabinet was sworn in. The number of ministers was reduced from 29 to 26 and of deputy ministers from 31 to 21 (six ministries were merged into three). Since the dissolution of the previous cabinet had been required under the constitution and did not reflect a desire on the part of Kikwete to undertake a full-scale ministerial shake-up, the new cabinet strongly resembled its predecessor. Only four new ministers or deputy ministers were appointed and only eight ministers and seven deputy ministers were not reappointed, two of them stepping down voluntarily for reasons of age. A number of big names were, however, among those dropped, including Finance Minister Zakia Meghji, Industries and Trade Minister Basil Mramba, Public Safety and Security Minister Bakari Mwapachu and Livestock Development Minister Anthony Diallo. The president also used the opportunity to reshuffle portfolios and returned only four ministers to their previous positions. Of the new cabinet's members, a quarter were female compared to 30% in the previous cabinet. Although the president was praised for his seemingly strong moves against corrupt leaders, questions began to arise by the end of the year in the absence of legal action against the suspects accused of having caused enormous damage to the country. Moreover, none of the suspects lost their prestigious party positions in the CCM. The speed of cabinet reshuffle was partly owing to the upcoming *state visit of US President Bush* (16–19 February), who praised Kikwete for his strong commitment to tackling corruption.

Another major financial scandal involved the central bank, the *Bank of Tanzania (BoT)*. In early January, Kikwete announced he had sacked BoT governor Daudi Balali after external audits revealed the bank had in 2006 paid more than TSh 130 bn from its External Payment Arrears (EPA) account to several companies on the basis of faked documents. Balali's suspension as well as the appointment of Benno Ndulu, a respected economist and former BoT deputy governor, as new governor were widely welcomed. Balali reportedly died of leukaemia on 16 May in the US, where he had gone for medical treatment in late 2007. Public opinion and the media reacted impatiently when there were no signs of further action against the culprits and when Kikwete announced that those implicated in the scandal had until the end of October to repay the illegally obtained money. It was suspected that after returning the money, they would escape punishment. Kikwete's announcement later appeared to have been a trap to restore confidence among the main suspects and encourage repayment of the money stolen from the account (75% of which was recovered). In early November, about 25 top business people and senior BoT officials were arrested and taken to court.

The anti-corruption campaign came to the fore again in mid-April over *graft allegations* involving another *political heavy-weight*. Andrew Chenge, infrastructure development minister and former attorney-general, stepped down following a story in a British newspaper alleging that he had deposited $ 1 m into an account on Jersey. Chenge was under suspicion of having been involved in the shady procurement in 2001 of an expensive traffic control system from the British defence and aerospace company BAE *Systems*, which transaction the British serious fraud office was investigating. The main suspect, a Tanzanian businessman, had been granted immunity in the UK in return for cooperation in the investigations into the case. Chenge's resignation was followed by another cabinet reshuffle, albeit minor. In late November, *two former cabinet ministers*, Basil Mramba (finance) and Daniel Yona (minerals and energy) were charged with *abuse of office* and causing the loss of over TSh 11 bn to the government by agreeing to have a private company sign and execute gold production assaying agreements in contravention of the law and guaranteeing unjustified tax exemptions to the company. A few weeks later, Gray Mgonja, former permanent secretary in the finance ministry, was arrested on the same charge. Yona and Mramba had been senior ministers under Kikwete's predecessor Mkapa and close allies of the former president. During his presidency, Mkapa was criticised for sparing influential politicians from prosecution. It was unclear whether the unprecedented prosecution of senior CCM politicians was the beginning of a new era in the fight against grand corruption or just a move to weaken Mkapa's faction in the *major power struggles* within the party. The same uncertainty applied to the *allegations against Mkapa* himself, who was suspected by MPs and the media of involvement in several cases of corruption and misuse of power while in office. He was accused of having bought a coal mine (together with then Minerals and Energy Minister Yona) at a give-away price and of thereby using the government's indigenisation scheme for personal enrichment. Pinda declared in parliament that Mkapa was among the government leaders being investigated for abuse of office. It was, however, not clear whether Mkapa as former president enjoyed immunity from prosecution. Mkapa denied all the allegations, declaring that they were part of a campaign by people whom he hadn't favoured when he was in office.

Corruption allegations also led to a prominently reported conflict in September in CCM's *youth wing*, UVCCM, when its deputy chairman Nape Nnaye not only implicated the organisation's leadership, but also pointed to links with Lowassa. Nnaye's expulsion from CCM was only prevented through Kikwete's personal intervention. During its mid-December congress, UVCCM elected a new chairman from Zanzibar, who promised that the party youth would be in the forefront of the fight against corruption.

Media, parliament and opposition parties played an important role in the campaign against corruption and misuse of public office. These issues were discussed much more openly, aggressively and impatiently than in previous years. In addition to the abovementioned cases, a good number of serious corruption allegations were made against leading politicians and high-ranking civil servants. This development was described by many observers as a sign of growing political emancipation, but doubts remained as to whether corruption allegations were sometimes false and made for personal benefit or to discredit potential rivals as the selection process for candidates for the 2010 elections got under way. Also, citizens reacted less tolerantly towards allegedly corrupt public leaders. The already *high level of discontent* rose even further. In a number of cases, government members were booed or even faced stone-throwing when they appeared in public. Opinion polls revealed the unpopularity of the government and the state administration. A survey published in August by the well-regarded university project REDET (Research and Education for Democracy) concluded that although Kikwete was still more popular than the government, public confidence was at a very low level. According to the REDET poll, Kikwete was – halfway through his first presidential term – the *most unpopular president* in Tanzania's history. This situation was all the more remarkable since he had only three years earlier entered State House on a wave of public sympathy and with high expectations for his presidency. Kikwete responded positively, stating that he took the public grievances seriously and promising to improve the performance of his administration. The openness with which people were able to air their discontent as well as the positive manner in which the government responded were a good indication of significant improvements regarding freedom of opinion and of the press. According to analysts, the deep public frustration mainly arose from the lack of perceived progress in three major areas that the president had during his electoral campaign promised to tackle: first, the continuing disclosure of corruption and theft by public leaders and the impression that the president was being inactive in addressing the issue; second, the persisting poverty of the majority of people and increasing hardship for the middle-class due to steep price increases; and third, the inability to resolve the Zanzibar crises.

The long-standing *crisis in Zanzibar* was marked by two developments: continuing talks between the rival CCM and Civic United Front (CUF, the strongest opposition party) to find a political solution for the deadlock and new discussion of the character of the statehood of the semi-autonomous islands. The *'muafaka' talks* (from the Swahili word for 'agreement') between the ruling CCM and CUF finally met with apparent success on 17 March, when CUF Secretary General Seif Shariff Hamad publicly announced that agreement had been reached between the two negotiating teams that envisioned a *government of national unity*. Hamad's statement soon proved premature. During CCM's party congress held in late March in Butiama, the village where Tanzania's founding father Julius Nyerere was born, the party organs rejected immediate implementation of the agreement, arguing that a CCM-CUF coalition government was such an important step that the population of Zanzibar should decide by means of a *referendum*. There was general disappointment with this decision, even within CCM. There were doubts that the Zanzibar authorities would be able to organise a free and fair referendum since they had never managed to organise general elections that were free of rigging and manipulation. It appeared that a small clique around Zanzibar's President Amani Karume had blocked a solution supported by even a majority within CCM. The CUF leadership was disappointed but reasonable in its responses. Although some CUF leaders cautioned that prolonged deadlock would strengthen radical forces within the party, the leadership declared it would continue to favour peaceful means for achieving CUF's aims. Leading CUF members suggested the UN should come and not only supervise but also organise the next elections in 2010 to guarantee a free and fair voting process and prevent violence. Although CCM invited CUF to return to the negotiations, CUF stated there was no sense in doing so since the accord already agreed had been rejected by CCM party organs.

Apart from the problems this decision posed for Zanzibar, it also clearly indicated that *Kikwete's power as party chairman was constrained* by strong politicians and rival groupings within CCM. He was known to favour a coalition government in Zanzibar, but was obviously not in a position to convince the party to follow this course. The Zanzibar wing of CCM and Karume in particular were assumed to have blocked the approval of the power-sharing agreement. CUF, however, increased pressure on Kikwete by stating they still counted on him to carry through with the implementation of the agreed coalition government. In his mid-term speech to parliament on 21 August, Kikwete announced that Vice President Ali Mohamed Shein, originating from Pemba, would play a stronger role in finding a solution to the Zanzibar problem. Since Karume's two terms in office under the constitution would end in 2010, moderates in CCM might try to select a presidential candidate who would handle the political problems on the islands in a more collaborative way.

The need to break the longstanding deadlock was underscored in mid-May when elders from Pemba demanded the *separation of their island from Unguja* in a letter to the UN representative in Tanzania. The seven initiators of the letter, said to be CUF members, were arrested on charges of treason. It appeared that the demand for separation was to draw public attention to the perceived marginalisation of Pemba Island by Zanzibari authorities. It seemed unlikely that the arrests were in any way helpful and they may have been another overreaction by the police. The 'Legal and Human Rights Centre', a reputable NGO, stated that the arrests had violated the right of freedom of expression guaranteed by the Tanzanian constitution.

In early July, a heated *debate on the character of Zanzibar's statehood* erupted. It was provoked by Pinda, who stated in the union parliament that Zanzibar was not a state (*nchi* in Swahili) and thus could not join the OIC. Reactions from Zanzibar were harsh. Some Zanzibari leaders within both CCM and the opposition insisted that Zanzibar was a genuine state, albeit within the union. Much of the debate stemmed from different understandings of the meaning of statehood, but the debate also exposed deep-rooted differences in the concepts of the union as well as the prevailing mistrust between both its parts. The debate continued for some weeks and Kikwete was called on to intervene. He initially declined the request on the grounds that such essential discussions should be allowed in a democratic society, but finally ended the debate by stating that Zanzibar had ceased to be a sovereign state with the creation of the United Republic of Tanzania in 1964. Demands by Zanzibar to be allowed to join the OIC were again rebuffed. Foreign Minister Bernard Membe, however, promised that the union government would examine the possibility of Tanzania's joining the OIC. This option had, however, been promised for over 15 years with no action being taken. On 24 October, the Christian Council of Tanzania called for Membe's resignation for allegedly violating the country's secular constitution by considering membership in a faith-based international organisation.

Despite the major internal conflicts within CCM and the high level of public frustration, the *opposition was unable to benefit significantly* from the situation. CUF focused its attention almost exclusively on developments in Zanzibar, while the other smaller opposition parties watched the developments apprehensively, fearing that close cooperation between CCM and CUF would further marginalise them. CHADEMA (Party for Democracy and Progress) had spearheaded the anti-corruption crusade in 2007. However, after the government and particularly Kikwete took the leading role, it became difficult for CHADEMA to maintain its image as the brave and honest David fighting Goliath in the form of the corrupt ruling party. CHADEMA mourned the loss of Chacha Wangwe, MP for Tarime and the party's vice chairman, who died in a car accident on 28 July. Members of his family and residents of his home region doubted the official version and rumours spread that he was the victim of political assassination. The tensions abated when his family confirmed the official version following an independent investigation. The *by-election* on 12 October to fill his seat was extremely fiercely fought by the main contenders from CCM and CHADEMA. *Violent clashes* between supporters of both parties and also involving security forces prompted observers to fear the worst for polling day. However, the day itself passed peacefully, presumably due to a strong police presence. CHADEMA won and CCM immediately accepted unconditional defeat. Although much of the violence resulted from poor and politically one-sided 'escalation management' by local security forces, the Tarime by-election suggested that Tanzania's record of peaceful elections could be jeopardised during the next elections in 2010.

The director and a leading journalist of '*MwanaHalisi*', a weekly newspaper known for strongly denouncing corrupt practices, were victims of a violent attack in early January. State authorities were praised by media organisations for condemning the assault and commencing immediate investigations. Five people were arrested. On 13 October, 'MwanaHalisi' was *banned for three months* after publishing a story about an alleged plot to oust the president allegedly spearheaded by certain senior CCM leaders and Kikwete's own son. The ban was strongly criticised by Western embassies and by media organisations and newspaper editors.

An increase in *killings of albinos* gave rise to negative international publicity for Tanzania. The belief that using body parts of albinistic people in rituals or potions would enhance the user's prosperity resulted in numerous killings of albinos or the hacking off of parts of their bodies. Most of these crimes were committed in regions bordering Lake Victoria where superstition was prevalent and 'witch-hunts' and the killing of elderly people had been reported for years. Numerous suspects were arrested and the president announced efforts to register and control traditional healers, who were thought to be the driving force behind the phenomenon. As a symbolic gesture, Kikwete appointed a woman from Zanzibar as the first albino MP.

The voluntary repatriation of *refugees* continued and almost 100,000 refugees from Burundi (who had come in the 1990s) returned home. Thus, the overall number of refugees was reduced to about 46,000 Burundians and 80,000 Congolese. In a separate repatriation exercise, launched in March, another 30,000 people returned from among the earlier wave of over 200,000 Burundians who had arrived in 1972. Tanzania offered full local integration, including naturalisation and citizenship, to those long-term Burundian refugees who wished to remain in the country. In 2008, 165,000 refugees submitted their citizenship applications.

Foreign Affairs

Excellent relations were maintained with all major international players. Kikwete's energetic response to corruption allegations pleased *Western donors* who had become increasingly impatient with the slow pace of cracking down on this problem. There were only minor instances of criticism by Western donors of the government, such as when it banned 'MwanaHalisi'. Tanzania's good reputation and growing international prestige earned some appreciation: on 31 January Kikwete was elected *AU chairman* for a one-year-term, and in early February Tanzania was one of five African states visited by US *President Bush*, who spent four out of six days (16–19 February) in Tanzania and signed the Millennium Challenge Corporation compact, a grant worth $ 698 m over five years. In early June, the 8th Leo Sullivan Conference for African-Americans interested in African business ventures was held in Arusha and attracted 4,000 participants. On 13 April, Tanzania was the first sub-Saharan African country to become part of the *Olympic torch relay route*, an obvious recognition of the friendly Tanzanian-Chinese relations dating back to the 1960s.

As in previous years, Tanzania played an active role in the *management of violent political conflicts* in Africa. The post-election violence in neighbouring *Kenya* early in the year was viewed with great concern, but the inflow of refugees from Kenya was unexpectedly low. The government declared itself neutral and refrained from acknowledging either of the two Kenyan rivals. A coalition of four opposition parties planned to hold a demonstration in Dar es Salaam on 5 January in support of Raila Odinga, but was banned from doing so by the police. In mid-January, ex-President Mkapa joined Kofi Annan's team of African mediators to find a solution to the Kenyan deadlock. On 28 February, Kikwete also became involved as AU chairman and contributed to the two parties' acceptance of a power-sharing arrangement. Although Kikwete earned international respect, the local press challenged him to not only resolve foreign conflicts but also to make the same effort to resolve the difficulties with Zanzibar.

Tanzania took the lead in the *AU-mandated invasion of Anjouan Island* in the *Comoros* on 25 March and contributed almost half of about 1,500 soldiers. The invasion was backed by the US and France and generally understood to be a legitimate move. There was no major national or international opposition to the invasion except from South Africa's President Mbeki, who tried to halt the invasion in a last-minute appeal to the AU. Tanzania and South Africa also followed different approaches in regard to *Zimbabwe*. While Mbeki, SADC's mediator, was extremely reluctant to criticise Zimbabwean

President Mugabe, Kikwete was one of the first African presidents to change his position and sharply condemned Mugabe. On 21 April, more than 100 African bar associations, human rights groups and other independent organisations met in Dar es Salaam and demanded that the AU become involved in Zimbabwe's crisis, saying that SADC was not doing enough. In contrast to the strong condemnation of Mugabe, Tanzania rejected ICC efforts to indict *Sudan's President al-Bashir* for genocide. The threatened indictment was viewed as untimely and as complicating efforts to implement a peace accord.

Tanzania continued its somewhat hesitant approach to EAC integration. During the third round of negotiations on the EAC common market protocol in Bujumbura in October, Tanzania finally appeared to be willing to lift restrictions on the right of residency for nationals of EAC member countries. This step would remove the need for work permits, a major hindrance to the free movement of labour within EAC. Tanzania, however, maintained its hard line on provisions in the draft protocol allowing nationals of other partner states to acquire land, stating that it was still too early to fully open its lands to other East Africans. Tanzania's clear reluctance on these issues antagonised the other four member states.

Socioeconomic Developments

Judged on the basis of most macroeconomic indicators, the economy continued to perform relatively well, as it had since the beginning of the decade, and this was positively acknowledged by the multitude of international donors active in the country. *GDP growth* was robust at 7.5% (7.1% in 2007), helped by favourable weather conditions and particularly good results in manufacturing, trade, construction and mining. The global financial and economic crisis did not have much of an impact, but projections for 2009 envisaged a limited slowdown. *Inflation* accelerated markedly, with an average of 10.3%

for the year and a peak of 13.5% in December, while the food price index surged to 18.6% by year's end. The agricultural sector grew by only 4.8%, and towards the end of the year some northern parts of the country experienced food shortages and threats of partial famine, but the national food reserve was sufficient to handle the situation. The *exchange rate* experienced normal fluctuations throughout the year, but on balance remained quite stable. The (preliminary) *trade deficit* widened further with imports growing substantially by 32% to $ 2,608 m and exports slightly less (by 29%) to $ 6,328 m. Thus, only about 40% of Tanzania's import bill was covered by exports. Apart from gold (benefiting from high prices), there was a sharp rise in exports of manufactured goods (mainly to African markets), which had become more valuable than the traditional range of agricultural exports. The (provisional) current account deficit of about $ 2.8 bn (equivalent to 14.2% of GDP) was a new record, but in the overall balance of payments was largely offset by inflows of foreign direct investment and aid. Gross *foreign reserves* decreased only slightly to $ 2.7 bn by the end of September, equivalent to 4.4 months of import coverage. While the *external debt* had in previous years, through debt cancellations, been substantially reduced, standing at $ 4.4 bn at the end of 2007, it surged again to $ 5.4 bn at year's end.

Despite almost a decade of fairly solid GDP growth, the reduction of the conspicuous *poverty* in the country was disappointingly modest. This became very evident in December with the release of the results of a new national household budget survey undertaken in 2007. The proportion of the population living below the national poverty line had only dropped from 35.7% in 2001 to 33.3%. Economic decision-makers were shocked that the effect of overall GDP growth on poverty reduction had been so marginal. The distribution of economic benefits had obviously remained highly uneven, with the lower strata of the population and most inhabitants of rural areas experiencing no improvement in their living conditions. The urban-rural gap was widening. It was evident that

Tanzania would not be able to achieve the MDGs by 2015. Despite all the macroeconomic successes and positive acclaim by the international donor community, Tanzania remained one of the poorest countries in Africa. In UNDP's 2007–08 Human Development Index, Tanzania was ranked 159 (out of 177), near the top of the low human development category. The 2005 GDP per capita was only $ 316 and in PPP terms ($ 744) only three other countries had a lower average income.

Despite these shortcomings, Tanzania continued to be regarded by practically all international aid agencies as among the most successful and consistent reform-oriented countries and to be fully supported with aid resources. *IMF* missions in February–March and in September undertook reviews of the *Policy Support Instrument* (*PSI*) that had been in effect since February 2007 as a new form of monitoring government's financial and economic policies aimed at sustaining broad-based growth and accelerating poverty reduction. The IMF's generally positive assessment of the policies pursued was a key element in maintaining the confidence of all 35 members of the Tanzania Development Partners Group. In both reviews, the IMF affirmed that the mutually agreed financial and other core targets (especially tax and customs administration reforms; local government, legal sector and public sector reforms) had by and large been met and that the PSI programmes were broadly on track. At the end of a visit on 29 February, the IMF managing director, Dominique Strauss-Kahn, also expressed himself very satisfied with Tanzania's strong macroeconomic performance and structural reforms and pledged continued full support. The government in a letter of intent to the IMF on 3 December reiterated its adherence to the agreed reform goals. The World Bank on 21 October approved its sixth PRSC for Tanzania to the value of $ 160 m.

Finance Minister Mustafa Mkulo on 12 June introduced the new *budget* in parliament, providing a confident outlook for the government's budgetary operations based on the successful fiscal performance of the previous financial year. Only minor changes to fiscal policies were announced in the budget speech. Preliminary assessment of budget performance for 2007–08 showed that consolidated targets in regard to revenue collection and expenditures had been very nearly met, thus indicating further improvement over previous years, particularly in respect of the government's capacity to implement planned projects. The strategy of decentralisation by devolution had been gradually extended and by and large brought positive results.

The *budget* for financial year *2008–09* foresaw an ambitious rise in expenditures of 19% to TSh 7.2 trn (about $ 6.1 bn). In accordance with the National Development Vision 2025 and the National Strategy for Growth and Reduction of Poverty (Swahili acronym: MKUKUTA), Tanzania's version of a second-generation PRSP, the six main priority areas (education, roads, health, agriculture, water, energy) were allocated 64% of the total budget. The overall thrust was positively received by the general public and the budget was acclaimed as a 'people's budget', although some critics felt that too little attention was still being given to the agricultural sector. Of the envisaged budget, 66% was expected to be raised from domestic sources, based on an enhanced tax ratio target of 18.5% of GDP (compared to 16.7% in 2007–08). All recurrent expenditures were to be entirely funded from domestic revenues, without recourse to domestic borrowing. Despite continuing efforts to substantially raise domestic revenue collection, it was clear that most development expenditures in the budget were still dependent on external funding. The share of foreign funding for the budget was expected to decline to 34% (compared to 42% in 2007–08). Most donor activities were more closely coordinated than in the past in the context of the Joint Assistance Strategy for Tanzania (JAST) established with the government in 2006. Almost 40% of all external aid was expected to be provided as general budget support, i.e., no longer in traditional project or programme form.

The Parastatal Sector Reform Commission (*PSRC*) that had since 1992 been in charge of *privatisation* of the roughly 400 state-owned enterprises or institutions was wound up in December 2007. Responsibility for finalising outstanding divestitures until 2011 was given to a reconstituted Consolidated Holding Corporation (CHC), but during its first year little further progress was made and only TSh 1.9 bn was collected from sales. The highly unsatisfactory performance of several semi-public corporations responsible for essential infrastructural services (ports, railways, airways, power) continued to create political problems and generate public anger. The management of Tanzania Railways (TRL) had only in 2007 been granted under a 25-year concession to RITES of India. Air Tanzania was still in deep trouble and in need of a new structure after the earlier 49% participation by South African Airways was reversed in 2007. Dar es Salaam's port management deteriorated considerably and became a burden on many economic sectors. The same was true of the Tanzania Electric Supply Company (TANESCO), which was still unable to guarantee a reliable power supply, although some improvements and expansion projects were under way. In April, an unusually heated debate erupted in parliament over the rationale for partial privatisation of TANESCO. Zanzibar was for months without regular electricity after the power cable from the mainland was damaged. Several months of controversy over petrol prices culminated in December, when government decreed a price limit after petrol companies refused to pass lower world market prices on to consumers. This led to the temporary unavailability of petrol on the market.

Effective 1 January, government raised the *minimum wage* significantly to TSh 150,000 (about $ 120) per month in the private sector and TSh 120,000 in the public sector. Following protests by employers, a compromise, immediately implemented by some, was negotiated that allowed private companies to lower the minimum wage under certain circumstances to TSh 80,000. This resulted in *strikes* in various sectors, such as transport services and the textile industry. In the public sector, a growing number expressed dismay at the economic hardships resulting from rising inflation and began to protest, particularly at the six-month delay in the higher wages promised in January. While most trade unions were too weak and ineffectual to mount mass action, the powerful Tanzania Teachers Union (TTU) with over 150,000 members was different. A general strike by teachers on 15 October was called off at the last moment due to government intervention, but the threat was at least successful in securing outstanding wages, but not further wage increases. University students also went on strike in November to protest the cost-sharing burden and insufficiency of bursaries, but the authorities did not budge and suspended the students for the remainder of the year.

Conflicts in the *mining sector* between small artisanal miners and large international mining companies continued to be sensitive but remained low-intensity. The presidential mining contracts review committee, chaired by a former attorney-general, Mark Bomani, submitted its report to parliament in early July. The committee suggested a number of measures to allow government to obtain a greater share of the benefits from the mining sector. Contracts between previous Tanzanian governments and mining companies had been widely criticised for strongly favouring companies to the detriment of the interests of the state, small-scale miners and communities living in the mining areas.

Tanzania in 2009

In a year without major political changes or excitement, political discussions mainly centred on several allegations of high-level corruption, ever clearer signs of deepening rifts between quarrelling factions of the ruling party CCM, and the continuing confrontation between the two leading parties, CCM and CUF, in semi-autonomous Zanzibar. The overwhelming dominance of CCM was not in serious jeopardy, while internal cracks were partly a forerunner of infighting for a rearrangement of power positions in the election year 2010. Local government elections were convincingly won by CCM, while all opposition parties remained relatively weak as opponents of the long-dominant governmental forces. Despite some reluctance, Tanzania finally accepted the next step in deepening the EAC into a common market. The economy remained surprisingly resilient to the negative effects of the global economic recession, but some fall in the growth trend of recent years was unavoidable. International financial institutions continued to support the government's economic policies, while the majority of the population became increasingly dissatisfied with not seeing any direct tangible improvements.

Domestic Politics

One year before the next general elections, the *ruling party 'Chama cha Mapinduzi'* (CCM/Revolutionary Party) maintained its dominant position despite severe internal rifts and the first signs of infighting about the nomination of candidates. Support for opposition parties, namely 'Chama cha Demokrasia na Maendeleo' (CHADEMA/Party of Democracy and Progress), increased slightly but without posing a serious threat to CCM's political dominance. Several opinion polls conducted throughout the year indicated a still significant but decreasing and by no means compelling degree of sympathy for *President Jakaya Kikwete*, and massive dissatisfaction with the performance of his government and the CCM. Public discontent resulted mainly from a perception of continuous and increasing hardship for the majority of Tanzanians while a small minority among the elite were seen to be benefiting excessively from government policies, mostly through corrupt practices, and – despite all the official anti-corruption rhetoric – without being prosecuted.

The campaign against *corruption* remained one of the hot issues. Numerous cases involving accusations against high-ranking politicians and civil servants had been revealed in previous years, but hardly any visible measures had been taken against the alleged culprits. Former prime minister Edward Lowassa, who had to resign in February 2008 in the wake of corruption allegations, creating the severest government crisis in more than 25 years, was never legally taken to task and also retained his powerful position on the CCM Central Committee. Two other former ministers, who had allegedly been involved in the same scandal – known as 'the Richmond-Saga' – and had stepped down with Lowassa, also got off scot-free. During the parliamentary budget session (June/July), Deputy Minister for Energy and Minerals Adam Malima submitted a government report that cleared three senior civil servants (former attorney general Johnson Mwanyika, former permanent secretary in the Ministry of Energy and Minerals Arthur Mwakapugi, and Director-General of the Prevention and Combating of Corruption Bureau Edward Hosea) of any wrongdoing in the scandal. Parliament firmly rejected the report and demanded clear answers to the outstanding questions, which, however, had not been provided before end-2009. Shortly after the parliamentary debate, the state house issued a detailed response to rumours that Kikwete had been directly involved in the scandal. The statement elaborated four areas in which the president had played a role in the deal, but rejected any involvement in corrupt practices.

In July, the government cleared *former president Benjamin Mkapa* of any accusation of misuse of political power regarding his purchase of Kiwira coal mine at the end of his presidency in 2005. The mine had been sold at a give-away price to a company co-owned by Mkapa, then energy and minerals minister Daniel Yona and some of their closest family members. In June, the Energy and Minerals Ministry announced it had taken over the mine, but a heated dispute emerged between the ministry and a parliamentary committee of enquiry about whether the owners would be required to refund to the government about TSh 17 bn, disbursed to the company for investing in the mine. The ministry, on the contrary, announced that it would have to reimburse the company for its investments.

Accused of corruption in another case, Yona had been arrested in November 2008, together with former finance minister Basil Mramba and former finance permanent secretary Grey Mgonja, over charges of abuse of office and having caused the loss of over TSh 11 bn to the government. The full hearing of the case started in September, when both ex-ministers accepted the allegations. Public opinion remained sceptical about the seriousness of *anti-corruption efforts* and visible actions such as prosecution of culprits were expected. It was feared that prominent politicians and civil servants in particular would be spared prosecution. In early September, Kikwete explained in an unprecedented question-and-answer-session with the general public on TV and radio that 578 corruption cases were currently in the courts, compared with 58 when he came to office, although he acknowledged that there were delays in prosecution due to the heavy caseload and a shortage of judges and magistrates. According to TI's 2009 Corruption Perception Index, Tanzania performed better than most other EAC member states (apart from Rwanda), but nevertheless dropped 24 places as compared with 2008 to rank 126 out of 180.

The fight against corruption also revealed *deep rifts within the CCM*. Rumours of factions and a probable split in the party had been discussed for years, especially prior to elections, but the party had always been able to reconcile these tensions internally. Together with the media, *parliament* had become the driving force in the fight against corruption. A group of CCM MPs constantly used parliament as a forum to criticise corruption in the government and in their own party and to demand that more vigorous measures be taken against the accused. This had apparently caused a defensive reaction among some other parliamentarians, who appealed to parliament speaker Samwel Sitta to discipline the critics. However, the speaker, known for his strong anti-corruption stance, allowed the outspoken MPs to continue. During a CCM National Executive Committee (NEC) meeting in mid-August, some CCM MPs tried to unseat Sitta, claiming that his way of dealing with the corruption allegations would harm the party. The attempt failed but unveiled a deep internal rift in the party. Immediately, an *ad-hoc committee of 'three wise men'* was set up, comprising former president Ali Hassan Mwinyi, former speaker of the East African Legislative Assembly Abdulrahman Kinana and ex-parliamentary speaker Pius Msekwa. The team was tasked with reconciling the conflicting groups and looking into ways that CCM parliamentarians could air their views and grievances without harming the party, but fears were expressed that the committee had only been established to discipline and silence the critics.

The deliberations conducted by the 'three wise men' revealed that the *conflict* was between a *reformist group*, including Sitta, Harrison Mwakyembe (chairman of the parliamentary committee on the Richmond Affair in 2007/08 that had forced Lowassa to resign) and some other MPs on the one hand, and a *group of influential politicians facing corruption allegations* on the other. The core of this group seemed to comprise Lowassa, former CCM treasurer Rostam Aziz, who was suspected of having played a major role in the Richmond Affair, former attorney-general and minister Andrew Chenge, who had to step down in 2008 following corruption allegations, and CCM Secretary General Yusuf Makamba. They were accused of trying to gain control of the party and sideline the reformers, who had attracted much public sympathy for their crusade against corruption. Despite the efforts of the 'three wise men' and CCM's long-standing experience of reconciling internal rifts, this conflict posed a severe *threat to the unity of the party* and its ability to continue to rule the country almost unchallenged. It appeared unlikely that a split would occur before the next elections in 2010, but it was nevertheless an indicator of the internal power struggles taking place in the run-up to the usually fiercely contested nomination processes for the party's parliamentary candidates, and thus the composition of the next CCM parliamentary faction. President and CCM chairman Kikwete remained remarkably silent in this important dispute. Observers argued that his position in the CCM was apparently too weak to enable him emphatically to support the reformers and intervene in the struggle between the factions battling for control of the party.

Despite this intense infighting in the ruling party, the *opposition* was hardly able to capitalise on the situation. *CHADEMA*, the main opposition party on the mainland, was also mired in a leadership conflict, indicating the existence of rival factions in the party. In late August, deputy Secretary General Zitto Kabwe, an aspiring and very popular young MP, announced that he wanted to challenge party chairman Freeman Mbowe in the party's forthcoming leadership elections. This came as a surprise, since Mbowe (chairman since 2000) had been generally credited with CHADEMA's growing importance over the previous few years. Mbowe welcomed Kabwe's candidacy as a sign of the party's political maturity, but party elders persuaded Kabwe to abstain from challenging the incumbent in order to maintain the unity of the party. Kabwe was reminded that, at 32, he was still very young and had ample time for a political career. Mbowe was re-elected unopposed with 93% of the votes. Kabwe had explained his move as arising out of a desire to strengthen the party in order to prepare it to play a leading role in the country. Despite the 'cease-fire' between the rival leaders, elections to the youth wing and elders' committees showed that their supporters were still divided. Allegations of bribery were made, Secretary

General Wilbroad Slaa announced the suspension of the elections, and the national anti-corruption agency PCCB was called in to investigate. Apart from partisan support for either Mbowe or Kabwe, the conflict was mainly between a more conservative wing on the Mbowe side and a rather leftist wing on Kabwe's side. Furthermore, the latter attracted younger party members, while Mbowe's powerbase were the well-established networks of party elders and business people, mostly from Kilimanjaro Region. On 25 February, party elections in the *Civic United Front (CUF)*, the strongest opposition party in Zanzibar, went smoothly. The two leading politicians, chairman Ibrahim Lipumba and Secretary General Seif Sharif Hamad were easily re-elected.

Several parliamentary *by-elections* were seen as a litmus test for the general election in 2010; elections in Mbeya Rural, Busanda (Mwanza Region) and Biharamulo-West (Kagera Region) on the mainland and in Magogoni in Zanzibar were all won by CCM. The Mbeya elections on 25 January were overshadowed by the disqualification of the CHADEMA candidate on formal grounds; voter turnout was extremely low at 35% and the CCM candidate won by 73%. Campaigns for the elections in Busanda (24 May) and Biharamulo-West (5 July) were tense, with some violent incidents. No major incidents occurred on polling days, but voter turnout was again very low (36% and 41%, respectively). CCM was able to win the polls against CHADEMA, its main rival – albeit by slim margins. While CHADEMA accepted defeat in Busanda, they complained about irregularities in Biharamulo, but refrained from filing a petition with the electoral commission, stating that the general elections were to be held in slightly more than one year anyway. The peacefully conducted and well organised by-election to the Zanzibar parliament in Magogoni constituency on Unguja Island (23 May) was won by the CCM candidate as expected.

In September, political parties began preparations for the *local government elections* held on 25 October. Voter registration took place from 4 to 10 October and candidates were allowed to campaign between 15 and 24 October. As in the by-elections, voter registration and turnout was very low. Various problems occurred during selection of candidates, voter registration and the voting process. Voters had to write the names of their preferred candidates on the ballot, a tiresome procedure which also allowed party agents to manipulate voting by 'assisting' voters who could not read or write. Although the government had increased the funds for the elections from TSh 1.4 bn in 2004 to TSh 13 bn, the electoral process was unsatisfactorily managed. Instances of bribery and manipulation and a few minor violent incidents were reported. In some cases, campaigns were dominated by incumbent MPs or individuals who wanted to stand for a parliamentary seat in the 2010 general election. CCM was the only party with a nationwide presence and easily won the poll by securing 93.9% of the votes. Only CUF (2.9%) and CHADEMA (2.3%) were able to win a somewhat significant number of seats; other parties got less than 1%. Despite this landslide victory, CCM had to accept a small loss in comparison with the 2004 elections, when it received 96% of votes.

A civic-education booklet by the *Catholic Church*, which was distributed to all Catholic parishes in May, caused a great controversy. The booklet was part of the church's comprehensive civic education project to raise citizens' awareness about the general election and the importance of identifying and electing committed leaders who were not corrupt. The church used the project and the booklet to criticise the growing gap between rich and poor and advocate a change of policies. The booklet caused outrage and numerous critics with various standpoints accused the church of influencing people to vote for the church's preferred leaders and of creating disunity in the country, as well as hostility between religious groups. The church entirely rejected these accusations and its booklet also received warm support from a number of popular politicians. A few weeks later, the *Council of Imams* ('Shura ya maimamu') launched its own booklet of guidelines in response. It called upon believers to elect candidates who loved Islam and would end the alleged suppression of Muslims in Tanzania. However, the Muslim Council of Tanzania (Bakwata), regarded as the official Muslim representative organisation, distanced itself from the text, stating that no religious body should produce such a political document.

In April, remarks by Zanzibar's Minister for Water, Works, Energy and Land, Mansoor Himid, brought *tensions between Zanzibar and the mainland* back to the surface. In a speech before the Zanzibar House of Representatives, he declared that his government would seek to remove the clause on oil and natural gas from the list of issues falling under the jurisdiction of the Union government. A British consulting company had been assigned by the Union government to ascertain how best to deal with potential oil revenues, if oil were found in Zanzibar waters. The company suggested sharing the potential incomes, but Zanzibar's government and parliament rejected the recommendation and insisted that all revenues from any oil found in Zanzibar would not be shared by any means. Representatives of the Union government gave a relatively relaxed reaction, probably owing to the fact that, despite more than 55 years of exploration, no oil had yet been found, and stated that any Zanzibari wishes could be discussed. These remarks should probably be understood in the context of the 2010 elections, in which the Zanzibar wing of CCM will have to compete not only with strong opposition from CUF, but also with internal divisions about who would have the final say in choosing the next presidential candidate for the islands, since the incumbent Amani Karume was constitutionally barred from standing again.

The highly sensitive issue of *voter registration* in *Zanzibar* led to chaos and violence. In February, the Zanzibar Electoral Commission (ZEC) announced that it would only accept Zanzibar ID cards as proof of identity for the registration process, although other official documents had been accepted for registration purposes in the past. The main opposition party, CUF, protested against this regulation, saying that many Zanzibaris did not hold ID cards and would be denied them by the local authorities because of their political affiliation. CUF alleged that CCM intended to use this as a means of reducing the number of people voting for the opposition in order to redesign constituencies in CCM's favour. CUF also suspected the government of planning to issue Zanzibar ID cards to their supporters on the mainland, with a view to shipping them to the islands in great numbers on election day. Registration started on 6 July on Pemba Island, the CUF stronghold, and was expected to conclude there on 14 December. Registration on the larger Unguja Island was meant to begin in September. Refusals to register numerous voters soon led to *violence* on Pemba. The media reported the planting of landmines, and some exploded, albeit without causing injury. Houses and offices were torched. Police opened fire and, on 3 August, injured two CUF protesters. On 7 August, the ZEC finally reacted by suspending the registration process. In a joint statement, the representatives of the major donor countries expressed serious concern about these developments and the obstacles Tanzanians on Pemba were facing to obtain Zanzibar ID cards, the principle means of registration. However, the ZEC resumed the registration process on Pemba on 12 September and started on Unguja the same day. Turnout on Pemba was very low and violent incidents were reported from Pemba as well as from a few areas on Unguja.

Amidst this highly charged atmosphere of conflict between the two rival parties, it came as a major surprise when it was revealed on 5 November that *CUF Secretary General Seif Shariff Hamad* and *Zanzibar President Amani Karume* had met behind closed doors. It was the first meeting between the two leading politicians since the controversial 2005 elections, when CUF had refused to recognise Karume as president. Both politicians said that they had agreed to *end the hostilities* between their parties and to cooperate in future for the benefit of the people of Zanzibar. However, it remained unclear what practical consequences this meeting might have with regard to the outstanding problem of voter registration and the likelihood of the establishment of a government of national unity. While Karume indicated that he did not rule out the idea of a CCM-CUF coalition government, two influential Zanzibar ministers spoke clearly against this option. This indicated that Karume's move was not supported by the whole of Zanzibar CCM, which was divided into at least two rival factions, namely the Karume camp and supporters of former Zanzibar chief minister Mohamed Bilal, who was among those tipped to succeed Karume in 2010. CUF followers also responded ambivalently to the agreement. In a number of gatherings immediately after his meeting with Karume, Hamad was booed and even called a traitor. The CUF leadership had, after all, long portrayed CCM and Karume much more as enemies than simply as rivals, and all the agreements that had previously been reached between the two parties had ultimately been blocked by CCM. These experiences had caused deep frustration among CUF supporters and their willingness to trust in new agreements was therefore very limited. Nevertheless, the temperature cooled significantly after CUF leaders had toured the islands and explained to their supporters their new policies regarding the government. Although the international community, as well as the Union government, praised the two leaders for their agreement, both insisted that there had been no involvement by anyone from outside Zanzibar. CUF even called upon the mainland CCM to stay out of the reconciliation process.

As in previous years, several violent clashes occurred in various parts of the country, in most cases caused by *land conflicts* between pastoralists and farmers. Clashes caused the deaths of several people and left many injured, and property including houses and farms was destroyed. Pastoralists were also in conflict with government authorities, whom they accused of violating their rights, complaining of detentions, expulsion from their land and the forced sale of their cattle. Land conflicts also arose between villagers and commercial investors. In June, hundreds of villagers invaded the land of a MP in Arusha Region, who had intended to establish a hotel there. They destroyed his property and blocked roads to prevent security forces from intervening. Six hours of fighting between villagers and police left one woman killed, and two other villagers and six policemen injured. Almost 400 villagers were reported to have fled to the forests of Mount Meru. The villagers declared that they were angered by government policies to allow rich people to own large tracts of land while poor villagers did not have enough land to farm. International attention was drawn to a conflict in parts of the Loliondo Game Controlled Area (Arusha Region), where in early July Maasai villagers were violently expelled from an area that the government had leased for game hunting to a company from the United Arab Emirates in 1992. The police field force unit conducted an operation in eight villages, torching about 200 homesteads, including food stores and maize fields. As a result, some 3,000 people were left without shelter, food or water and more than 50,000 cattle were pushed into areas hit by extreme drought with no water or grass. The authorities denied that any houses had been burnt, but justified the operation by stating that the villagers were illegal immigrants and were damaging the environment. The incident provoked an outcry from Tanzanian and international NGOs. The Danish ambassador, who travelled to Loliondo with four other ambassadors, called upon the government to stop evictions and to investigate what he described as inhuman acts. Denmark had just handed over a 15-year development project in the area. The African Commission on Human and Peoples' Rights also requested Kikwete to intervene. Parliament decided to investigate the issue through one of its committees. In mid-September, Minister for Natural Resources and Tourism Shamsa Mwangunga announced in Ngorongoro that fresh demarcations of land in Loliondo Game Controlled Area were planned in order to avoid property conflicts in the future.

Severe clashes between *conflicting clans* of the *Wakurya* in Mara Region had been causing loss of life and property for about two decades, and this continued in 2009. According to Home Affairs Minister Lawrence Masha, 136 people were killed between 2001 and April 2009, 336 people were wounded and 2,421 houses burnt down. Theft of cattle, conflicts about land and cultivation of cannabis were seen as the main causes of the conflicts. Former minister Philemon Sarungi accused rustlers from Kenya of having caused the problems and demanded compensation from Kenya for 3,500 cattle and the deaths of 40 people. In late March, a 44-member committee was formed, including representatives from the warring clans. It was the first time members of the two clans had held peace talks without the presence of senior central government leaders. The elders, who were held responsible for triggering the conflicts, promised to preach peace instead of hatred. However, in May the situation escalated again and more than 60 people were killed. In July, the government declared Tarime and Rorya districts special regional police zones and deployed a large number of police officers and since then reports of violence have decreased dramatically.

The government continued its endeavours to repatriate *refugees* from Burundi. On 30 September, all refugee camps in Kagera Region were officially closed. Only two camps in Kigoma Region were still operating, hosting fewer than 100,000 refugees for the first time in 15 years. According to reports from human rights organisations, the authorities exerted considerable pressure on the refugees, enforcing repatriation by allowing degrading living conditions in the camps. Tanzanian officials were accused of denying about 37,000 refugees in Mtabila camp access to basic services such as medical care and primary education, and also of routinely harassing, beating and threatening refugees who declined to return to Burundi. In contrast to this heavy-handed approach to refugees who had fled Burundi in the 1990s, 3,568 Burundian refugees who had escaped from Burundi in 1972 were granted Tanzanian citizenship on 4 August. They were the first of a total of 162,000 Burundian refugees who had accepted Tanzania's offer of naturalisation. This was the first large-scale naturalisation of this kind in Africa and was expected to be completed by early 2010.

Foreign Affairs

On 2 February, Kikwete completed his one-year term as *AU chairman*, during which he had earned international commendation for efforts in various conflict-resolution exercises in Africa (specifically Kenya, Comoros and Zimbabwe). However, during the hand-over ceremony to Libya's leader Kadhafi, he criticised the weak position of the AU chairman and suggested reforms.

Despite some minor disputes, peaceful and cordial international relations were generally maintained. *Western aid donors* were pleased by the government's commitment to curbing corruption, although more decisive action against culprits was expected. Finance Minister Mustafa Mkulo expressed dismay at a public statement by the World Bank that Tanzania was not doing enough to fight grand corruption. Minor rows occurred over several incidents, such as Western concerns about manipulation in the voter registration process in Pemba and the violation of human rights in Loliondo. In July, the Dutch government threatened to withhold $ 42 m of direct budget support, following a commercial dispute between the Tanzanian government and a Dutch investor. However, by November the conflict was resolved and Finance Minister Mkulo declared that the support had been released.

The generally high standing of the government's reputation in the Western community was also reflected by the fact that, on 22 May, Kikwete became the first African head of state to be received by the new US President Barack Obama. According to the White House, the two presidents exchanged ideas about intensifying bilateral cooperation, improving development policies in the fields of health, education and agriculture, and solving conflicts in Africa. During his week-long working trip to the US, Kikwete visited various organisations, companies and financial institutions.

On 10–11 March, Dar es Salaam hosted an international conference on the impact of the global financial crisis on African states, organised by Tanzania and the *IMF*. More than 300 high-ranking financial sector delegates from all over Africa adopted a joint declaration calling for enhanced support to help Africa cope with the effects of the crisis. Kikwete and Foreign Minister Bernard Membe were among the few African leaders invited by British Prime

Minister Gordon Brown to participate in the Pre-G20 Summit Africa Outreach Consultative Meeting in London on 16 March. The meeting was intended as a forum to discuss African leaders' views concerning the world economic crisis and have them reflected in the G20 Summit on 2 April.

Over 45 years of cordial relations between *China* and Tanzania were celebrated during a visit by Chinese President Hu Jintao on 15–16 February. Tanzania was one of four African countries Hu toured on his "journey of friendship and cooperation". The Chinese president attended the official launch ceremony of the Chinese-built national stadium in Dar es Salaam. He announced a new $ 22 m aid package and invited Tanzanian students to China, offering more scholarships.

Tanzania remained a somewhat reluctant supporter of the *EAC integration process*. During the final round of lengthy negotiations about the EAC Common Market Protocol in April, the Tanzanian delegation delayed the signing because of its continued concern about three main issues, namely the use of ID cards as travel documents between member states, the right to permanent residence for all East African citizens, and access to land. Access to land appeared to have been the most contentious issue because of already existing land conflicts in Tanzania and differences in land ownership laws compared with those in other EAC countries. Furthermore, there was fear that sparsely populated Tanzania could witness a massive influx of migrants from its neighbours, especially Uganda, Rwanda and Burundi, which were among Africa's most densely populated countries. Although the disputed issues were not resolved, the protocol was finally signed on 20 November, allowing future free trade and movement of people in the EAC common market, to be effective from 1 July 2010.

On 6–23 September, Tanzania hosted an *EAC field training exercise* conducted by military units from all five EAC countries and fully funded by the member states. The exercise was meant to train a Combined Joint Task Force of 1,556 personnel in planning and conducting combined joint operations and civil-military cooperation activities in the three areas of peace support operations, counter-terrorism and disaster management.

On 12 August, Tanzania deployed an advance party of 200 soldiers to the *UN/AU peacekeeping mission in Sudan (UNAMID)* in Darfur. They joined some 60 Tanzanian military observers, staff officers and police advisers who had been deployed earlier. In a change of attitude, the government promised to contribute a total of 875 personnel, although it had in the past been reluctant to participate in UN peacekeeping exercises.

Socioeconomic Developments

The global economic and financial crisis had a destabilising effect on Tanzania's economy, mainly due to reduced foreign investment, trade and tourism, but in the end the *slowdown* turned out to be much less pronounced than had initially been feared. Most economic activities proved to be surprisingly resilient, and the financial sector was affected very little because of its limited exposure to the toxic elements of global financial markets. The 2009 *GDP growth rate* was forecast to finally attain 5.5%, better than projected earlier, but below the 7% average for recent years (7.4% in 2008). Consumer price *inflation* was persistently high, with monthly rates hovering around the year's average of 12%. This was largely due to elevated food prices, partially the effect of adverse weather conditions (drought in northern regions early in the year) and substantial exports to neighbouring countries. The *exchange rate* experienced normal fluctuations throughout the year, but on balance remained relatively stable (vis-à-vis the dollar). The structural *trade deficit* narrowed somewhat, with exports (over 40% gold) growing slightly by 6% to $ 3,227 m and imports, as a result of a slackening of new investments and lower oil prices, even contracting by 2% to $ 6,294 m. Thus, roughly half of Tanzania's import bill was covered by its own exports, the highest ratio for many years. This improved situation enabled a reduction of the (provisional) current-account deficit to about 9.4% of GDP (down from 11.4% in 2008). Gross *foreign reserves* reached a new high of $ 3.2 bn at year's end (compared with $ 2.8 m at end-2008), partly the effect of an injection from the IMF; this was sufficient for an astounding import coverage of about six months. While the *external debt* had in previous years, through concerted debt cancellations, been substantially reduced to a low of $ 4.2 bn in 2006, this continued to rise again and the debt stock attained a volume of $ 7.1 bn at year's end.

Several IMF missions reviewed Tanzania's macroeconomic performance in the framework of the *Policy Support Instrument* (PSI) that had been in effect since February 2007 (and was extended until May 2010) as a form of monitoring government's financial and economic policies aimed at sustained broad-based growth, but without the need for IMF financial assistance. All the agreed benchmarks were by and large met, thus gaining for the government the IMF's positive stamp of approval, which was in turn crucial for maintaining the confidence and support of the many other donor countries and institutions that provided various forms of aid programmes for the country. On 29 May, the IMF approved a new 12-month $ 336 m arrangement under its *Exogenous Shocks Facility* (ESF), intended to bolster Tanzania's foreign reserves and to support its balance of payments, which were assessed to have reached a precarious status. The ESF was specifically meant to cushion from the effects of the global crisis countries that were in principle eligible for the PRGF, but did not currently have a PRGF-supported programme. Under the ESF, $ 244 m were made available immediately, and a second disbursement of $ 63 m on 24 November upon the completion of a first review. Earlier plans for issuing a sovereign eurobond to raise funds for public investments were dropped in the prevailing financial circumstances, as a precautionary measure against the dangers of new commercial borrowing.

Despite its praise for Tanzania's strong macroeconomic performance, the IMF nevertheless noted that progress on *poverty reduction* was mixed. In its assessment, there were substantial improvements in education and health outcomes, but the incidence of income poverty had declined only modestly. It was evident that Tanzania would not be able to achieve the MDGs by 2015. Despite all the macroeconomic successes and positive acclaim from the donor community, Tanzania still remained one of the poorest countries in Africa. In UNDP's 2009 HDI (based on 2007 data), Tanzania was ranked 151 (out of 182), near the end of the medium human development category. GDP per capita was only $ 400 and in PPP terms it was given as $ 1,208, a considerable upward revision over previous calculations.

The *fiscal outturn* for the financial *year 2008/09* (July–June) was characterised by a shortfall in revenue collection and underspending in foreign-financed development expenditure. Total domestic revenue collection of TSh 4,293 bn was 18% higher than in 2007/08, but a shortfall of 10% against the original budget estimate, mainly caused by the impact of the global financial crisis and the resulting slowdown of domestic economic activities. To compensate, the government had resorted to higher domestic borrowing. Recurrent expenditures were broadly in line with budget estimates and showed a marked improvement in budget execution. Development expenditures were, however, 14% lower than budgeted due to non-disbursement of foreign project funds. The overall effect of this situation was a sharp widening of the fiscal deficit to 4.4% of GDP (against 0.8% in 2007/08).

Faced with somewhat gloomy economic prospects, just prior to the release of the new budget, Kikwete announced an ambitious *economic stimulus plan* with a financial volume of about $ 1.3 bn (roughly 6% of GDP). The main components entailed large infrastructure programmes, financial support for crisis-affected ailing companies and help for small farmers. It was, however, not altogether clear to what extent these programmes were included in the state budget or were to be handled by public financial institutions. A concurrently released new government document (*medium-term public investment plan*) outlined a public investment strategy with a focus on the agricultural sector and on strengthening Tanzania's role as a sub-regional logistical hub, wherever this was feasible in the form of public-private partnerships.

On 11 June, Finance Minister Mkulo presented to parliament the *2009/10 budget*, with an overall 30% volume increase. The key focus was a substantial increase for agriculture, raising its share of the budget from 4% to 7%. This was in line with the government's new 'Kilimo Kwanza' (agriculture first) strategy, officially launched by Kikwete on 4 August, to give much more energetic support to small farmers, but to also pursue opportunities for more large-scale farming (including irrigation) and to initiate a dynamisation of agriculture over the medium term, the agricultural sector having long been grossly neglected. Other sectors receiving priority attention were education, health and infrastructure. Domestic revenue was rather conservatively projected to grow only from 15.9% to 16.4% of GDP, thus lowering earlier more ambitious forecasts and effectively relying on a further rise in donor funds, thereby quietly dropping all plans for a reduction of ingrained aid dependency. About 12.5% of the budget volume was expected to come under the general budget support scheme, supported by eleven bilateral and three multilateral donors. A reduction of VAT from 20% to 18% was intended as a stimulus to economic activities, but created obvious budget risks. The projected total revenue of TSh 9,513 bn was expected to be generated from domestic revenue (56%), foreign loans and grants (33%) and domestic borrowing (11%). By the middle of the financial year at end-December, it emerged that domestic revenue was 10% lower than targeted and that there might be a need to look for supplementary funding.

The World Bank in its 2010 Doing Business report assessed that there had been a considerable slippage in respect of further improvements in the *general business environment*. No significant reform measures were recorded in the preceding year and Tanzania was consequently downgraded by five places to rank 131st. Several government spokespersons expressed concern and pledged to remain on track in the pursuance of favourable market-friendly conditions. For most of the year, intensive discussions were held in parliament and government about revising the existing *mining legislation* with the aim of raising more government revenue in royalties from the international mining companies, whose activities had increased tremendously over the last decade, but the new mining bill was not ready by year's end. The volume of *foreign direct investments* was expected to have declined by about 10% compared with 2008 (with a record $ 744 m, mostly for mining ventures) due to delays of several new projects as a result of the global crisis. Apart from gold, new prospects for uranium mining appeared to be very promising. *Tourism*, the second foreign-exchange earner after gold, also experienced a set-back, with visitor numbers declining by about 10% compared with 2008.

Weaknesses in key parastatal service institutions continued to be a burden on the economy and to create hardships for the population. *Electricity* supply remained insufficient to meet the growing demand, due to maintenance problems in existing facilities and delays in planned new power projects, thus necessitating the repeated introduction of power cuts. On 10 December, the power cable from the mainland to Zanzibar broke, causing an electricity blackout on the island well into 2010, with strong negative effects on the local economy, especially in the tourist sector. Operations of *Tanzania Railways Ltd*, operated and 51% owned by RITES from India since 2007, continued to be very poor and workers protested vehemently against management in November, while the government was contemplating looking for a new arrangement. The *TAZARA railway line* to Zambia similarly continued to be in deep operational trouble and in permanent deficit; discussions were underway to obtain new assistance from China for a major rehabilitation. The future of *Air Tanzania* was also uncertain, with a sharp reduction of staff in December and government efforts to find new investors.

Climatic conditions were unfavourable for most of the year. The northern and central regions as well as the coast were hit by exceptional drought, causing severe problems for agricultural production and for the provision of an estimated 1 m needy people with food and water. The government supplied food from southern regions, which had produced a surplus, and duty on imported food was temporarily waived. Heavy rains in December flooded several areas in various regions and led to loss of life and severe damage to infrastructural facilities (including the closure of the central railway line for several months), houses and agriculture.

Tanzania in 2010

General elections in October both for the Union and for Zanzibar fully occupied public attention through most of the year. As generally expected, President Kikwete was re-elected for a second term and the long-ruling party, CCM, easily defended its dominant role in the Union parliament, albeit against a strengthened opposition in a prevailing climate of political apathy and discontent about the government's achievements. A new president was elected in semi-autonomous Zanzibar and a novel power-sharing government was installed, thus bringing to an end years of conflict and confrontation between two almost equally strong political parties. Despite unavoidable campaign confrontations, Tanzania's reputation as exceptionally stable and peaceful was never seriously challenged. The EAC integration process advanced one step further with the start of a common market, a move still regarded with some scepticism by many Tanzanians. The macroeconomic indicators showed a quite satisfactory performance, and the country continued to receive good marks from international institutions and donor agencies. For the overwhelming majority of the population, however, noticeable material improvements remained elusive.

Domestic Politics

The run-up to and conduct of *presidential, parliamentary and local elections* on 31 October dominated internal affairs during the year. The National Electoral Commission (NEC) was responsible for the organisation at Union level on the mainland and in Zanzibar and of the mainland local council elections, while the Zanzibar Electoral Commission (ZEC) organised the elections to the Zanzibar presidency, the Zanzibar House of Representatives and the islands' local councils. The continuation of incumbent *President Jakaya Kikwete*'s mandate and the confirmed but reduced dominance of the *ruling party* 'Chama cha Mapinduzi' (CCM, Party of the Revolution) were expected on the mainland. The situation in Zanzibar was dominated by two topics: first, the end of President Amani Karume's second term and the selection of a successor, and second, the surprising agreement between CCM and it's main competitor the Civic United Front (CUF) to end their long-lasting conflicts and form a government of national unity after the elections.

Preparations for the elections had already started in 2009 with the updating of the *NEC's permanent national voters' register*. This was done without major incident, but incurred some complaints about inconsistencies. *Voter registration in Zanzibar* (executed by the ZEC) was carried out in separate rounds. The first round, which had mostly started in 2009, was boycotted by CUF in protest against the requirement for potential voters to show the new Zanzibar ID card (ZAN ID) in order to be registered. CUF complained that many of their supporters had been denied the ZAN ID because of their political affiliation. This phase was marred by mistrust and violence and even had to be suspended by the ZEC. The second round, subsequently conducted after the reconciliation agreement between the two parties' leaders, took place smoothly. CUF called off the boycott and the ZEC now appeared very cooperative. However, unclear procedures, insufficient voter education, poorly trained staff and continuing attempts by some *shehas* (appointed local-level state representatives) to prevent eligible voters from registering remained a source of contention.

On 12 July, a CCM Special National Congress with almost 2,000 delegates nominated *Kikwete* as *CCM presidential candidate* for a second (and final) term by an overwhelming 99% vote. Kikwete, also doubling as CCM chairman, was the sole contender after a competitor had withdrawn his candidature before the nomination congress began. Such undisputed support had not been unreservedly expected, first, because of the massive tensions between various party factions that had come into the open in 2009, and second, because various opinion polls had revealed growing public discontent with Kikwete's leadership. He nevertheless remained popular enough to ensure strong support for his party, and CCM had long experience of bridging internal rifts in order to remain in power. Upon his nomination, Kikwete named former Zanzibar chief minister Mohamed Gharib Bilal as his running mate. Among other *amendments* to the *CCM constitution*, the Congress introduced some changes concerning the nomination of candidates for parliamentary elections. Formerly, the party's two top-level committees had been instrumental in selecting the final candidates. The new mechanism allowed a higher degree of party members' participation in the preferential nomination of parliamentary and local council candidates through primaries, held on 1 August. A good number of prominent politicians lost in these primaries, among them former prime minister and CCM powerbroker John Malecela, six cabinet members and more than 75 MPs. The final decision on the candidates was made on 14 August by the National Executive Committee, which approved most of those proposed. However, some of those whose nomination was not confirmed defected from CCM and joined various opposition parties.

The *Election Expenses Act*, promulgated on 17 March, aimed at increasing the transparency of funding for candidates and political parties at all stages of the electoral process, and at reducing corruption. It also restricted 'foreign' funding for election expenses and limited the amount permitted to be spent by parties and candidates on election-related expenses in the constituencies, depending on their size and population. The registrar of political parties (a political appointee) was granted substantial power in electoral matters. Opposition parties criticised the act, fearing that the restrictions would affect them much more than the wealthy and well-connected CCM.

Altogether *18 political parties contested the elections*. Other than CCM, only five had already been represented in previous parliaments. CUF and 'Chama cha Demokrasia na Maendeleo' (CHADEMA,

Party of Democracy and Development) had emerged as the strongest parties within a generally weak and divided opposition camp. The Tanzania Labour Party (TLP), United Democratic Party (UDP) and National Convention for Construction and Reform – Change (NCCR-Mageuzi) were expected to play at least a perceptible part in the elections. None of the other parties had ever played a significant role, but all of them were able to field at least a handful of candidates for the parliamentary as well as the local council elections. Some attention was drawn to a newly-created party 'Chama cha Jamii' (CCJ, Party of the Society). It was widely suggested in the local media that CCJ, founded when internal rifts within CCM came into the limelight, was created to receive prominent CCM reformers and anti-graft activists in the case of a split, which might have left CCM in the hands of a faction widely perceived as being involved in corrupt and greedy practices. There was much speculation about which CCM heavyweights might soon defect to CCJ. In the end, only one MP moved to CCJ, but it failed to obtain full registration for technical reasons and the only convert joined CHADEMA. The amount of attention given to a party that ultimately never came into existence indicated how severe the internal CCM rifts were at least perceived to be by the public.

For the selection of their *parliamentary candidates*, only CUF applied a system similar to that of CCM, while CHADEMA and NCCR-Mageuzi candidates were nominated by the party leadership on the basis of preferential votes by party delegates. Smaller parties' candidates were usually selected by the party leaders. Only CCM was able to field candidates in all 239 constituencies, and in 17 constituencies CCM candidates stood uncontested. The number of uncontested constituencies had doubled in comparison with 2005, in some cases clearly as a result of deliberate CCM efforts to enable prominent members to stand unchallenged. CHADEMA fielded 182 candidates, CUF 170, NCCR-Mageuzi 64, and TLP 64. Of the 1,036 candidates only 191 were women.

On 27 June, CUF's national congress nominated party chairman Ibrahim Lipumba as their *presidential candidate*. Lipumba, supported by 89% of the delegates, was vying for the presidency for the fourth time. After his defeat in 2005, the party had discussed whether somebody else should lead CUF into the 2010 elections, but nobody emerged to replace the popular and widely respected party leader. More surprising was CHADEMA's decision to field its secretary-general Wilbroad Slaa in the race for the presidency. Party chairman Freeman Mbowe had stood in 2005 and was expected to run again. His position had possibly been somewhat damaged in 2009 when deputy secretary-general and MP Zitto Kabwe, a young and popular politician, declared that he would challenge Mbowe for the chairmanship. Kabwe was dissuaded from this move by party elders. Slaa's nomination could thus be seen as a compromise between Mbowe and Kabwe. Slaa himself, however, had already gained popular recognition and support as a result of his vocal anti-corruption campaigns. TLP strongman Augustine Mrema preferred a safe seat in parliament to another futile attempt to beat the CCM candidate for the presidency. For the first time since his 1995 defection from CCM, he did not contend for the top position and a little-known former MP was nominated instead. Three other parties also nominated relatively unknown presidential candidates.

The *electoral campaign* started officially on 20 August and generally took place in a peaceful and unrestricted manner, which in most cases enabled opposition parties to hold their rallies freely, although there were a few localized cases of clashes between supporters of different parties, which left at least one person dead. However, there was not a level playing field, since CCM took extensive advantage of its incumbency and its access to state resources and the administrative structures. Opposition parties' efforts were also restricted because of their poor financial and organisational resources. Media coverage slightly favoured the ruling party, but was not explicitly biased. The issues addressed during the campaign were rather general and did not indicate significant differences between the contending parties' policies, which mainly focused on the fight against corruption, the need to sustain peace, the improvement of the economy and the education system, and promises to empower poor Tanzanians. Despite the generally peaceful conduct of the campaigns, numerous incidents of verbal abuse, mud-slinging and the exploitation of ethnic and religious affiliations were reported.

Although there were numerous minor instances of disorder, missing polling materials and even violence in individual constituencies, *election day* itself was by and large *peaceful* and procedures were adhered to. In seven of the 239 constituencies (and 20 of the 2,358 polling stations for the council elections) voting had to be suspended because ballot papers were missing and candidates' names were misspelled, and the poll was postponed to 14 November. *Delayed announcements of results* and somewhat *chaotic vote-counting procedures* led to confusion in a number of constituencies, allegations of manipulation and protests, which in some areas turned violent. In Mwanza and Dar es Salaam riot police used tear gas to disperse protesting youths.

Kikwete and CCM *won the elections* by wide margins, but had nevertheless to *accept losses*, mainly to CHADEMA, and the *emergence of a real opposition*. Kikwete got 61.2% of the votes, followed by Slaa with an unexpected 26.3% and Lipumba with a disappointing 8.1%. Various opinion polls conducted throughout the year had already revealed substantial disappointment with CCM and Kikwete and shown that CHADEMA would be the main beneficiary. *CCM also lost significantly in the parliamentary elections.* Only 186 seats (206 in 2005) were won by their candidates. CHADEMA managed to increase their number of seats significantly from five in 2005 to 23. Their candidates were successful in various parts of the country, especially in Shinyanga, Mwanza and Kilimanjaro Regions. CHADEMA's success was owed more to its urban followers than to support on grounds of regional affiliation, but they also gained in rural areas. CUF was also able to increase its number of seats from 19 to 24. It won all constituencies in its stronghold Pemba, four on Unguja and two on the mainland (towns in Lindi Region). NCCR-Mageuzi, the strongest opposition party in 1995 but which had since declined after internal conflicts and failed to win even a single seat in 2005, managed to take four seats, all in Kigoma Region. The chairmen of TLP and UDP each won a seat in their home constituencies. CCM took an additional 67 *'special seats' for women*, CHADEMA 25 and CUF 10, allocated from their party lists in accordance with the share of constituency seats.

The *majority vote system* had clearly *favoured CCM*. With 60.4% of the votes, they took 77.8% of the seats (apart from the 'special seats' for women, which further increased CCM's majority), whereas CHADEMA was most disadvantaged and took only 9.6% of seats despite receiving 24.8% of the votes. The *opposition* was nevertheless able to *reverse its recent gradual decline* owing to sharply increased popular dissatisfaction with the ruling party and its government, as well as recurring reports of severe infighting within CCM. CHADEMA's aggressive style of campaigning also had an important impact. CCM won an overwhelming 85% of the 3,325 *council seats* (CHADEMA 10%, CUF 4%) and thus controlled most district and municipal councils. CHADEMA managed to take the majority of seats on Kigoma and Moshi municipal councils and in Mwanza city council. Almost 600 seats (18%) were secured unopposed by CCM candidates. *Mayoral elections* on 18 December were hit by chaos in a number of councils, mostly due to unclear rules about who was allowed to participate in the polls, and had to be suspended and postponed in Tanga, Mwanza and Kigoma. In some other cases, as in Dar es Salaam and Arusha, CHADEMA protested about the decisions of the electoral officers.

Voter turnout (43% of the roughly 20 million eligible voters) was by far the lowest since the introduction of the multiparty system. Analysts attributed this to a growing frustration with politics and a general distrust of politicians. National and international *election observer missions* praised the peaceful and orderly conduct of the elections, which, despite some shortcomings, were characterised as widely complying with international standards. *CHADEMA*, however, did *not accept the results* of the presidential elections and demanded a re-run or at least an independent investigation. They alleged that the presidential elections had been flawed and said they would not recognise Kikwete as legitimate president. CHADEMA MPS stressed this when they ostentatiously walked out of parliament during Kikwete's inaugural speech. Chairman Mbowe explained the intention of this move (decided after a controversial internal debate) as being to put pressure on the government to reform the constitution and several electoral laws, which the party considered not to be in accordance with the requirements of a multiparty system. CHADEMA formed a shadow cabinet in the National Assembly without attempting cooperation with CUF.

Much attention focused on the election of a new *parliamentary speaker*. From a number of applications, CCM's central committee (CC) selected three women whose names it proposed to parliament. Parliament overwhelmingly elected *Anna Makinda*, a respected MP for 35 years, former minister and former deputy parliamentary speaker. Makinda's predecessor, Samwel Sitta, had earned much credit by running the house's affairs quite independently and encouraging a new style in parliament. His strong stance against corruption, even in his own party, had in 2009 led to an unprecedented (but failed) 'parliamentary coup attempt' by some influential CCM members. Sitta's bid for re-election to the post and the CC's preference for three others were seen by many as the party leadership's concession to the demands of a group of corrupt powerful politicians.

Kikwete nevertheless demonstrated unbowed support for Sitta and appointed him minister for East African cooperation in the new cabinet. Having been sworn in on 6 November, Kikwete re-appointed *Mizengo Peter Pinda* as *prime minister*. The new *cabinet* of 29 ministers and 21 deputy ministers was a demonstration of great continuity, as most of the key ministers were re-appointed to their former posts. A good number of previous ministers were given new ministries and the cabinet also saw the promotion of former deputies to full ministers. Of the 24 new cabinet members, two appointments were most remarkable. By appointing former UN-HABITAT executive director Anna Tibaijuka as minister for lands, housing and human settlement, Kikwete was able to include a high-ranking international figure in his cabinet. Former Zanzibar chief minister Shamsi Vuai Nahodha became minister of home affairs, a step obviously owed to internal developments in Zanzibar and intended to integrate the Karume-Nahodha faction into the government (just as the choice of Bilal as Union vice president was meant to integrate the Salmin-Bilal faction). Kikwete had appointed Nahodha as member of the Union parliament after he had not been considered in the new Zanzibar government.

The situation in *Zanzibar remained peaceful* after president Amani Karume (CCM) and CUF strongman Seif Shariff Hamad had met behind closed doors in November 2009 and agreed to end the long-standing hostilities between the two parties. In January, CUF's leader in the House of Representatives put forward a private motion, asking the government to amend the Zanzibar constitution in order to allow the formation of a *government of national unity* (GNU) and also proposing a referendum. This was remarkable, since CUF had always rejected the idea of a referendum because of their distrust of the ZEC, which they presumed to be controlled by CCM. The motion was discussed for two days and then passed. The Zanzibar government formulated a corresponding bill, and the ZEC organised a *referendum* on 31 July that asked Zanzibaris whether or not the constitution should be amended to allow the creation of a GNU. Both parties campaigned massively for a 'yes'-vote. There was nevertheless some underground campaigning for 'no', allegedly by CCM members who were suspected of being close to the faction around former president Salmin Amour and former chief minister Bilal, both strong adversaries of Karume. No incidents overshadowed a peaceful and orderly voting process and the ZEC's successful handling of the referendum increased the hope that the coming elections would also be organised well and impartially. A two-thirds majority accepted the government's proposal for a GNU. Voter turnout was 71.3% of the 407,669 registered voters. On 8 August, the House of Representatives formalised the voters' decision and *amended the constitution* accordingly.

The GNU would be led by a directly-elected president and two vice presidents, with the first vice president coming from the second strongest party in parliament and the second vice president (also leader of government business) from the strongest party. The post of chief minister was abolished. Cabinet ministers would be appointed from all the parties represented in parliament, in proportion to their numerical strength. Smaller opposition parties criticised the new set-up, accusing both main parties of sharing the cake and sidelining smaller competitors.

The selection of the *CCM candidate* for the *Zanzibar presidency* became crucial in a situation where CCM Zanzibar was sharply divided between an 'incumbent' camp of Karume and his chief minister, Nahodha, on the one hand and a camp of Karume's predecessor Salmin Amour and his chief minister, Bilal. Eight candidates submitted their names to CCM's NEC, among them the two main exponents of the rivalling factions, Bilal and Nahodha. Unexpectedly, the NEC chose none of them, but *Union Vice President Ali Mohamed Shein*. After two terms as vice president, Shein was barred from another term, but hardly anyone expected the friendly but low-profile politician to continue his political career in the top job in Zanzibar. He had never played any significant role in Zanzibar politics and was more perceived as a Tanzanian than as a Zanzibari politician. Thus it was expected that he would guarantee the implementation of the GNU agreement (which was fully supported by Kikwete and the Union government). In addition, he became the *first Pemban* to be nominated as the CCM presidential candidate. Since CUF nominated its secretary-general, *Seif Sharif Hamad* (five other candidates were nominated by smaller parties), it became clear that the next president would hail from the politically much neglected northern island. The CCM NEC, however, avoided sidelining the powerful

Zanzibar factions. Bilal was rewarded with the Union vice presidency, which also gave him responsibility for Union matters. To him, expecting to become Zanzibar president, the post as Union vice president was cold comfort rather than a promotion. Nahodha was later appointed Union minister of home affairs.

Unlike in previous elections, which had been marred by violence, and unlike the 2009 registration process, both campaigns and elections were conducted in a *peaceful atmosphere* of cordiality, despite an increased security and military presence. Some turmoil arose only among CUF supporters when the ZEC announced the results, declaring Karume to be the winner with 50.1% of the votes against Hamad with 49.1%. Tension calmed, as Hamad immediately accepted the verdict, congratulated his rival and promised a fruitful cooperation with the new president. As expected, CUF won all 18 seats on Pemba as well as four on Unguja. CCM was successful in the remaining 28 of the 50 constituencies. CCM took 11 additional seats for women and CUF nine (the number of 'special seats' for women having been increased from 30% to 40%). Only three women entered parliament through a direct vote in a constituency, all on the CCM ticket. None of the other ten competing parties received a significant number of votes. The newly-elected president used his right to appoint up to ten additional members at a very early stage – appointing six men and two women from CCM and one man and one woman from CUF. The high voter turnout of almost 90% reflected the expectations of the populace (compared with 43% in the Union elections). CCM won 69 of the 114 local council seats (CUF took 46 seats, mainly on Pemba).

On 15 November, Shein appointed *19 ministers* and *six deputy ministers from both parties* (CCM 13, CUF 6), with seven former ministers re-appointed. All deputy ministers came from CCM. Hamad was appointed first vice president, while the experienced CCM politician and deputy foreign minister in Kikwete's cabinet, Seif Ali Iddi, was made second vice president. Thus, it was not only the first time that a Pemban had become Zanzibar president, but also, and even more strikingly, *all three top posts were occupied by Pembans*. Through a deliberate selection of the key personnel, CCM had laid the foundations for leading the GNU to success. However, the real test still remained: how would the rival parties work together in the new government, how would the sidelined CCM factions react, and would the people of Zanzibar feel they were benefiting from the GNU?

Strong calls went out soon after the elections from opposition parties, civil society organisations and academics for a *review of Tanzania's constitution*. This matter had been raised at least since the introduction of the multiparty system in the 1990s. For the first time, leading CCM politicians from the mainland indicated that they were willing to deal with the issue – including Prime Minister Pinda, who stated in late November that he was advising the president on the subject. On 28 December, a CUF delegation handed a *draft constitution* to the ministry of constitutional affairs and justice. According to CUF, the draft had been prepared during the past three years in a process involving civil society groups. The police banned a demonstration that was to accompany the CUF delegation from its headquarters to the ministry. The demonstration nevertheless took place, but the police over-reacted and fired into the air to disperse the demonstrators and arrested at least four people. In his televised New Year address on 31 December, Kikwete announced the formation of a Constitutional Review Commission tasked with gathering the views of experts, political parties and representatives of the society concerning a new constitution.

Corruption was a *key issue* during the electoral process, both as a topic in the campaigns and as the main cause of power struggles within CCM, which were primarily about who would gain control over the party and thus over access to the country's resources. It appeared that Tanzania had come to the crossroads between turning into a 'clean' state seriously fighting corruption and a thoroughly corrupt state controlled by greedy criminals. And as in previous years, the fight against corruption was one of the hottest public topics. While a good number of cases involving allegations of grand corruption were still under investigation, remarkable developments took place in three of the major cases. On 5 February, the *British Serious Fraud Office* (SFO) reached an agreement with Europe's biggest defence contractor, BAE Systems, to close the long-standing investigation into allegations of corruption against the company. BAE had, inter alia, been accused of having overcharged Tanzania for an *air traffic control system* in 1999, allegedly using corrupt practices. Under the deal with the SFO, BAE agreed to pay fines in the UK and the US, and also to give an ex-gratia payment of £ 30 m to Tanzania. While BAE preferred to pay the compensation to charitable organisations, Foreign Minister Bernard Membe insisted that it should be paid to the government. Although one aim of the SFO-BAE agreement was to finally settle the case (without investigating the corruption allegations), Tanzania's Prevention and Combat of Corruption Bureau (PCCB) stated that it would continue its own investigations. In late December, local newspapers reported a *Wikileaks revelation*, quoting a diplomatic cable sent by a US diplomat to his government in 2007. The diplomat reported on a meeting with PCCB director Edward Hoseah, at which the latter painted a mixed picture of Tanzania's anti-corruption efforts. According to the cables, Hoseah had highlighted legal reforms and the anti-graft efforts by parliament and the media, but also expressed concern about Kikwete's resolve to allow the law to be applied in corruption cases involving top-level personalities, including former president Benjamin Mkapa and politicians in his inner circle. He was also said to be pessimistic about the high level of corruption on the part of the Zanzibar government and was quoted as being concerned about his personal safety and fearing his life was in danger. The PCCB director immediately denied the reports, emphasized the willingness of the president to fight grand corruption and declared that the US diplomat had quoted him out of context.

On 24 May, a former director of the Bank of Tanzania (BoT) was sentenced to two years imprisonment on charges of abuse of office, causing the government a TShs 221 bn loss during the construction of the *BoT twin tower* headquarters. It remained unclear, however, whether the massive overrun of construction costs was caused by corruption or just by poor project management. A new controversy arose in the so-called *Richmond saga*, a scandal about the purchase of electric power plants that had led to the forced resignation of then prime minister Edward Lowassa and other ministers in 2008. On 15 November, the International Chamber of Commerce ruled that the Tanzania Electric Supply Company should pay about TShs 95 bn ($ 65 m) for breach of contract to a company called Dowans, which had been involved in the dubious deal. Although the government quickly stated that it would follow the order, opposition and civil society spokespersons, the media and even Minister Sitta criticised the government, demanded information about the owners of the company and their relations to allegedly corrupt politicians, and also questioned the Chamber's legal right to issue such an order.

An international outcry was caused in late July, when Kikwete announced that the government was pursuing plans to build a *road* through the *Serengeti National Park* to connect the towns of Arusha and Musoma. Foreign governments, national and international NGOs and environmentalists strongly criticised the plan, saying it would disturb the great wildebeest migration and thus destroy an important aspect of the World Heritage Site Serengeti. The government, however, insisted that the road would only be built with gravel – like existing roads through the national park – and that the authorities would take care that the environment and the great migration would not be harmed.

In mid-April, the government naturalized *162,200 Burundian refugees* who had fled their home country in 1972 and settled in Tanzania. From September, a number of attacks by *Somali pirates* on ships in Tanzanian waters were reported. In some cases, the attacked ships were able to escape or were defended by members of the Tanzania People's Defence Forces. Fear increased that Somali pirates might have shifted their areas of operation southward into Tanzanian territory to escape international surveillance.

Foreign Affairs

The government's ambivalent stance on corruption also affected Tanzania's external relations. *Western donor countries* strongly supported the government's reforms and praised it for the peaceful and orderly conduct of the elections. However, pressure became more vocal to intensify the fight against corruption. In early March, the US ambassador demanded stronger measures against grand corruption, including jail sentences for leaders and confiscation of their unlawfully acquired property. In mid-May, a group of donors announced a substantial reduction in their general budget support contributions in reaction to the slow pace of economic reform and the government's reluctance to fight high-level corruption. During the June budget session, it became known that Tanzania had agreed to refund TShs 2.8 bn to the Norwegian government. A 2009 audit had revealed that funds of TShs 44 bn, given to a ministry of natural resources and tourism programme, had been misused or at least poorly accounted for. The affair had caused considerable irritation between the two governments and the refund was seen as an effort to normalize relations with an important donor country.

Cordial relations with all *neighbouring countries* were maintained, despite Tanzania's reluctant approach towards the EAC integration process. Although the government remained somewhat cautious about several aspects (such as land ownership and residence rights), the *EAC common market* protocol nevertheless came into force as of 1 July. In December, 106 police officers joined the UN/AU peacekeeping mission in Darfur, Sudan, to which the government had committed a battalion of about 1,000 soldiers.

Relations with *China* intensified further. On 15 January, the two governments signed four agreements for grants and loans of TShs 239 bn for projects including infrastructure projects such as upgrading the Zanzibar airport and support for the ailing TAZARA (Tanzania Zambia Railway) line. Kikwete visited *Turkey* in mid-February and signed agreements on commercial and economic cooperation. Turkish Airlines started to operate direct flights to Dar es Salaam in June. While Kikwete had in previous years often been criticised for spending too much time on foreign trips, he now cut short his external engagements to concentrate fully on the domestic election campaign.

On 5–7 May, Dar es Salaam hosted the 20th *World Economic Forum on Africa*, the first in East Africa, under the theme "Rethinking Africa's Growth Strategy", with more than 1,000 participants from 85 countries, including 12 African heads of state and government. Eight international companies declared support for Tanzania's 'Kilimo Kwanza' agricultural reform programme.

Socioeconomic Developments

The economy continued to perform significantly better than had initially been expected in face of the adverse effects of the global economic and financial crisis. The GDP *growth rate* for 2010 was estimated to attain 6.9%, compared with an upwardly revised figure of 6.6% for 2009. Despite some slowdown from the earlier average of around 7.0% in recent years, these figures were proof of the economy's astounding resilience and provided ground for a continued optimistic macroeconomic outlook. The good performance was mainly due to a rebound in agriculture resulting from improved weather conditions (although the agricultural sector was still lagging considerably behind other sectors), continued expansion of the mining sector, and the impact of the government's 2009 economic rescue plan and public investment programme, which were intended to provide an extra growth stimulus.

Consumer price *inflation* was successfully reined in to an average of 7.2% for the year, compared with 12% in 2009. The September inflation rate of 4.5% was the lowest for the last five years, largely the result of a general good harvest and low food prices. This also permitted a partial lifting of the food export ban that had been decreed in earlier drought years. The national food reserve (maize and sorghum) reached its highest level of 211,000 tons at year's end. The *exchange rate* experienced normal fluctuations, with a gradual decline of about 10% vis-à-vis the dollar during the course of the year. The *structural trade deficit* was narrowed slightly further, with exports growing by 18% to $ 3,970 m and imports by 15% to $ 6,730 m (preliminary figures). Thus, almost 60% of Tanzania's import bill was covered by its own export revenues, the highest ratio ever achieved. Gold accounted for 40% of exports, while manufactured goods exports to regional markets rose strongly. In contrast, the relative share of traditional agricultural exports declined further. Almost one-third of the import bill was needed for oil and oil products, and somewhat more than one-fifth for food and consumer goods. The situation permitted the stabilisation of the (preliminary) *current-account deficit* at around 8.5% of GDP (similar to 2009). Gross *foreign reserves* reached a new high of $ 3.65 bn at year's end (compared with $ 3.2 bn at end-2009). This was sufficient for a very satisfactory import coverage of more than six months. While the *external debt* had previously, as a result of concerted debt cancellations, been substantially reduced to a low of $ 4.2 bn in 2006, it then continued to rise again, reaching $ 7.6 bn at year's end (compared with $ 6.8 bn at end-2009). *Tourist* numbers were estimated to have recovered to 794,000.

IMF missions in March and September reviewed Tanzania's *macroeconomic performance* in the framework of the on-going IMF support programmes and showed themselves generally very satisfied with the results achieved, by and large commending the government for the policies it had pursued. In June, the IMF Board completed the final review of the 12–month $ 320 m *Extended Shocks Facility* (*ESF*) that had been approved in May 2009 and released a final disbursement of $ 29 m. The ESF had been specifically intended to bolster Tanzania's foreign reserves, to support its balance of payments and to serve as a cushion from the effects of the global financial crisis. In the meantime, the situation had greatly improved. Simultaneously the Board completed the seventh performance review under the *Policy Support Instrument* (PSI) operative since February 2007, and approved a new three-year PSI. The PSI was designed as a quality seal for obtaining other aid funds, with special attention given to poverty reduction strategies adopted in a participatory process involving both civil society and external development partners. In December, the Board completed the first review under the new PSI, which concluded that all quantitative assessment criteria had been met and important progress made with regard to the agreed structural reform benchmarks in the area of public financial management and poverty reduction policies.

The current PRSP (generally known by the Swahili acronym MKUKUTA) for the 2005–2010 period was to end officially in June. Work on a successor MKUKUTA II, covering 2010–2015, began in January, but formal government approval was delayed until mid-October due to comprehensive consultation processes. The new strategy continued to be in line with the National Development Vision 2025. It focused on accelerating pro-poor growth in a sustainable manner by ensuring adequate prioritisation and coordination of policies and harnessing public-private-partnership potentials (based on a new act passed in July). Highest priority was accorded to agriculture under the 'Kilimo Kwanza' initiative, since it was identified as a growth driver supporting the majority of the poor rural population and with the potential of lifting them out of poverty. Greater emphasis was also given to infrastructure, with expectations of attracting more private investment, while progress was also to be maintained in education and health, with specific focus on improving the quality of social service delivery. A National Social Protection Framework was to be developed to improve the implementation of measures on social protection designed to ameliorate the lives of the extremely poor and most vulnerable groups in society.

At the UN's MDG summit in September, Tanzania received a performance certificate for meeting the education targets. Good progress was also made with regard to maternal and child mortality rates and water access, but hardly any noticeable achievements were evident in bringing down the incidence of income poverty. The obvious shortcomings in this regard were also reflected in various opinion polls, which showed the growing dissatisfaction of the populace with the government's social and economic policies. Despite praise for a successful macroeconomic performance, Tanzania still remained one of the poorest countries in Africa. In the 2010 HDI (based on 2008 data), Tanzania was ranked 148 (out of 169 countries) in the low human development category. GDP *per capita* was only $ 496 and in PPP terms $ 1,344.

On 10 June, Finance Minister Mustafa Mkulo presented a highly ambitious expansionary *2010/2011 budget* to parliament. With the announced cuts in the volume of external budget support, it was in danger of being underfinanced. Total expenditure was planned at TShs 11.1 trn, with 71% needed for recurrent expenditure and 21% for development purposes. Four priority sectors (agriculture, infrastructure, education, health) were allocated one-half of total funds. Domestic revenue sources (taxes, customs, fees) were expected to cover 54% of the budget, with only 25% coming from foreign assistance (compared with over 40% in recent years) in an effort to cut donor dependence. In December, the government was faced by a budget deficit as a result of considerable shortfalls in revenue collection and unexpected cost overruns, but Mkulo allayed fears that a supplementary budget would be needed. Extensive discussions between the treasury and the donor community then aimed at finding new common ground for an improved policy dialogue.

A new *Mining Act* was passed on 23 April after controversial public and parliamentary debates. It had long been widely presumed that existing contracts concluded with big international mining firms during Mkapa's presidency were highly disadvantageous to Tanzania. The new act provided for a removal of tax breaks, an increase in royalties and new calculation formulas, and was to apply retrospectively. However, complete control over the important mining industry still remained uncertain. Separate legislation was under preparation for the envisaged start of uranium mining.

No satisfactory solution was yet in sight for the ailing *Tanzania Railways Ltd.* (TRL) and *Air Tanzania*. In March, the cabinet decided to repossess a majority share in TRL from RITES of India in response to its extremely disappointing management performance. A Tanzanian interim management team was installed in June, but the divorce negotiations with RITES dragged on into 2011. No new investor was found for the over-indebted and practically dysfunctional national airline after an expected deal with a Chinese company did not materialise. The provision of *electricity* and *water* by the respective public corporations encountered serious problems for months, creating a severe burden for both private consumers and commercial operators. While the government planned to divest from a number of remaining parastatal companies, it was also contemplating the possible repossession of failed privatised public firms. Similarly, idle land not utilised by commercial developers was also threatened with repossession. Generally, there were no major concerns about known 'land-grabbing' ventures by foreign investors like those taking place elsewhere in Africa.

A serious *labour dispute* arose between government and the Trade Union Congress of Tanzania (TUCTA) when the latter called for a general strike on 5 May, which was declared illegal. The official minimum wage was doubled by government decree to about $ 75 per month as of 1 May, but this was considered insufficient by TUCTA. Subsequent to talks with government authorities, the strike was finally called off.

Tanzania in 2011

As a result of the October 2010 elections, President Kikwete and his dominant Revolutionary Party ('Chama cha Mapinduzi', CCM) were faced by a substantially strengthened political opposition and by vocal criticism by civil society organisations, but nevertheless remained fully in control. Much attention focussed on discussions about a review of the constitution, but these centred on procedural aspects and did not yet go as far as dealing with the substance of a new constitution. The parliament became much more assertive in attempts to control and criticise the government. Internal power struggles between various CCM factions were evident as the party tried to regain some of its lost public credibility. Zanzibar issues were much less in the limelight than in previous years. Macroeconomic performance remained relatively satisfactory and continued to be commended by international institutions, but the population saw little concrete progress and was increasingly dissatisfied with the services provided by state institutions. There was, however, no sign of a popular uprising.

Domestic Politics

Throughout the year, the *constitution review process* was at the centre of heated political debates and became a trial of strength between the government on the one hand and opposition parties, civil society organisations and wide sections of the public on the other. President Jakaya Kikwete announced this review in his new-year address in response to growing demands from various parts of the society after the 2010 elections. While this initiative was broadly welcomed, criticism was quickly levelled against the government's attempt to take firm control of the process. On 11 March, the government published a draft *Constitution Review Bill*, which it wanted to rush through parliament under a certificate of urgency in order to have it implemented by June. The bill proposed the establishment of a Constitutional Review Commission, tasked to establish and assess public opinion. The bill furthermore elaborated on the announcement of the formation of a Constituent Assembly, which was to be set up to make provisions for the new constitution, and finally proposed a referendum on the new constitution.

Major *concerns of opposition parties* and civil society included the inordinate powers vested to the president throughout the entire process and the perceived attempt to tightly control the proceedings and to restrict public debate and participation by fast-tracking the bill. Fears were also expressed that the government was attempting merely to amend the current constitution rather than allowing the formulation of a genuinely new one. Any restrictions on the debate were heavily criticised. It was claimed that so-called "contentious issues", such as the Union between Zanzibar and the Mainland and some fundamental constitutional principles, were to be excluded from public debate. The criticism was also raised that the draft bill had only been presented in English, although a Kiswahili version was seen as essential for a fully-comprehensive debate.

The Parliamentary Committee on Constitution, Justice and Good Governance conducted *public hearings* on the proposed bill in order to solicit opinions from the general public. Hearings in Dodoma, Dar es Salaam and Zanzibar on 7 and 8 April were chaotic and had to be extended until 10 April. In Dodoma, thousands of people reportedly arrived but were denied entry to the consultation for lack of space. When the confrontation became violent, police used tear gas to disperse the crowds. Similarly in Dar es Salaam, angry crowds demanded entry and the hearings had to be temporarily suspended. In Zanzibar, even representatives of the Zanzibar government rejected the bill, complaining that Zanzibar had been side-lined in the drafting process. Freeman Mbowe, chairman of the main opposition party CHADEMA (Party for Democracy and Development), declared that the fate of 44 m Tanzanians should not be decided by a few people in Dar es Salaam, Dodoma and Zanzibar, and called for countrywide demonstrations to force the government to halt the fast-tracking of the bill. Extensive coverage in the media and criticism from opposition parties, NGOs and academia made the government finally give in and *abandon its fast-tracking approach*. Parliamentary hearings scheduled for 18 April were called off, as were protest demonstrations by CHADEMA. A Kiswahili version of the bill was gazetted in late April. In late June, Prime Minister Mizengo Pinda declared that the government planned to launch the new constitution on 26 April 2014, the 50th anniversary of the Union between Zanzibar and the Mainland.

Civil society played an important role in the process. A variety of organisations (including the Tanganyika Law Society, Legal and Human Rights Centre, Tanzania Retired Judges Association, Policy Forum, University of Dar es Salaam Staff Association, Tanzania Media Women Association, Tanzania Women Lawyers Association, Tanzania Gender Networking Programme, HakiArdhi, and others) took active part in the discussion of the bill and the constitution. They published leaflets and booklets for public information, organised workshops in various parts of the country to discuss the issue, analysed the proposed bill and the current constitution and came up with their own recommendations. They cooperated closely with other NGOs, as well as with academicians, and formed the network 'Jukwaa la Katiba' (Constitutional Forum), representing more than 100 NGOs country-wide.

In late October, Minister of Justice and Constitutional Affairs Celina Kombani presented a *revised bill* to be tabled in parliament for its second and third reading. CHADEMA, NGOs, 'Jukwaa la Katiba' and faith-based organisations immediately rejected the bill, claiming that it did not incorporate many of their recommendations. When it was introduced in parliament on 14 November, CHADEMA's shadow minister for constitution and legal affairs, Tundu Lissu, read a statement on the opposition's views and left the house, accompanied by most opposition MPs. They declared that they would boycott the debate and stage demonstrations instead, but these were immediately banned by the police. Parliament nevertheless passed the bill (after introducing some changes) on 18 November on the strength of the undisputed majority of the ruling CCM. On 27 and 28 November Kikwete quite surprisingly met a *CHADEMA delegation*, which presented him with their recommendations on the issue. The meeting took place in a friendly atmosphere and both sides agreed that the bill needed to be amended. Kikwete emphasised that the government would continue to collect views on the bill and to review the process, but Kikwete nevertheless gave his assent to the disputed bill the following day. Although CHADEMA's public reactions were harsh, analysts argued that a typical Tanzanian compromise seemed to have been reached between the government and the major opposition party, which allowed the passing of the bill but also provided for the incorporation of CHADEMA's views in a later amendment.

CHADEMA's new role as the *first significant opposition party* in Tanzania's history, a result of its impressive performance in the October 2010 elections, led to tensions with state organs throughout the year. Invigorated by its electoral success and by opinion polls that indicated that the party's secretary general and 2010 presidential candidate, Wilbroad Slaa, would emerge as the clear winner in presidential elections, CHADEMA tried to extend its political leverage against the dominance of the ruling CCM, and also against the claims of the previously strongest opposition party, the Civic United Front (CUF). CHADEMA followed a mixed approach of confrontation with CCM and the state on the one hand, and constructive contributions to the public debate on the other. However, it also repeatedly embarked on a populist approach, mobilising support in public rallies where party officials built on widespread dissatisfaction with the government. Its leaders demanded an investigation into the 2010 elections, which they claimed were flawed, and refused to recognise Kikwete as the legitimate president. Hinting at the effects of mass actions in Egypt and Libya, they threatened to use public support to cause the government serious problems.

On 5 January, *five people died* and numerous others were injured in Arusha during clashes between CHADEMA *supporters* and *police*. CHADEMA had called for demonstrations to protest against the election of the chairperson of the Arusha City Council (serving as City Mayor) in December 2010. After initially granting permission, police banned demonstrations but allowed a rally to be held. CHADEMA nevertheless staged its demonstration, which provoked an overreaction by the riot police, who responded to stone-throwing demonstrators with tear gas and live ammunition. More than 40 CHADEMA members, among them the national party leaders, were arrested and charged with unlawful assembly, but were released on bail. Government leaders, including Kikwete, Minister of Home Affairs Nahodha and Foreign Minister Membe, spoke of "unfortunate" incidents and criticised at least indirectly the harsh response of the police. Although the escalation was mainly due to the overreaction of the security forces, CHADEMA was also blamed for going ahead with the demonstration despite the ban. Further demonstrations brought thousands of people to the streets in Arusha, Mwanza and other towns, and were conducted peacefully, but not without incident. In Kahama, secretary general Slaa was one of three senior party leaders who were detained for addressing a party rally without permission. On 5 June, CHADEMA chairman Mbowe was arrested in Dar es Salaam, after an arrest warrant was issued against him and six other CHADEMA leaders who had failed to appear before the Arusha court in May. The same day, CHADEMA MP Zitto Kabwe was arrested in Singida for having allegedly extended a political rally beyond the permitted time. Godbless Lema, MP for Arusha, and 19 other people were arrested on 31 October for unauthorised assembly. CHADEMA announced a seven-day vigil and set up a tented protest, calling for his release. On 8 November, Slaa and other party leaders were arrested after they had extended to early morning a permitted public assembly staged to demand Lema's release. Again, police used tear gas and live ammunition to disperse the crowd. The following day, the party leaders were charged with unlawful assembly and released on bail. Lema was released two weeks later.

Parliament also became an arena for the display of CHADEMA's increased self-confidence, and debates became more heated and emotional. While some observers saw these developments as an indication of a lively democratic atmosphere in the National Assembly, others were concerned that parliamentary rules were being violated and that the quality of debate was falling, focussing more on party interests, polemics and personal accusations than on solving the country's problems. Some *CCM parliamentarians*, however, refrained from pure partisan politics and fulfilled their responsibility to *control the government*. This became most obvious when MPs denounced corruption, especially during the budget sessions in June. The budgets of several ministries came under intense fire. The ministry of energy and minerals' budget was initially rejected and only passed three weeks later after the minister had explained in detail how his ministry intended to tackle the severe energy problems. The budgets of two other ministries were also only passed after amendments and the prime minister's intervention.

CHADEMA's Zitto Kabwe opened a new and popular debate by *questioning additional daily allowances* of TSh 150.000 for MPs. The system of allowances had always attracted much criticism from donors, as well as from within Tanzania. Kabwe argued that it was the duty of parliamentarians to participate in meetings and to discuss public affairs and that they were paid their regular salaries in order to do so. He asked the parliament's secretary to stop paying allowances to him, and said he would otherwise donate them to development projects in his home constituency. Kabwe's popular initiative was supported by some opposition MPs, but also earned criticism, even from MPs of his own party, who accused him of being motivated by personal ambition.

Relations within the opposition camp were somewhat cold. CHADEMA, as the largest opposition faction in parliament, broke with an unwritten tradition and formed a shadow cabinet without including members of the other opposition parties, particularly the CUF, which CHADEMA accused of no longer belonging to the opposition after forming a Government of National Unity (GNU) in Zanzibar. The CUF and the other smaller opposition parties appealed in vain for the formation of a joint bloc of all five opposition parties. Towards the end of the year, two smaller *opposition parties were shaken by internal conflicts*. In mid-December, NCCR-Mageuzi (National Convention for Construction and Reform – Change) expelled one of its only four elected MPs, accusing him of undermining the party. In late December, an influential CUF member was threatened with expulsion, together with 13 others, for violating the party constitution.

The arrival of a serious political alternative to the CCM posed new challenges for the long dominant party. CHADEMA's strong showing, its persistent campaigning and the continuing popularity of its 2010 presidential candidate, as well as widespread dissatisfaction with the CCM government and perceptions that the CCM had mainly become the home of corrupt politicians, put the ruling party under stress. Internal factionalism and power struggles in the run-up to crucial party elections in 2012 increased the need to act. During the CCM's 34th anniversary celebrations in February, Kikwete, in his role as party chairman, announced that the CCM would undergo a *purge*, introducing reforms and freeing itself of corrupt members. In early April, a *major reshuffle of the top leadership* was undertaken during meetings of the top party organs – the National Executive Committee (NEC) and Central Committee (CC). Several members of the CC, the most important decision-making organ, and the complete seven-member party secretariat stepped down on 9 April. Two days later, new members were chosen. The most significant changes included the replacement of secretary general Yusuf Makamba by the experienced public servant Wilson Mukama, and that of ideology and publicity secretary John Chiligati by former youth wing leader Nape Nnauye, who became mainly responsible for the purge process, popularised under its Kiswahili name 'kujivua gamba' (skin-shedding). Welcomed as a *first step to clean up the party* was the removal of two formerly influential but highly controversial politicians from the CC, Rostam Aziz and Andrew Chenge, who, together with former prime minister Edward Lowassa, were alleged to have been involved in major corruption scandals in previous years and were seen by many as symbolic of major corruption in the CCM. They remained members of the NEC, however, where Lowassa in particular was still able to mobilise support. The composition of the CCM's new top team indicated that Kikwete was able both to fill the main party organs with supporters of his reform policies, and to satisfy the interests of influential competing factions associated with Lowassa, Chenge, Aziz, Makamba and others. On 13 July, *Aziz resigned* unexpectedly as MP for Igunga constituency and as NEC member, explaining that he was tired of "gutter politics" and intended to focus more on his private business. He also wanted to allow the CCM to concentrate on more important issues.

Observers argued that changes in the CCM's leadership were no more than a first step, which would have to be followed by a revitalisation of the party structure down to grassroots level if the party wanted to regain public confidence. In addition to changes in personnel, *structural reforms were introduced*, such as the establishment of an advisory board of elders, a professionalised secretariat and changes to the mechanisms for the election of NEC members.

By-elections in Igunga on 2 October were heavily contested between the CCM and CHADEMA due to the *highly symbolic* nature of the vote. CHADEMA was keen to take the seat from CCM as a demonstration that it was already on its way to take over power from the ruling party. To the CCM, it was important to bring to a halt what could otherwise be seen as CHADEMA's continuous triumphal progress. Both parties deployed leading personnel during the campaign to ensure victory. The CCM's campaign was headed by former president Benjamin Mkapa and even supported by the ousted Aziz. CHADEMA's top brass appeared in the constituency, including chairman Mbowe and other prominent members. The campaigns were dominated by mud-slinging and aggressive behaviour. The *CCM secured the seat by a small margin* (55.5%) and the CHADEMA candidate finished second with 44.3%. Despite its victory, the CCM suffered a significant fall in support compared with the 73% of votes that Aziz had won only a year before, and CHADEMA had gained, finishing second in a constituency where the CUF had been number two in October 2010. CHADEMA refused to accept the result and claimed that electoral standards had been violated. The media presence and coverage was high, but voters seemed to have been alienated by the ferocity of the campaign, as turnout was only 31.4%.

CCM top-level meetings on 20–27 November raised expectations, mainly in the press, that the party would speed up its cleansing process and expel party cadres widely associated with corruption, namely Lowassa, Chenge and Aziz. Nnauye, who had involved himself in a months-long battle against Lowassa and friends, declared, however, that the popular demands to remove a few individuals from the party would reduce the comprehensive purge to a mere symbolic action. Lowassa and Chenge remained influential NEC members and Lowassa in particular seemed even to strengthen his position. Some observers assumed that Nnauye and other reformers had underestimated the Lowassa faction's power basis. To avoid an open conflict between the competing factions, the purge seemed to have been quietly abandoned.

Zanzibar had come *out of the limelight* somewhat. The GNU, formed after the 2010 elections between the equally strong CCM and CUF, apparently worked smoothly, without any obvious disruptions. The question remained of whether the new arrangement would simply allow the former opposition party, the CUF, to participate in the exploitation of state resources or whether it would also lead to positive developments for the Zanzibari people. The new arrangement at least contributed to reducing tensions among the Zanzibari population. It was reported that party affiliation stopped playing a segregating role in daily activities as it had before the parties' compromise. On the other hand, because it united formerly divergent forces, the GNU contributed to the growth of a *pronounced Zanzibari nationalism*, at least in the context of the debate on the new constitution. Prospects of offshore oil discoveries in Zanzibar waters also led to an emphasis on Zanzibar's nationalist ambitions.

Corruption, irrespective of the government's commitment to curbing it, remained an issue throughout the year, although no major developments were revealed. In May, the Prevention and Combating of Corruption Bureau published its National Governance and Corruption Survey, but the long-awaited report contained hardly any new or surprising information. It named institutions most prone to corruption, such as the police, the judiciary, the education sector and water and electricity supply agencies. This perception was largely shared by TI's *East Africa Bribery Index* in late October. The Index ranked Tanzania the third most corrupt of the five EAC member states, taking the place of Kenya, which now ranked fourth. The BAE scandal about the supply of an air traffic control system in 1999 rumbled on. In early 2010, the British Serious Fraud Office had ordered the arms manufacturer BAE Systems to pay almost £ 30 m to Tanzania. The Tanzanian and UK governments had agreed in late 2010 to invest most of the money in the education sector. BAE, however, insisted on having a say and suggested that a British NGO should supervise the use of the money. This was strongly rejected by the Tanzanian government. The relevant UK House of Commons committee advised BAE to transfer the money to Tanzania as soon as possible.

Celebrations for the *50th anniversary of Tanzania Mainland's political independence* started in July, with numerous small events. The celebrations were themed "We dared, we succeeded, and we are still forging ahead". The main celebrations on Independence Day, 9 December, were attended by many international representatives, including five African heads of state. The absence of the presidents of the other four EAC member states (which did, however, send representatives) was speculated to have been an expression of dismay at Tanzania's absence at the signing of an agreement *for the establishment of the* EAC *Political Federation two weeks earlier*. During the festivities, the government highlighted achievements of 50 years of independence, comparing the country's current situation with conditions in 1961, and focussing on education, infrastructure and the economy. These positive views were largely shared by the media, which also questioned, however, the limited extent of these successes as well as the degree of the country's independence, with it being still one of the poorest nations in the world and highly dependent on foreign aid. Some members of opposition parties complained that the costs of the celebrations, reportedly TSh 64 bn, were too high and that the money could have better been invested in the country's development.

Much public attention was given to a *healer* from a village near *Loliondo* in northern Tanzania. The retired Lutheran pastor, Ambilikile Masapila, nicknamed 'Babu' (Grandfather), claimed that the Almighty had revealed to him the recipe for a miracle cure that could treat several diseases, including HIV/AIDS, cancer, diabetes and asthma. About 4 m people, including cabinet ministers and other prominent politicians, reportedly went to his remote village to drink from '*kikombe cha babu*' (Grandfather's cup), causing traffic jams for up to 50 km. People even came from abroad by plane and helicopter, and the authorities had to introduce special regulations to control the traffic. Prime Minister Pinda ordered the district authorities to improve the infrastructure and to establish sanitation facilities and large health centres, as well as cemeteries for the many sick people who died while queuing. The government analysed the brew, consisting mainly of the boiled roots of a certain tree, and found that it did not have any negative effect on the human body, but stated that it was too early to say whether it had any curative properties. However, there were press reports about patients whose conditions had worsened or who had even died, since they had stopped taking their prescribed medication after drinking from 'Grandfather's cup'. Following Babu's success, numerous other self-declared healers claimed that they had also been given secret recipes by God. After several months' excitement, the hype about "Babu's cup" subsided significantly.

Plans to close the remaining two *refugee camps* by the end of the year were postponed to 2012. The government's programme to relocate to other regions refugees who had been naturalised in 2010 proved difficult, because most of these early Burundian refugees (from 1972) had established themselves over decades and refused relocation. Strong competition for jobs and increased immigration from China, South Asia and African countries prompted intensified efforts by the state authorities to *control and reduce illegal immigration* but also led to *increasing xenophobia and economic nationalism.*

Foreign Affairs

Numerous high-profile visitors reflected Tanzania's excellent international relations. In May, *India*'s Prime Minister Manmohan Singh signed bilateral agreements, including a $ 190 m credit for water supply projects in Dar es Salaam and $ 10 m for capacity-building projects in the social and education sectors. Another agreement was signed to construct a heart surgery hospital in Dar es Salaam with Indian aid. Singh offered support for Tanzania's 'Kilimo Kwanza' (agriculture first) programme and envisaged the intensification of trade relations, focussing on small and medium-sized industries, healthcare and human resource development. US Secretary of State *Hillary Clinton* paid a short visit on 11–12 June on her way back from a Libya Contact Group meeting in the UAE. Tanzania was one of only four countries to take part in the first set of the new US 'Partnership for Growth' initiative. Clinton spoke with Kikwete *inter alia* about security threats posed by Somali pirates along the East African coast. She visited some US-funded development projects and the memorial site for victims of the US embassy bombings of 1998, only one day after Somali officials stated that soldiers had killed Fazul Abdullah Mohammed, the suspected mastermind behind the bombings. Clinton also co-hosted a high-level forum on the fight against global hunger and malnutrition, together with *Irish* Deputy Prime Minister Eamon Gilmore, who, on a four-day visit, met Prime Minister Pinda and senior members of government, representatives from Irish NGOs and members of the business community.

Somalia's interim president, Sheikh Sharif Sheikh Ahmed, accompanied by several ministers, arrived on 9 August for a two-day visit. Kikwete pledged to donate 300 tonnes of maize as food aid to combat famine and promised further support for Somalia in fighting its manifold problems, including eradicating the al-Shabaab militias and piracy activities. Both phenomena were increasingly perceived as a threat to Tanzania. The authorities reported increased acts of piracy and illegal Somali immigration and alerted the public to the possibility of al-Shabaab terror attacks. Kikwete backed Kenya's military operation against al-Shabaab.

On 6 November, the UK's *Prince Charles* and his wife Camilla arrived for a four-day official visit on Kikwete's invitation as part of the 50th anniversary celebrations of Tanzania Mainland's independence. Although they were warmly received in Dar es Salaam, Zanzibar and Arusha, their visit coincided with threats by British Prime Minister David Cameron to withhold UK aid from governments that would not reform legislation banning homosexuality. Several Tanzanian government leaders, along with religious leaders and the media, sharply rejected these demands, calling them a neo-colonial attempt to impose Western ideas on poor countries in violation of their own values and declared that the country would rather go without British funding than legalise homosexuality. The UK High Commissioner tried to smooth the waters, explaining that Cameron had been quoted out of context. Britain would neither enforce acceptance of homosexuality nor cut development aid.

The *donor community* remained concerned about Tanzania's problems in effectively fighting corruption, and doubted the government's willingness to enhance the anti-graft crusade. However, this only slightly affected the generally good relations, which were characterised by continuous support for Tanzania's development efforts.

Despite generally cordial relations with all neighbouring countries, Tanzania's cautious attitude towards faster far-reaching EAC integration remained a source of contention. After long-disputed land and security questions re-emerged during a November meeting in Bujumbura, Burundi, the Tanzanian delegation refused to sign an agreement for moves towards an EAC Political Federation, but subsequently agreed to a reformulated text.

The government strongly opposed NATO's intervention in *Libya*, alleging that the UK and France had exceeded the mandates of the UN and the Arab League. Tanzania condemned the killing of Khadhafi as a human rights violation and warned of uncontrollable violence. It initially refused to recognise the National Transitional Council as Libya's new government.

Socioeconomic Developments

The overall *macroeconomic performance* continued to be fairly robust and generally in line with the strong growth trend of the past decade. In this period, Tanzania had become one of the best and most consistently performing countries in Africa, albeit still characterised by a very low absolute level of material wealth. The economy had largely been shielded from the adverse effects of the global economic and financial crisis. The *GDP growth rate* for 2011 was estimated to attain around 6.5%, quite similar to the preceding two years. Expectations for an acceleration of growth were mainly quashed by the effects of severe drought in parts of the country and the resulting power shortages. The agricultural sector again only grew by about 3%, barely higher than the population growth rate.

The deliberate growth stimulus through the government's 2009 rescue plan and extensive public investment programmes had clearly had a positive effect, but also greatly increased the fiscal deficit and now necessitated a return to a tighter monetary and fiscal policy. *Inflation* increased alarmingly throughout the year and was a major cause for growing popular discontent. Consumer price inflation climbed steadily from 6.4% in January to 19.8% in December, with an average for the year of 12.7%. The food price index in December had risen by 25% within a year. The *exchange rate* remained relatively stable during the first half of the year, but then depreciated sharply by 14% against the dollar to a new low in October, before recovering to an annual depreciation of 8% by year's end. The *structural trade deficit* narrowed slightly further, with 63% of Tanzania's import bill now covered by its own export revenues, the highest ratio ever achieved. While imports had grown by 21% to $ 8,650 m, exports had leapt by as much as 26% to $ 5,432 m (preliminary figures). Gold accounted for the bulk of exports (about 40%), but manufactured goods exports to regional markets also featured strongly, while the relative share of traditional agricultural exports declined further. The situation permitted the stabilisation of the (preliminary) *current-account deficit* at around 9.7% of GDP, slightly higher than in 2010. Gross *foreign reserves* also remained largely stable at $ 3.7 bn by the year's end, sufficient for a comfortable import coverage of over five months. While the *external debt* had previously been substantially reduced to a low of $ 4.2 bn in 2006 as a result of concerted debt cancellations, it had crept up again since then, reaching $ 9.7 bn at year's end (compared with $ 7.6 bn at end-2010). In the 2011 HDI, Tanzania marked some slight improvement and was ranked 152nd (out of 187 countries) in the low human development category. *GDP per capita* was estimated at about $ 525 and in PPP terms at $ 1,328.

IMF missions in March and October/November conducted the second and third reviews under the current *Policy Support Instrument* (*PSI*) operative since June 2010. They were generally satisfied with the overall macroeconomic performance and with progress in implementing agreed structural reforms, but stressed the need for a return to a tighter fiscal policy and for reducing inflation. In June, the *World Bank* formulated a new country assistance strategy for the 2012–2015 period, largely in line with support for Tanzania's own current PRSPs (generally known by their Swahili acronyms as MKUKUTA II for the mainland and MKUZA II for Zanzibar). In addition to these documents, a Five-Year Development Plan for 2011–2016 was launched by Kikwete on 7 June, creating some confusion about an abundance of policy documents, with the National Development Vision 2025 and the CCM election manifesto also still being used as guidelines.

As common declared principles, all documents focused on accelerating *pro-poor growth* in a sustainable manner by ensuring adequate prioritisation and coordination of policies and harnessing public-private-partnership potentials. Highest priority was accorded to agriculture under the '*Kilimo Kwanza*' (agriculture first) initiative, since it was identified as a growth driver supporting the majority of the poor rural population and offering employment opportunities to the youth. In January at the World Economic Forum in Davos, Switzerland, Kikwete outlined highly ambitious plans for a Southern Agricultural Growth Corridor in Tanzania, with expected investments of $ 3.4 bn over a 20-year period. Visions about more such corridors were also discussed. The government welcomed foreign agricultural investors and offered large tracts of land in little publicised deals. Despite looming problems of unresolved changing land rights, public criticism about 'land grabs' remained largely subdued for the time being. In the plans, greater emphasis was also given to infrastructure, with expectations of attracting more private investment, while progress was also to be maintained in education and health.

On 8 June, Finance Minister Mustafa Mkulo presented the 2011/2012 *budget* to parliament in conjunction with a review of the previous financial year's (provisional) outturn. Both revenue and spending figures had again been below the original budget projections, and the overall *fiscal deficit* had been lower than expected at about 6.9% of GDP. Domestic revenue shortfalls of 7.1% indicated an apparent slackening of revenue collection efforts, while received external grants were as much as 18.1% lower than had been expected, adding up to an overall revenue shortfall of 9.8%. This led to substantially reduced capital (development) expenditure (by 28%), while recurrent spending was only 4.3% below target. Only 23% of the total revenue had by then arrived from foreign donors, a noticeable reduction compared with the situation only a few years earlier (with over 40%). The domestic revenue quota of 16.3% of GDP had remained comparatively low, with a target of 17.9% set for 2015/2016. On the expenditure side, 71% was allocated for recurrent expenses, and only 29% for investments.

The *mining sector* (mainly gold) continued to contribute significantly to overall growth and exports, but by and large remained an enclave activity without substantial linkages to the rest of the economy and without much employment generation. Even the IMF was critical of the fact that the gold mining companies were still not contributing enough to the government's revenue and it called for a review of mining taxes. After lengthy debates, agreement was reached in October to raise royalty payments from 3% to 4% in line with the 2010 Mining Act, to become effective in 2012.

On 22 June, Minister for Natural Resources and Tourism Ezekiel Maige sent a letter to the UNESCO World Heritage Centre, clarifying that the government had abandoned plans to build a *highway* through the *Serengeti National Park*. According to the letter, tarmac roads would only be constructed to towns close to the eastern and western borders of the park. The 53–km section running through the Serengeti would remain a gravel road and be used mainly for tourism and administrative purposes. The government was also seriously considering the construction of an alternative road south of Serengeti and Ngorongoro, which had been suggested by critics of the Serengeti Highway. Environmentalists welcomed the decision, but pointed out that even a gravel road would increase traffic through the Serengeti. Only a few days later, Transport Minister Omari Nundu emphasised that the proposed *railway project from Tanga via Arusha to Musoma* would also be built around the southern end of the Serengeti, thus avoiding the park. On 23 December, Nundu announced that a Chinese company had been commissioned to conduct a feasibility study. Construction of the railway line and ports in Tanga, Musoma and Kampala was envisaged to be completed by 2015. Ecologists were worried that the Tanga port was planned to be built in the Marine National Park at Mwambani Bay. The government asked UNESCO to allow changes to the boundaries of *Selous Game Reserve* so that *exploration of uranium deposits* could go ahead without its World Heritage Site status being affected. Preparations for uranium mining in Ruvuma Region and in Bahi and Manyoni Districts in central Tanzania made progress. Opposition to the uranium mining activities came from various national and international NGOs, scientists, the media, members of opposition parties and affected villagers.

Towards the end of the year, the government was faced with considerable *liquidity problems* and was contemplating cutting a number of planned and budgeted development projects. This was mainly the result of considerable disbursement delays on the part of external donors, who contributed substantially to the regular budget through the General Budget Support scheme, while revenue collection was quite normal. Public employees in local government structures were allegedly only being paid after considerable delays.

Tanzania was less severely affected by *drought* than Kenya and the Horn of Africa, but was nevertheless confronted by serious problems. There was temporary fear of famine in about 42 districts, but the situation was by and large contained with the release of 115,000 tonnes from the Strategic Grain Reserve. In May, the government banned all food exports as a measure to constrain food price inflation, but this was lifted in October, after a good harvest and a grain surplus of 1.7 m tonnes.

The lack of rainfall also led to a lowering of water levels and to renewed *power generation* problems, which affected many industries and the urban population. In May, power-rationing measures had to be introduced and remained in force throughout the year. An emergency power plan aimed to install additional thermal plants (with a capacity of about 220 MW), but this would need time to be realised. The power problems negatively affected economic growth, but also contributed to anger and political frustration among the population. With effect from January 2012, electricity tariffs would be raised by 40% to cover some of the extra costs for the emergency installations, although the power company TANESCO had applied for an even higher increase. In August, the Energy and Water Utilities Regulatory Authority decreed the reduction of *fuel prices* by 8%–9% in an attempt to control sharp price escalations, but this seriously backfired when the oil companies stopped the sale of fuel, causing immediate severe shortages and public anger. After two weeks, the Authority had to backtrack and allow price hikes.

There was growing optimism, based on good longer-term prospects for commercial *oil and gas production*, that the perennial energy problems would soon be overcome. Exploration activities both on-shore and off-shore seemed to indicate a promising future, most concretely in the existing Songo Songo gas-producing area along the coast and around Mnazi Bay on Lake Nyasa. It also seemed that long-existing plans to exploit the Mchuchuma *coal reserves* in the south-west for power generation would become a reality in the near future, with the signing of an investment agreement with a Chinese company.

No viable longer-term solution was yet in sight for either the ailing *Tanzania Railways Ltd.* (TRL) or *Air Tanzania*. In July, the last personnel from RITES of India left the TRL operations after the government's decision in 2010 to terminate the Indian shareholding and management involvement in TRL following a clearly disappointing performance. TRL continued to function very unsatisfactorily under local management, while prospects for extensive upgrading remained uncertain. The same was the case with the national airline. A possible recapitalisation, with public money and a (partial) privatisation, was still contemplated, but the airline remained inoperative throughout the year. The private Precision Air had in the meantime become the leading local airline and started to offer shares in October, with 51% reserved for Tanzanians.

On 11 September, more than 200 people died in a *ferry accident in Zanzibar*, and over 600 people were rescued. The heavily overloaded ferry was apparently hit by a strong current on its way from Unguja to Pemba Island. Only a few weeks later, in late December, the nation was shocked by heavy seasonal rains which caused *flooding* in various parts of the country. Dar es Salaam experienced the heaviest rainfalls for 57 years and was seriously affected, and many parts of the city were flooded for several days. At least 40 people died and thousands lost their homes or other property. The government provided an area of land for the resettlement of almost 3,000 of the more than 4,500 flood victims. Earlier in the year, on 16 February, Dar es Salaam had already been the scene of a tragic accident. More than 25 people died when a military arsenal exploded, and about 400 were injured. The government was criticised for keeping ammunition too close to residential areas.

Despite Tanzania's consistently high GDP growth rates, a better overall socioeconomic development continued to be restrained by a combination of major contributing factors, such as poor education, unproductive agriculture, permanent energy and infrastructural weaknesses, ineffective government structures and cumbersome bureaucracy. In the World Bank's Doing Business 2012 Tanzania was ranked 127th (of 183 countries), thus showing no improvement at all.

Tanzania in 2012

President Kikwete and his long-ruling dominant Revolutionary Party ('Chama cha Mapinduzi', CCM) were faced by an ever more assertive political opposition and by vocal criticism from civil society organisations, but nevertheless remained fully in control of all state institutions. Rising social and religious tensions led to unrest and demonstrations and raised fears about a possible end of Tanzania's hitherto typically stable and peaceful political climate. Internal power struggles between various CCM factions were evident as the party tried to regain some of its lost credibility and was already gearing up towards the next elections in 2015. Countrywide public hearings were held to solicit views on the content of an envisaged new constitution, but no firm conclusions had begun to emerge. Highly divergent views on the delicate issue of the structure of the Union between Zanzibar and the mainland were prominently raised and created an element of uncertainty. Tanzania was poised to shoulder more responsibility for various sub-regional conflicts in the near future, while an old border conflict with Malawi escalated into a diplomatic confrontation. Macroeconomic performance remained relatively satisfactory and continued to be commended by international institutions and donors, but the population still saw little concrete progress and was by and large dissatisfied with the services provided by state institutions. Many large infrastructural investments were in the planning stage, and high expectations centred on prospects for Tanzania becoming a major gas producer.

Domestic Politics

The *government* and the *CCM* were faced throughout the year by growing pressure from the main opposition party, *CHADEMA* (Party for Democracy and Development), which continued its efforts to increase its political weight and gain popular support. For the first time in Tanzania's multi-party history, the CCM *lost a parliamentary seat in a by-election* to the steadily growing CHADEMA. The by-election on 1 April in Arumeru constituency (Arusha Region) had become necessary upon the previous MP's death. Despite some minor incidents in the weeks before election day, the election itself was conducted in a peaceful atmosphere and without major problems. However, voter turnout reached barely 48%. CHADEMA's candidate, Joshua Nassari, won comfortably with 54% against his CCM competitor (44%), the son of the deceased MP. Many observers highlighted the significance of CHADEMA's historic victory as a harbinger of regime change in the general elections due in 2015. On 21 August, the Tabora High Court, in a judgment following a CHADEMA challenge, nullified the CCM's victory in the October 2011 Igunga by-election on the basis of bribery of voters. And on 27 December, the Court of Appeal reinstated CHADEMA's Godbless Lema as MP for Arusha, thereby overturning an earlier High Court ruling that had nullified Lema's win in the 2010 elections.

Hardly three weeks after CHADEMA's Arumeru victory, several *ministers came under fire* when the National Assembly debated the reports of three parliamentary oversight committees, which revealed gross misuse of public funds. In addition, the tabled annual report of the Controller and Auditor General disclosed details of massive fraud. Several MPs demanded the resignation of seven cabinet ministers and one deputy minister, including the finance minister. On 19 April, the deputy leader of the official opposition and chairman of the parliamentary Parastatal Organisations Accountability Committee, CHADEMA MP Zitto Kabwe, threatened to initiate a *vote of no confidence against Prime Minister Mizengo Pinda* unless the accused ministers stepped down. It was the first time in Tanzania's parliamentary history that the instrument of impeachment had been used. Kabwe made it clear that he was not targeting the prime minister himself, but the said ministers. Since the National Assembly's members did not have the constitutional right to remove individual ministers, the motion was directed at the prime minister as the leader of government business. Opposition parties put aside their rivalries and supported the motion, and at least five CCM MPs also signed. By 22 April, the motion had the support of the required quorum of at least 20% of all MPs. However, Parliamentary Speaker Anne Makinda ruled out the possibility of a no confidence motion during the current parliamentary session for technical reasons. On 4 May, *President Jakaya Kikwete carried out a cabinet reshuffle* and dropped six of the embattled ministers and two deputy ministers; two of the accused ministers were shifted to other ministries. Three new ministers and ten new deputies were appointed, increasing the cabinet by five to 55 members and giving it a somewhat more technocratic appearance.

In the aftermath of the political crisis, which had further increased popular distrust in the CCM and added to CHADEMA's credibility, the government increased its efforts to *fight corruption and bad governance.* On 29 May, the director of the Tanzania Bureau of Standards was suspended. In June, Pinda sacked 12 local government district executive officers in response to allegations of misappropriation of public funds. On 15 July, the managing director of Tanzania Electric Supply Company (TANESCO) and at least three other senior officials were suspended following allegations of embezzlement and abuse of office. A number of high-ranking officials from the Ministry of Natural Resources and Tourism were sacked in August in connection with smuggling live animals and other dubious activities. Transport Minister Harrison Mwakyembe suspended seven high-ranking Tanzania Port Authority (TPA) officers in August, including the director general, and disbanded the TPA board. In December, 12 other TPA officials were sacked following allegations of mismanagement. MPs were not spared either. On 2 August, Speaker Makinda appointed a subcommittee to investigate corruption allegations against several legislators in connection with the budget of the Ministry of Energy and Minerals.

The CCM held its *8th National Congress* in Dodoma on 10–13 November to elect a new leadership to serve for the next five years – and to prepare the party for the general elections in 2015. The Congress was the culmination of internal party elections from district to national levels and of party wing leaders, which had been conducted in several steps over a six-month period. The Congress aimed at giving the party a new image and burnishing its tattered public reputation, but was overshadowed by widely reported allegations of many cases of fraud and corruption in rivalry for leadership positions. *Kikwete* was *re-elected as chairman* with the votes of 99.9% of the almost 2,400 delegates. Zanzibar President Ali Mohammed Shein replaced his predecessor Amani Karume as CCM vice chairman for Zanzibar, as expected, and former secretary-general Philip Mangula became vice chairman for the mainland. Party veteran Abdulrahman Kinana was entrusted as new secretary-general with the clear task of reconciling the various feuding factions, while former UN deputy secretary-general Asha-Rose Migiro was given responsibility for political and foreign affairs as member of CCM's secretariat. Kikwete surprisingly deferred the crucial decision on the composition of CCM's new Central Committee, explaining that he needed time to acquaint himself with the newly-elected members of the National Executive Committee (NEC).

Earlier, in February, the NEC had at Kikwete's instigation decided on important *changes* to the *CCM constitution*. In the future, NEC membership was to be a full-time post, no longer to be held concurrently with other public positions (even that of MP). This was intended to make NEC membership more secure, but also easier for the party chairman to control. A new Advisory Council, made up of former party chairmen and vice chairmen, was also instituted.

According to an *Afrobarometer survey*, conducted between May and June, Kikwete still enjoyed a relatively high level of popularity, but his approval ratings had gone down from 90 points in 2008 to 71 points in 2012. The decline was seen as related to lack of progress in the fight against corruption. About two-thirds of those interviewed expressed their confidence in the likelihood that the central government would solve the most important problems, despite complaining about the state authorities' poor performance in reducing poverty.

The *constitution review process*, started in 2011, was a significant issue throughout the year. After the government's attempt to control the entire process had failed in 2011 as a result of pressure from opposition parties (namely CHADEMA) and civil society, the process sailed into calmer waters in 2012. At the heart of the debate was the *Constitution Review Bill*, which Kikwete had assented to in late November 2011, just one day after meeting a CHADEMA delegation. Although Kikwete had apparently ignored opposition concerns, some observers stated that a typical Tanzanian compromise might have been reached, allowing both the passing of the bill and a later incorporation of CHADEMA's views – and the bill was indeed amended in early February, after lively parliamentary debates had taken place and the demands of CHADEMA and civil society organisations were met. The amended bill ensured transparent and comprehensive public participation. A *Constitutional Review Commission* was assigned to canvass public opinion regarding a revised constitution, prepare a draft constitution, call for a constitutional assembly to discuss the draft and finally organise a referendum on the revised draft. The Commission was given powers to act independently and the president's office invited numerous societal groups to propose members. The Constitutional Forum (Jukwaa la Katiba), a coalition of more than 180 civil society organisations (CSOs), and two national NGO umbrella organisations called for a CSO convention in mid-March to decide on joint CSO representation on the Commission. The convention in Dodoma was attended by over 170 CSOs from all regions of the country. A list of 30 names was reduced to five and then to three, and was finally sent to the president's office. Altogether, about 550 people were proposed to the president by various stakeholders.

On 6 April, Kikwete announced the composition of the 30-member Constitutional Review Commission. The well-respected judge, former attorney general and prime minister Joseph Warioba was appointed as its chairman and former chief justice Augusto Ramadhani was named as his deputy. The members, half from each part of the Union, were selected from among well-known lawyers, academicians and representatives of civil society and the business sector. Despite some minor criticism, Kikwete was widely applauded for the wise selection of the Commission members.

The Commission began its work on 2 July and completed the first phase in early January 2013. Groups of two Commission members each were formed and toured the country to conduct *hearings* to collect the views of the people. According to Commission Chairman Warioba, more than 1,700 meetings were held in all 30 regions; over 1.3 m people attended the hearings, almost 65,000 individuals made verbal contributions, and some 250,000 people made written submissions. The Commission also received electronic contributions by e-mail and SMS. The hearings took place in a generally peaceful atmosphere and hardly any incidents were reported. In some cases, however, citizens complained that they had not been properly informed or that members of the public did not feel free to speak their mind in the presence of members of the local administration. Media coverage was high and the press reported frankly about criticisms of the government and the ruling party. The second phase, scheduled for January 2013, would serve to gather the views of organised groups, including state and non-state institutions, NGOs and political parties.

As expected, a number of *controversial issues* were discussed, among them the status and structure of the Union between Zanzibar and the mainland, the powers of the president and the system of government and public administration, as well as some questions regarding the electoral system. Other issues were arguments against gay rights, arguments in favour of and against the death penalty, complaints about corrupt practices and mismanagement, and concerns about disunity and increasing crime and violence. Some hearings developed into broad discussions of general political issues and causes of discontent and concern. In Zanzibar, the two political parties that formed the Government of National Unity (GNU), the CCM and *Civic United Front* (CUF), *disagreed on the format of the Union*. Whereas the CCM called for the continuation of the current two-tier government structure, the CUF proposed a treaty-based structure, whereby an autonomous Zanzibar would be linked to the mainland through contractual agreements.

The hearings also revealed a number of *shortcomings* in the *constitutional process*. It became clear that most people did not understand the role of the constitution in the political administration of their country. Thus, expectations were widespread that a new constitution would improve socioeconomic conditions for the people and ease daily hardships. It also was evident, that the frequently referred 'views of the people' were far from homogeneous. CSOs such as the Constitutional Forum argued that the whole process lacked a consensus-building mechanism to deal with differing opinions and work out solutions that would be acceptable to all.

Several separate developments indicated a general societal *tendency towards increasing conflict* and a growing readiness to use violence as a means of conflict resolution. *Violent conflicts* between CHADEMA and state organs, between Muslims and Christians and between the government and a newly emerged Islamist group, 'Uamsho' ('Awakening'), in Zanzibar cost the lives of several people and caused fears that the long-lasting peace in Tanzania was in serious danger.

On 24 March, *CHADEMA* launched its *M4C (Movement for Change) campaign*, which aimed at increasing the party's financial base and expanding its presence beyond its current strongholds. As in 2011, the party's efforts to increase its political reach provoked overreaction by the police. One person was killed on 27 August when anti-riot police tried to disperse a CHADEMA rally in Morogoro. On 2 September, Daudi Mwangosi, a well-known television reporter and chairman of the Iringa Press Club, was shot dead by police at close range when he was reporting on clashes between CHADEMA and police during a political rally in a village in Iringa Region. According to eyewitnesses and photographic material, police officers attacked Mwangosi after he confronted them about an assault on another journalist. It was the first time Tanzania had witnessed a *journalist killed while working*. The killing was widely condemned both inside and outside the country, and the government was called upon to investigate. Three separate investigation committees – set up by the Ministry of Home Affairs, the Commission for Human Rights and Good Governance and jointly by the Media Council of Tanzania and the Tanzania Editors Forum – determined that the police had used excessive force. While the Ministry of Home Affairs' committee stated that the police were not responsible for Mwangosi's death, the other committees found evidence that the journalist was deliberately killed by police and urged the government to take strong measures against those involved. The Legal and Human Rights Centre filed a case against the government at the ICC and submitted a petition to the UN Special Rapporteur on extrajudicial, summary or arbitrary executions and to the African Commission on Human and Peoples' Rights. Although one police officer was arrested and charged with murder, it remained unclear whether the authorities were willing to investigate the case thoroughly.

The activities of *'Uamsho'* in *Zanzibar* contributed to *increasing tensions* between its followers and the state and between *Muslims* and *Christians* – albeit on a comparatively minor scale. Registered in 2001 as a religious group, 'Uamsho' came up with a political agenda in 2012 and emerged as one of several groups campaigning for Zanzibar's full autonomy. Demonstrations by 'Uamsho' supporters on 26 and 27 May turned violent, after police forces used tear gas. Groups of rioting youths blocked roads and destroyed shops, bars and other property, mainly belonging to Christians and mainlanders, and three churches were torched. 'Uamsho', which was accused of being behind the riots, distanced itself, however, and called for calm. The authorities reacted strongly, with an increased police presence and a ban on all religious demonstrations. When 'Uamsho' members met on 21 July in a Zanzibar mosque to mourn the victims of a disastrous ferry accident, riot police violently dispersed them, accusing 'Uamsho' of exploiting the prayers for purposes of political agitation. According to the police, 43 'Uamsho' members were arrested following clashes with the police in Zanzibar's Darajani area. The situation escalated again on 17–18 October, after 'Uamsho' leader Sheikh Farid Hadi Ahmed was reported missing. Supporters of the group demanded information from the police about the Sheikh's whereabouts, blocked streets and looted bars and shops and fought with the police, who used tear gas. One policeman was hacked to death on his way home, but 'Uamsho' denied any involvement in the murder or in any kind of violence. Police arrested about 50 people, including Sheikh Ahmed, who had reappeared a few days after the riots.

Many observers agreed that the riots were primarily caused by *young hooligans* and were motivated by socioeconomic rather than religious or political factors. However, 'Uamsho''s taking up a political agenda – and the support its secessionist and Islamist propaganda enjoyed – indicated that the group was able to fill a political gap that had opened up with the creation of the GNU after the 2010 elections. The GNU forced the former opposition party, the CUF, into a more moderate stance towards the Union and towards the CCM. In the absence of any other strong political party, 'Uamsho' was clearly able to attract disaffected individuals who felt betrayed by the CUF. However, the latter was accused of having informal links with 'Uamsho', allegedly using the organisation as an instrument to work for CUF's assumed anti-Union aims, which the party itself, as part of the government, could no longer campaign for. Whether 'Uamsho' supported anti-Christian actions or not, the attacks on churches indicated a radicalisation of a section within the Muslim society of Zanzibar and a *deterioration* in the usually good *relations between*

Christians and Muslims, including increased suspicion between the two groups.

The combination of rivalry between various Muslim groups, mutual distrust between Muslims and Christians in an already heated atmosphere, and a frustrated and violence-prone mostly young mob, joined by criminal gangs, led to a situation in which a minor incident was enough to cause *riots* in the *Dar es Salaam suburb* of *Mbagala* in mid-October. On 12 October, an angry mob stormed a police station and demanded that the police hand over a 14-year-old boy, who had been accused of desecrating the Qur'an. The Christian boy had urinated on a copy of the Qur'an during an argument with a Muslim friend about the assumed power of the Qur'an to turn anyone who defiled it into a snake. Police refused to hand over the boy and several 100 mostly young people started looting at least five nearby churches, destroying several cars and clashing for about five hours with the police. More than 120 people were arrested and a few days later 36 were charged in court with violence and vandalism.

Dozens were injured on 19 October, when police used tear gas and water canon to disperse a group of about 200 people who had planned to demonstrate for the release of Secretary General of the Council of Muslim Organisations Sheikh Ponda Issa Ponda. Ponda and almost 50 of his followers had been arrested on 17 October on charges related to a land dispute with the National Muslim Council of Tanzania ('Bakwata'). Ponda was also charged with inciting chaos and breaching the peace by allegedly calling for the violent demonstrations in Mbagala. Ponda and his organisation had for years been involved in power struggles with the state-affiliated 'Bakwata' over control of and influence on the Muslim community. Just a month before his arrest, Ponda had threatened to force the government-appointed Mufti Issa bin Simba and 'Bakwata' leaders to step down.

Shortly after the October fracas, *two clerics* were *severely injured* in Zanzibar. On 6 November, the secretary of the Mufti of Zanzibar was injured by a liquid believed to be acid which was thrown on his face and body, and a Catholic priest was shot and seriously wounded on Christmas Day.

Despite the different political contexts and the complex backgrounds of the events in Zanzibar and Dar es Salaam, the coincidence of two religiously-linked violent events within a short period of time raised fears that Tanzania's record on inter-religious harmony, one of the main pillars of Tanzania's self-image, was in danger. Leading Christian and Muslim representatives, as well as representatives of the state, strongly condemned violence and hatred, called for calm and expressed their deep concern about the fragility of Muslim-Christian relations and hence of peace in the country.

Strikes and demonstrations indicated the population's *growing readiness* to *protest* against at least perceived injustice and to *risk conflict* with the state. In January, *medical doctors employed in public hospitals* went on *strike* for about three weeks, demanding improvements in the health sector and an increase in their salaries. After the government agreed to meet their demands, doctors resumed work. In early March, they called for the resignation of the health minister and her deputy, because their demands had not been met. After a meeting with Kikwete, doctors announced the end of the strike to give the government more time, but took strike action again on 23 June, complaining that nothing had been done. This time, the government reacted harshly, declared the strike illegal, expelled about 300 assistant doctors and sent military doctors and retired medics to the clinics. The strikes were unpopular among wide sections of the population. Many people who were interviewed by the press expressed little sympathy for the doctors, accusing them of breaking their oath for selfish motives, despite already being relatively privileged. Activists from various NGOs announced that they were preparing to take legal action against striking doctors for causing the deaths of innocent people.

On 26 June, one of the *strike organisers*, Stephen Ulimboka, was *abducted, tortured and left for dead* in a forest near Dar es Salaam. He was found severely injured by a passer-by. The government asserted that it had not been involved and offered to pay for Ulimboka's medical treatment in India, but the doctors' organisation rejected the government offer and flew him to a hospital in South Africa. Police arrested a Kenyan who admitted that he and other members of a criminal gang had been hired to attack Ulimboka. After his return from South Africa, Ulimboka accused the government of being behind the assault.

After negotiations between the government and the Teachers Trade Union (TTU) about a rise in salaries failed, a *teachers' strike* started on 30 July. In Dar es Salaam, pupils from several primary schools went onto the streets calling for the government to guarantee their right to a good education and to resolve the stand-off immediately. Police used tear gas to disperse the children. On 2 August, the High Court declared the strike illegal for technical reasons and the TTU called it off.

The government decision to construct a *gas pipeline* from gas fields in the southern Mtwara region to Dar es Salaam provoked strong opposition from several thousand people demanding a share in the natural resources found in their region. A peaceful demonstration on 27 December was organised jointly by several political parties. The protesters wanted the government to construct energy plants and industries in their region in order to create local jobs, instead of taking the gas to Dar es Salaam. The government insisted on its plan to transfer the gas to the commercial capital and reminded the residents of the south of the fact that all the resources of Tanzania contributed to the wealth of the nation as a whole. Prime Minister Pinda toured the region for three days and held discussions with stakeholders to explain the government's plans. However, public pressure was such that even CCM politicians from the south opposed their own government's decision. The demonstrations revealed a *deeply-rooted distrust* of the government's willingness to care for the neglected south.

On 31 December, Kikwete announced the results of the *population census* conducted in August. According to the data, Tanzania had a population of 44.9 m, with 43.6 m on the mainland and 1.3 m in Zanzibar, compared with the 34.4 m recorded in the 2002 census. This gave an annual growth rate of 2.6%, compared with 2.9% between 1988 and 2002. Kikwete urged Tanzanians to use more effective family planning measures. The census was also an issue in the *power-struggle between Islamic organisations*. Some Muslim organisations, such as 'Uamsho' and Ponda's Council of Islamic Organisations, called on Muslims to boycott the census, since they believed that it was not conducted freely and fairly. They called for the census to ask the religious affiliation of Tanzanians, which was not part of the census questionnaire, in order to establish the number of Muslims, Christians and followers of other religions. However, 'Bakwata' and other Muslim organisations supported the census.

Foreign Affairs

The long-standing *border dispute with Malawi* over *Lake Nyasa* resurfaced in July, after a meeting of a joint committee that had been formed in 2010 to resolve the dispute. The Tanzanian government called on Malawi to stop exploration for gas and oil in the northeastern part of the lake until the stand-off between the two counties over the ownership of the lake and the demarcation of the border was resolved. The conflict had been simmering since independence; but escalated after the Malawian government contracted with a British company in 2011 on exploration for the large oil and gas deposits that were expected to be found beneath the lake. Since independence, Malawi had claimed the entire northern part of the lake (while the southern part was shared by Malawi and Mozambique), referring to a colonial treaty between the German Empire and Great Britain. The 1890 treaty ruled that the border between the two territories lay on the Tanzanian shore of the lake, but Tanzania insisted that, under international law, the border was in the middle of the lake.

When the Malawian authorities restated in late July their claims to the entire northern lake and their right to exploration, aggressive statements by Tanzania's Foreign Minister Bernard Membe and Chairman of the Parliamentary Committee on Defence, Security and International Relations, Edward Lowassa, a former prime minister, raised *fears of war*. Their statement that – although a diplomatic solution was preferred – the Tanzanian Defence Forces were prepared to defend the country, was extensively reported and commented upon in the media. Generally, media and public opinion was strongly against any military option and called for a diplomatic solution. To calm the growing fears, numerous high-ranking politicians argued against a recourse to arms. During a SADC meeting on 18–19 August, Kikwete finally assured Malawian President Joyce Banda that Tanzania had no plans to go to war with Malawi.

Despite subsequent meetings of the joint committee from 20 to 27 August, the rhetoric escalated again in September, when Malawi accused Tanzania of intimidating Malawian fishermen and called off a further scheduled meeting. While Tanzania claimed to prefer to continue with bilateral negotiations, Malawi wanted to take the issue to the International Court of Justice (ICJ). Talks resumed on 17 November and resulted in an *agreement to disagree* and to seek *mediation from the SADC* Forum of Former Heads of State. Both countries also agreed to take the issue to the ICJ if SADC mediation failed. On 21 December, the two countries submitted a joint application for mediation to the Forum's chairman, former Mozambican president Joaquim Chissano.

Tanzania played an active role in the search for a solution to the renewed escalation of armed *conflict in eastern DRC*. At an ICGLR summit on 7–8 September in Kampala, the government offered to contribute about 800 soldiers to the proposed 4,000-strong 'neutral' intervention force that was intended to be deployed under an AU and UN mandate along the Rwandan-Congolese border. In a joint statement with the presidents of the DRC, Kenya and Uganda, Kikwete called upon the M23 rebel movement to leave Goma, cease hostilities and stop talking about overthrowing an elected government. The statement, issued at an ICGLR emergency meeting in Kampala on 24 November, also called on the DRC government to respond to the grievances of the M23. At an extraordinary SADC summit meeting on 8–9 December in Dar es Salaam, the community decided to deploy the SADC Standby Force in eastern DRC under an as yet undeclared AU and UN mandate, and endorsed Tanzania's offer to lead the force.

In August, Tanzania took over the chairmanship of the *SADC Organ on Politics, Defence and Security Cooperation ('SADC-Troika')* from South Africa. As troika chairman, Kikwete was also involved in searching for a solution to the political deadlock in Madagascar, trying to persuade the two competing politicians not to stand in the expected 2013 elections, as the SADC roadmap had recommended. After talks with Kikwete, ousted president Ravalomanana declared on 11 December in Dar es Salaam that he would not stand but his rival, Rajoelina, left Tanzania after consultations with Kikwete without making a clear statement. On 20 November, Kikwete launched the Revised Strategic Indicative Plan for the SADC Organ on Politics, Defence and Security (SIPO II).

Apart from the border row with Malawi, Tanzania maintained *cordial relations* with all its *other neighbours*, with a major focus on the further intensification of the EAC integration process. The *donor community* remained concerned about problems in effectively fighting corruption and doubted the government's willingness to enhance the anti-graft crusade. However, this only marginally affected generally good relations, which were characterised by continuous substantial support for Tanzania's development efforts. In May, Kikwete was one of only four African leaders to attend the *G8 summit* in Camp David (USA), taking part in a symposium on global agricultural and food security and soliciting support for Tanzania's own ambitious agricultural investment programmes.

On 25 June, the Bloomberg news agency reported that *Iranian oil tankers* had been re-flagged by *Zanzibar*, thus enabling Iran to evade the oil embargo imposed by the EU and US. After some diplomatic embarrassment and an investigation, the Zanzibar authorities stated that they would deregister the 36 Iranian tankers, which had been registered through a Dubai-based agent without Zanzibar's knowledge.

Socioeconomic Developments

The overall *macroeconomic performance* again continued to be quite robust and generally in line with the strong growth trend since the early 2000s. In this period, Tanzania had become one of the fastest growing and most consistently performing economies in Africa, albeit still characterised by a very low absolute level of material wealth. In the 2012 HDI, Tanzania remained ranked 152nd (out of 185 countries) in the low human development category. GDP *per capita* was estimated at about $ 540 and in PPP terms at $ 1,383. In the face of the continued global economic and financial crisis, Tanzania's economy proved to be remarkably resilient. The GDP *growth rate* for 2012 was estimated at 6.9%, slightly higher than in 2011 and largely in accordance with the growth trend of most preceding years (range of 6%–7%). Climatically it was an average year, which allowed the agricultural sector to grow by about 4.5%, the highest rate for five years.

Inflation had increased alarmingly in 2011 and remained high throughout the year, although with a slowly declining trend from 19.7% in January to 12.1% in December, underpinned by higher food output, a fall in global oil prices and a tight monetary policy. The average 16% consumer price inflation for the year (compared with

12.7% in 2011) was, however, a major cause of growing popular discontent. The *exchange rate* was unusually stable during the entire year, with practically no change in relation to the dollar (TSh 1,572: $ 1). This stability was interpreted as a clear sign of widely prevailing confidence in the economy's prospects. The *structural trade deficit* apparently declined by 8% to $ 4,345 m, equivalent to 14% of GDP (based on preliminary figures that are normally substantially revised). Imports grew only modestly, by 5% to $ 10,325 m, with oil alone accounting for one third. Exports, by contrast, surged substantially by 17% to $ 5,980 m, despite a small decline in the value of the main export, gold (accounting for 36% of total exports). Traditional agricultural exports experienced a strong recovery, but manufactured goods exports to regional markets also did well with more than 20% growth. On balance, 58% of Tanzania's import needs were covered by its own export revenues. The (preliminary) *current-account deficit* was nevertheless estimated by the IMF to have grown considerably, to around 15% of GDP, the highest percentage for several years. Gross *foreign reserves* were somewhat strengthened at $ 4.0 bn by the year's end, sufficient for a comfortable import coverage of almost five months. While the *external debt* had previously been substantially reduced to a low of $ 4.2 bn in 2006 as a result of concerted debt cancellations under the HIPC initiative, it had been creeping up again since then, reaching $ 10.6 bn at year's end (compared with $ 10 bn at end-2011).

IMF missions in March and September conducted the fourth and fifth reviews under the current *Policy Support Instrument (PSI)* operative since June 2010. In July, the IMF approved a new 18-month Standby Credit Facility for $ 225 m as a precautionary measure against potential downside risks of a global slowdown. Completing the fifth PSI review, the IMF commended the Tanzanian authorities for their prudent policy management and progress in stabilising the economy. The overall macroeconomic outlook remained favourable, with buoyant growth and declining inflation. Continued tight fiscal and monetary policies were considered crucial for securing sustainability. In the IMF's view, the budget for 2012/13 appropriately balanced the country's development and social spending needs with the debt-stabilising objective. Following a debt sustainability analysis, the IMF granted Tanzania an increase of its *non-concessional debt* ceiling from $ 1.77 bn to $ 2.86 bn, since the government had demonstrated a commitment to sound fiscal policies. Total external debt was given as 37% of GDP, while public external debt (30.4% of GDP) was well below the IMF's threshold of 50%. New non-concessional loans were only intended for massive planned infrastructure projects. Plans for an entry into the international sovereign bond market did not yet materialise, however.

On 14 June, new Finance Minister William Mgimwa submitted an upbeat 2012/13 *budget* to parliament in conjunction with a review of the previous financial year's (provisional) outturn. Both revenue and spending figures in 2011/12 had again been below the original budget projections, and the overall *fiscal deficit* of about 5% of GDP turned out to be lower than predicted. In the IMF's assessment, revenue collection had been strong and government spending was well-contained. In the new financial year, the government expected to raise a total TSh 15.1 trillion, an increase of 11.8% over the previous year. Of this total, 58% would be generated as domestic revenue, 15% from grants and concessional loans for development projects, 6% from general budget support by external donors and 8% from non-concessional borrowing. Domestic revenue was expected to attain a quota of 18% of GDP, compared with an anticipated 16.9% for the year to June 2012. On the expenditure side, only 30% was budgeted for development (down from 38%) and the rest for recurrent government operations. In a heated parliamentary debate, many MPs expressed concern about a narrow tax base and wanted the share of the development budget to be raised to 35%, but after five days of tension the budget was passed with an overwhelming CCM majority against all opposition legislators. No major changes to the tax regime were planned, but a strengthening of the traditional areas of revenue generation was proposed. The budget's main objectives were geared to an improvement of economic infrastructure (particularly power and transport), which was perceived to be a key bottleneck hindering faster economic growth. The general budget thrust was in line with the priorities of the Development Vision 2025, the current PRSP (known by the Swahili acronym as MKUKUTA II) and the MDGS.

An agro-business investment forum organised by the Tanzania Investment Centre (TIC) in November was intended to attract potential investors for *commercial agricultural ventures*, in particular the highly ambitious plan for a Southern Agricultural Growth Corridor, with expected investments of $ 3.4 bn over a 20-year period. This had for some time been promoted by Kikwete, including at the G8 summit in May, but response had so far remained quite restrained. The TIC identified 300,000 ha of land as available for local and foreign investors. Under the '*Kilimo Kwanza*' initiative, launched in 2009, the government continued to accord high priority to the modernisation of all aspects of agricultural development, including traditional smallholders. An agitated parliamentary debate in November, however, turned public attention to a prevailing concern about the fast-rising number of land conflicts and '*land grabs*', involving both foreign and local investors. As an appeasement measure, the government decreed ceilings for land deals to be effective from January 2013 (10,000 ha for sugar estates, 5,000 ha for rice farms).

Recurring *power failures*, although not quite as bad as in 2011 when drought curtailed hydro-power generation, continued to be a restraining factor on the economy and a nuisance to private households. Electricity tariffs were raised by 40% in January, but were still far too low to end the continuous losses of the state-owned power utility TANESCO. An application for further badly needed tariff increases was withdrawn in the face of strong consumer and industrial opposition. TANESCO accumulated outstanding debts to various independent power producers for resources needed to complement its own generating capacity. In July, the government had to clear a $ 30 m debt to Songas that threatened to terminate the supply of gas. TANESCO had long been badly managed and severely under-resourced. Only 14% of the population were estimated to have access to electricity.

The deficient *transport system* had also increasingly been identified as a serious impediment to faster economic growth. After years of delay, the astonishing level of congestion in the commercial capital Dar es Salaam was at least partially tackled by the introduction of a rail commuter service and the start of construction of a bus rapid transit system. Many road sections in various parts of the country were upgraded, financed by either donor funds or commercial loans. Discussions again resurfaced about a complete upgrading of the central railway line, possibly including an extension to Rwanda and Burundi, and a new railway link from Tanga via Arusha to Musoma on Lake Victoria, but this all remained vague and inconclusive. In October, China offered a $ 42 m interest-free loan for the revival of the long ailing TAZARA railway link to Zambia.

Optimistic expectations of an upturn in the economy gained further momentum in response to promising prospects for Tanzania's *mining sector*, based in particular on the rapidly rising confirmation of substantial viable *natural gas* and *oil* finds. Some exploration work had been undertaken since the 1950s without apparent success, and the first extraction of gas had only begun in 2004 on Songo Songo Island. Since then exploration had intensified, mainly in Lindi and Mtwara regions and off-shore, and the confirmed volume of proven gas reserves was rapidly updated to presently around 33 trillion ft^3. By June, 26 production-sharing agreements with 18 exploration companies were in existence, with more under discussion. Tanzania seemed poised to become a major gas producer in the near future, raising high expectations, but also fears of the well-known resource curse experienced in many other cases. The production and export of liquefied natural gas was foreseen as potentially feasible in 2021. In June, construction began of a 532-km gas pipeline from Mtwara to Dar es Salaam, financed by a $ 1.2 bn concessional Chinese loan.

Tanzania's first petroleum and gas conference in mid-October provided little clarity on the industry's future, since only a draft version of a national *natural gas policy* was presented by the relevant ministry. A substantive policy paper was to go to parliament in April 2013. One key point was the expected split of the present Tanzania Petroleum Development Corporation into a regulatory body and a revenue management fund. Due to the upsurge in exploration activities, the inflow of FDI had in 2011 almost doubled to $ 854 m, with over $ 300 m going into gas exploration and the rest into other mining projects and other ventures. The general East African excitement about oil and gas prospects also affected *Zanzibar*, but had also been the source of a fundamental dispute between the Zanzibar and Union governments since 2009. Although responsibility for the sector was not stated unambiguously in the Union constitution, Zanzibar adamantly insisted on full control over its potential oil and gas resources. In a surprise disclosure, Kikwete and Shein reached agreement in October on Zanzibar's claims, thus paving the way for exploration activities in Zanzibar's waters and at the same time removing one of the most contentious points in the constitutional debate.

Gold production continued to contribute significantly to overall growth and exports, despite some slight setbacks. African Barrick Gold, the largest company, finally agreed in May to pay a higher royalty (4% instead of 3%), which the government had set in 2011, while the other two main producers still disputed this. An attempt by a Chinese state-owned firm to acquire a 74% share in African Barrick met resistance and did not succeed. Initial work began on the ambitious $ 3 bn project for the exploitation of the Mchuchuma *coal reserves* and Liganga *iron-ore deposits* in the south-west, which had been signed up to in 2011 by the National Development Corporation (NDC) and a Chinese firm. However, there was also growing resentment of the expanding presence of small Chinese traders, who were perceived by local businessmen and traders to be unfair competitors. Work started on setting up a *uranium mine* within two years, after strong environmental concerns and resistance in parliament had been overcome and UNESCO had granted a boundary revision of the Selous Game Reserve to separate off the mining area. Tanzania was poised to soon become a major uranium producer.

Tanzania in 2013

Throughout the year, most political attention was absorbed by discussions over the progress of the constitutional review process that had been initiated in 2012. A first draft of an envisaged new constitution was published in June and served as a reference point for all ensuing debates. Most contentious was the delicate issue of the future structure of the Union between Zanzibar and the Mainland. The draft somewhat surprisingly proposed a new three-tier set-up in contradiction to the position of the ruling Revolutionary Party ('Chama Cha Mapinduzi'; CCM), which favoured the continuation of the current system. Final decisions on the constitution were left for a Constitutional Assembly, to be convened in early 2014. Internal power struggles between various CCM factions continued as the party tried to regain some of its lost credibility and was already gearing up towards the next elections in 2015. In reaction to revelations of massive human rights violations during an anti-poaching campaign, four ministers were sacked. Continuing social and religious tensions led to unrest and demonstrations and raised fears about a possible end to Tanzania's hitherto typically stable and peaceful political climate. Two newspapers were temporarily suspended, indicative of government nervousness.

State visits by the Chinese and US presidents underscored Tanzania's enhanced international recognition as both an influential political actor in Africa and a resource-rich country with a projected positive economic future. As part of a new UN peace enforcement operation in the DRC, a military battalion was deployed and engaged in battles. Relations with Rwanda deteriorated markedly, while there was also a noticeably increased crisis of confidence between Tanzania and its EAC partners. Macroeconomic performance remained quite satisfactory and continued to be commended by the IMF, the World Bank and donors, but the majority of the population still saw little concrete progress despite a moderate decline in the measured poverty incidence. Many large infrastructural investments were underway or planned, and high expectations centred on prospects for Tanzania becoming a major gas producer.

Domestic Politics

In continuation from 2012, much of the year's political attention centred on the *constitution review process*. In early January the *Constitutional Review Commission* (CRC) completed the first phase of collecting views of citizens regarding a new or revised constitution. According to CRC chairman Joseph Warioba, the commission had conducted more than 1,700 public hearings all over the country in which over 1.3 m people had participated. More than 300,000 written or oral contributions were made, including statements made by mobile phone, and via the CRC website or Facebook. In a second phase in January/February, representatives from more than 160 societal groups (civil society organisations [CSOs], political parties, governmental and non-governmental institutions, etc.) were heard by the CRC. Numerous CSOs had conducted workshops with stakeholders to analyse the current constitution and to formulate their demands for a new mother law. Despite generally positive attitudes towards the process, CSOs as well as opposition parties followed the CRC's activities with great suspicion. It was widely feared that the *long-ruling Revolutionary Party* ('Chama cha Mapinduzi'; CCM) would not allow the CRC to operate independently, and would at some point or another 'hijack' the process, trying to use its power to manipulate the process to meet the party's (or some influential individual's) interests, regardless of the benefits for the country or the will of the people.

In May, the debate gained momentum when CSOs and opposition parties demanded new regulations concerning the composition of envisaged *district constitutional forums*. These forums were designated by law to discuss and amend the CRC's first draft of a new constitution, again involving the opinion of the populace. Critics, however, voiced concern that the forums were to be assembled by district authorities, most of which were controlled by CCM members. CSOs and opposition parties criticised the process for forming the district forums as marred by irregularities, alleged favouritism and corruption, upon which the CRC reacted by publishing guidelines for the forums that explicitly allowed CSOs and others to independently convene their own forums and come up with their own recommendations for a second draft.

The detailed *first draft* of a new *constitution*, formulated by the CRC and published on *3 June*, was received with surprise and mixed feelings by the general public. Whereas most CSOs, opposition parties and academics welcomed the proposal, it was strongly rejected by the CCM. The draft text, consisting of 240 sections, proposed a *fundamental change in the country's polity* towards a federal system by introducing a separate government for the Tanzanian mainland in addition to the already existing Zanzibar government, and a reshaped union government ("three tier government"). Matters to be dealt with by the union government were to be reduced from the present 22 to only seven. Changes were also proposed with regard to the union cabinet and parliament. The number of ministries was to be reduced from about 30 to 15, and ministers should no longer be selected from among MPs. By reducing the number of constituencies, the number of MPs was also to be drastically reduced to 75 (from about 360), and the allocation of special seats for women was to be discontinued; instead, each new constituency would be represented in parliament by one man and one women. Tenure for MPs was limited to three terms, and voters would have the right to re-call their MP at any time. With a view to increasing the political impartiality of the office, the speaker of the National Assembly would no longer be an MP.

Although the draft only made provisions for a new constitution for the United Republic, it implicitly proposed the creation a *new entity of Tanzania Mainland* (or *Tanganyika*), with responsibilities formerly vested in the union being split between the union and that new entity (and its counterpart Zanzibar). Whereas Zanzibar already had existing institutions, such as a parliament, a president and a constitution (although they would also have to be adjusted to the new set-up), such institutions needed to be established for the new entity on the mainland. The proposals concerning the new union structure naturally attracted most attention. However, the draft included numerous other changes, many of which had long been demanded by CSOs and opposition parties. Most importantly, the draft reduced the powers of the president, allowed for independent candidates in elections, introduced a modern bill of rights, and removed many restrictive regulations.

Although CSOs, academics and opposition parties criticised some aspects (such as keeping the death penalty, removal of land ownership from the matters under union jurisdiction, the doubtful independence of the Electoral Commission and the inconsistencies and vagueness of some clauses), the *draft was widely welcomed* by representatives of *civil society* as a progressive and people-centred foundation for the country. The CCM turned out to be the only relevant force that *rejected the draft*, primarily because of the proposed new government structure. CCM strongly favoured the existing asymmetrical set-up with two governments. However, the party's official position was challenged by some prominent CCM members who were willing to accept the CRC's proposal as an expression of the people's will. CCM's Zanzibar wing even actively supported the proposed structure as the best setting for Zanzibar. Since the ruling party's stance on the union question had long been known, it came as a surprise to many observers that the CRC proposed a draft that was evidently against the CCM's will. The CRC explained that in designing the draft it had been strongly influenced by the statements citizens had made in the hearings. According to CRC chairman Warioba, the proposals in the draft reflected citizens' wishes and were assented to unanimously by all 30 CRC members, despite and regardless of their differing political backgrounds and preferences.

The CRC's draft changed the interactions between all main actors significantly. Opposition parties and CSOs (especially the very outspoken Constitutional Forum) no longer regarded the CRC with suspicion, but perceived it as their ally and shifted their attempts to influence the CRC's second draft (due in December) from the district forums (which were conducted without much attention) towards the decisive *Constituent Assembly (CA)*. The CA was to debate and improve the second, revised draft in early 2014 and come up with a final proposal that would be put to all eligible Tanzanians in a referendum. However, the envisaged *composition of the CA* raised concerns that it could conceivably reject the CRC's draft for "egoistic reasons". After a heated debate, amendments to the *Constitution Review Bill* were endorsed by parliament on 6 September. However, opposition MPs protested against the bill and walked out of the house. According to the bill, the CA should be composed of all members of the National Assembly, all members of the Zanzibar House of Representatives and 166 members of societal groups, appointed by the president. Since the CRC draft had proposed regulations that would directly affect MPs (drastic reduction in the number of seats, limitation of tenure, threat of recall by voters, no appointments of MPs to ministerial posts), it was feared that the CA, being made up overwhelmingly of MPs, would reject these provisions. Furthermore, it was feared that the CCM would use its majority to block the proposed three-tier government structure. Although the inclusion of 166 civil society representatives was welcomed, there was vehement criticism that they were too few and that they were to be hand-picked by the president. On 21 September, the main opposition parties CHADEMA (Party of Democracy and Progress), CUF (Civic United Front) and NCCR-Mageuzi (National Convention for Construction and Reform – Change) staged a joint rally against the bill in Dar es Salaam and announced plans to hold countrywide demonstrations. They demanded an equal representation of Zanzibar in the CA and clear rules for the appointment of the additional 166 CA members. To reduce tension, *President Jakaya Kikwete* met representatives of six opposition parties on 15 October and agreed on a compromise. Consequently, parliament *amended the bill* again in early November, increasing the number of civil society delegates to 201 and stipulating clear rules on how and from which sectors of society they should be selected. Despite this compromise, MPs and CCM members would still constitute the clear majority in the CA.

After the CRC's deadline to complete its work and submit a second draft had been twice extended by the president, the Commission unveiled its *second draft on 30 December*. Despite attempts from the CCM to influence the CRC to change the contentious crucial provisions, the second draft did not differ much from the earlier version. However, it added some 31 further clauses (and increased the matters under union jurisdiction to eight), not all of which were welcomed by CSOs and opposition parties. Among other points, some of the newly introduced provisions were criticised as restricting the freedom of independent candidates.

During the entire process, the *CCM* never managed to control the developments or set the agenda. Its refusal to support changes that were supported by majority public opinion made the party appear a destructive force, more guided by egoistic motives than by public interest. Corruption allegations, theft of public funds and various scandals, the beginnings of infighting for positions in the run-up to the 2015 presidential elections, and what was widely perceived as an unsatisfactory government performance, further *tarnished CCM's reputation*. Its preparations for the next general elections had begun in 2012 with changes in the party constitution, the formation of a full-time secretariat and elections to the National Executive Committee (NEC). In June, the NEC finally elected the remaining 14 members of the influential Central Committee (CC); this step had been deferred since the National Congress in November 2012, while only the ex-officio members occupied their posts. The CC was expected to play the important role of choosing the party's presidential candidate for the next elections in late 2015. Given that President Kikwete was not allowed to stand again after two terms, the selection of his successor was expected to become an extremely sensitive issue, especially in a situation in which the opposition was vigorously gaining ground and the splits between various feuding CCM factions were threatening the party's dominance. However, the leadership's modest attempts to reform the party appeared not to be very successful. In his opening remarks at a party workshop in late October, Kikwete accused party leaders of being "agents of fuelling corruption" and warned that the party could lose the forthcoming elections if it continued its corrupt practices. In early June, a joint workshop of UNDP and the National Assembly revealed that *20% of the government's budget* was eaten-up by *corruption.* In TI's corruption assessment, Tanzania dropped slightly from 102nd in 2012 to 111th in 2013.

In a seeming repetition of a cabinet reshuffle that had become necessary in May 2012 due to allegations of ministerial corruption, misuse of funds and incompetence, the *government again came under parliamentary fire* towards the end of the year. In reaction to national and international pressure to deal with the increasing problem of *elephant and rhino poaching*, the government had in early September started *'Opereshi Tokomeza' (Operation Wipe-Out)* to contain this evil. The operation was a joint effort by four ministries and involved soldiers, policemen, game rangers and forestry officers. However, after only two months 'Tokomeza' was called off by the National Assembly, following reports of *rampant human rights violations* in the course of its operation. A parliamentary inquiry uncovered the murder of 13 civilians, arrests of over 1,000 people, torture, rape, sexual harassment, seizure of property and other abuses by agents of the operation. Upon the presentation of the report in parliament on 20 December, MPs demanded the *resignation* of *Prime Minister Mizengo Pinda* and the *four ministers* of the ministries involved in the operation.

Only a few days earlier, MPs had already demanded that the Prime Minister and the Minister of State for Regional Administration and Local Government step down for allegedly not reacting to the *misuse and theft of public funds in local authorities*, which were revealed by three parliamentary oversight committees. On 14 December, even the CCM's CC and secretariat presented a list of seven ministers and deputy ministers to Kikwete and recommended that they should be taken to task for underperformance. On 20 December, Kikwete *dismissed the four ministers* whose ministries were involved in 'Operesheni Tokomeza' (Defence, Home Affairs, Tourism and Natural Resources, and Livestock Development). Pinda and the other ministers who were criticised by the CCM organs remained untouched, but Kikwete announced a cabinet reshuffle for early 2014.

Apart from the challenges caused by its internal problems, CCM's position was also threatened by the activities of the *main opposition party CHADEMA*. Buoyed by growing popularity, the party continued with its efforts to win more public support – but at the risk of confrontation with the security agencies. In the struggle for a revised constitution, CHADEMA emerged as a driving force that was able to pressurise the government to give in to popular demands. Long-smouldering leadership conflicts erupted rather surprisingly on 22 November, when the party's CC announced that it had *deposed* the party's *deputy secretary-general Zitto Kabwe* and two other prominent leaders. Kabwe, CC member Kitila Mkumbo and former Arusha regional party chairman Samson Mwigamba were accused of planning a plot against the current party leadership to be enacted at the next internal party elections and were stripped of all their leadership positions, except their party membership. On the same day, CHADEMA's vice-chairman for the mainland, Said Amour Arfi, resigned. The three ousted leaders were given two weeks to explain why they should not be expelled from the party. Kabwe declared the accusations baseless and appealed against his deposition to the party's Executive Council (the highest party organ). The young and charismatic Kabwe, an MP for Kigoma North, deputy leader of the opposition in the National Assembly, shadow finance minister and chairman of the influential Public Accounts Committee, had for many years been one of the party's most prominent and popular figures, and CHADEMA owed much of its success to his activities. However, his personal ambitions had long been a source of contention and had led to leadership struggles in previous years. A lengthy internal conflict was likely to weaken the party's prospects in the forthcoming elections of 2014 and 2015.

As in previous years, *political, religious and socio-economic conflicts* posed a *threat to security*. On 17 February, a Catholic priest was shot dead in *Zanzibar*; two days later, a church was burnt down. On 7 August, two young female British volunteers were attacked with acid by two men on a motorcycle, and on 13 September, acid was thrown on a Catholic priest. Several people were arrested, but the culprits were not found. It remained unclear whether there was a connection to suspected al-Shabaab activities in the region or whether these attacks were a result of growing religious intolerance or anti-Union and anti-Mainland sentiments, since the growth of Christianity in Zanzibar was perceived to be the result of the influx of Mainlanders. On the *Mainland*, in Geita Region, a pastor of the Assemblies of God church was beheaded on 11 February. In early April, riots between Christians and Muslims in Tunduma, on the Zambia border, about slaughtering rituals prompted the authorities to temporarily close the border. At least two people were severely injured and a mosque under construction was destroyed. A bomb attack on a Catholic church in Arusha killed at least three people and injured 60 on 5 May, during a visit by the Vatican ambassador to Tanzania and the Archbishop of Arusha. Media reports that nationals from Tanzania and Saudi Arabia had been arrested raised concern about a possibly growing Wahhabi influence in Tanzania. However, the Arabs were soon released when it became clear that they were just tourists. Arusha was again shocked by a bomb blast on 15 June during a CHADEMA rally. The bomb, thrown at CHADEMA chairman Freeman Mbowe and the local MP, killed two people and injured several others. Both politicians were unhurt. A few days later, CHADEMA supporters clashed with the police. Arusha, having emerged as a CHADEMA stronghold in the 2010 elections, had since then witnessed several violent incidents involving security forces and party supporters. Politicians, religious leaders and members of CSOs expressed their deep concern at the alarming increase in violence between members of different religions and called for mutual tolerance and respect.

The conflict over government plans to construct a *gas pipeline* from the natural gas fields near the southern town of *Mtwara* to Dar es Salaam resulted in *violent clashes* between protesters and security forces on 26 January, which left four people dead and a dozen injured. The government arrested more than 50 people and put Mtwara under tight security control. Protests had started in late December 2012 with peaceful demonstrations jointly organised by several opposition political parties, followed by further demonstrations in January. Demonstrators protested against the planned pipeline and demanded to see local benefits from the natural resources found in their region. On 1 February, Kikwete announced plans for several *development projects in the region*, including a power station, expanded ports, factories and others. According to him, there were plans to pipe only 16% of the Mtwara gas to Dar es Salaam, with the remainder staying in the region. Prime Minister Pinda and five ministers visited Mtwara to hold discussions with residents and political and religious leaders and called for calm. Despite these efforts, the situation escalated again on 22 May, when protesters demolished a bridge, attacked several government and party offices and set some on fire. At least one person died and several were injured, most likely as a result of a heavy-handed response by the police. More than 90 people were arrested, and the government deployed the army to Mtwara to restore calm. Pinda visited Mtwara again and promised that several factories would be built and 1,000 jobs created in the region. The protests were an immediate reaction to a televised parliamentary statement by the energy and minerals minister that the pipeline would be built as planned.

The annual *human rights report* of the Legal and Human Rights Centre and the Zanzibar Legal Service Centre, published in April, indicated an increase in human rights violations in 2012. Mob justice and gender-based violence, including female genital mutilation, were among the major human rights problems. *Restrictive actions against the press* continued to occur during the year. On 8 January, community radio journalist Issa Ngumba was found murdered in a forest in Kigoma Region. Ngumba had been working on an investigation into the murder of a local shepherd. It was unclear whether he was killed because of his reporting or for other reasons. Two local radio stations in Morogoro and Mwanza, run by religious institutions (one Christian and one Muslim), were banned by the Tanzania Communications Regulatory Authority for six months for broadcasting statements that allegedly violated the law and broadcasting ethics, and a programme by the popular Clouds FM radio station was banned for allegedly promoting homosexual marriage. On 27 September, the government announced a 14-day ban on 'Mwananchi' newspaper and a 90-day ban on 'Mtanzania' newspaper. The *bans* on these two reputable *newspapers* were criticised by national and international media stakeholders and human rights activists as a restriction of the right of press freedom.

Foreign Affairs

Tanzania's growing importance as an emerging economy with vast natural resources, especially gas and uranium, an entry point to Eastern and Central Africa and the most peaceful and stable country in the region was reflected in two high-ranking state visits that seemed to be an expression of global competition and were regarded with envy by Tanzania's neighbours. For newly-appointed *Chinese President Xi Jinping*, Tanzania was only the second country he had visited, after Russia, and the first on his three-country Africa tour. During his visit (24–25 March), he signed a number of agreements on new development projects and on economic, trade and cultural cooperation. Among them was the planned construction of an entirely new port near Bagamoyo with an envisaged capacity 20 times that of the chronically congested Dar es Salaam port. A high-ranking delegation of ministers, regional commissioners, senior government officials and businesspeople, led by Prime Minister Pinda, participated in the *first Tanzania-China Business Forum* in Guangzhou in early November as part of a nine-day tour of China to bolster trade and investment links between the two countries.

During his visit to Tanzania (1–2 July) as part of an Africa tour, US *President Barack Obama* announced the launch of two new initiatives aimed at bolstering trade and increasing access to electricity. 'Trade Africa' was intended to increase internal and regional trade within Africa, with an initial focus on the EAC member states, and to expand trade and economic ties between Africa, the USA and other global markets, and the 'Power Africa Initiative' aimed at doubling electrical power generation and supply. Obama was accompanied by a 700-member delegation, mostly business people. He and his predecessor, George W. Bush, who was attending a conference in Dar es Salaam, laid a wreath to commemorate the victims of the al-Qaeda attack on the US embassy in 1998.

Generally good relations with the *donor community* were overshadowed by continuing misuse of donor funds and corruption. In late November, the Netherlands, Sweden, Finland, Ireland, Japan and Germany suspended their support to the Local Government Reform Programme and demanded a refund of more than $ 370,000. The six donors accused government officials of stealing the money. In early December, the government closed the programme's secretariat and dismissed several officials who were accused of embezzling the funds. Relations with Germany were temporarily shaken after Tanzania in mid-September rejected the back-to-back posting of the German ambassador to Kenya to the same position in Dar es Salaam. Although no reason was given by the Tanzanian authorities, it was widely believed that the unprecedented move was caused by the former envoy's close relations with the political opposition in Kenya.

Tanzania continued to play an active role in the search for a solution to the armed *conflicts in eastern* DRC. On 24 February, together with ten other African countries (all except South Africa ICGLR members), it signed a UN-sponsored agreement in Addis Ababa (Ethiopia) to bring peace to the region, which paved the way for the deployment of a regional military brigade to eastern DRC to complement the long-installed UN Stabilization Mission in DRC peacekeepers. Between May and June, Tanzania deployed at least 1,300 soldiers to the *UN Force Intervention Brigade (FIB) in the DRC*, which was established on 28 March and tasked with a robust mandate to carry out offensive operations against armed rebel groups in eastern DRC, mainly targeting the M23 rebel group, but also other so-called "negative forces". Tanzania, South Africa and Malawi contributed to the 3,069 strong force, commanded by the Tanzanian General James Aloisi Mwakibolwa. Tanzanian troops were involved in direct combat with the M23, which finally surrendered on 5 November. In another international mission, seven Tanzanian peacekeepers of the *UN-AU mission in Darfur* (UNAMID) were killed and 17 others injured while on patrol on 13 July. Tanzania had contributed more than 1,000 soldiers, police personnel and experts to the mission in February 2012. On 4 June, the Tanzanian Lieutenant General Paul Ignace Mella was appointed UNAMID Force Commander.

Relations with *Rwanda* worsened considerably in late May in reaction to Kikwete's suggestion during the AU summit in Addis Ababa that the DRC, Rwanda and Uganda should initiate direct talks with their respective rebel groups in the Great Lakes region. This was most strongly rejected by Rwanda, which accused Tanzania of thus implicitly recognising and backing the DRC-based FDLR rebels, held responsible for the 1994 genocide in Rwanda. Kikwete was viciously attacked in Kigali's state-controlled media. Although Rwanda had signed the February UN peace framework for the DRC, Tanzania's leading role in the FIB was hardly conducive to reducing the tension. The FIB fought against the M23 rebels, which Rwanda was supposedly supporting. The war of words between the two countries accelerated further, when Tanzania expelled thousands of Rwandans in late July and August. While Rwanda interpreted this as an unfriendly action, Tanzania justified it as an effort to cleanse the country of "illegal immigrants". On 25 July, Kikwete issued an order that *"illegal immigrants"* and "criminals" should leave the country by 11 August. The authorities forcibly expelled 7,000–8,000 Rwandans and at least 15,000 Burundians, many of whom had been living in Tanzania for decades. Malawians living in Tanzania reported xenophobic attacks against them, presumably due to the border dispute between the two countries. About 1,000 'illegal' Malawians were temporarily arrested, but also offered the opportunity to regularise their status in Tanzania by applying for residence permits. In October, Tanzania was still hosting 102,000 officially registered refugees.

This crackdown on residents from neighbouring countries contributed to long-standing irritations about Tanzania's apparent reluctance towards a deeper and faster *EAC integration* process. Tanzania felt side-lined when a so-called *Coalition of the Willing* (*CoW*), comprising the presidents of Kenya, Rwanda and Uganda, met in June, August and October to discuss several joint infrastructural projects in the so-called 'Northern Corridor'. Burundi, initially excluded, was invited to join the CoW, but decided to remain aloof, while a delegation from the EAC-aspirant South Sudan did participate in the meetings. Tanzania strongly ruled out joining the CoW, and insisted that the trilateral talks contravened EAC protocols and were a threat to EAC integration. On 30 October, Minister for East African Co-operation Samwel Sitta told parliament that Tanzania was considering leaving the EAC and initiating a closer alliance with the DRC and Burundi. In an eagerly awaited televised speech, Kikwete declared on 7 November that Tanzania was clearly determined to stay in the EAC; however, he sharply criticised the CoW and insisted that all EAC member states should follow the agreed regulations. This self-assured statement, two days after the defeat of the M23, was interpreted by some observers as an expression of Tanzania's 'victory' over Rwanda. On 10 November, Kenya's foreign minister paid a visit and promised that Kenya would work closely with Tanzania. During the regular EAC summit on 30 November in Kampala (Uganda), the conflicts appeared to have been sorted out; the five partner states reaffirmed their commitment to close cooperation and signed a protocol on a future Monetary Union. According to observers, the apparent split between the diverging EAC groups was rooted in three issues: first, the CoW's impatience for further and faster integration, which was perceived to be blocked by Tanzania; second, the conflict between Rwanda and Tanzania about their respective roles in the DRC and their alleged support for rebel groups; and third, economic competition between Kenya and Tanzania over control of the transport routes from the Indian Ocean to the landlocked countries and attracting (Chinese) investments.

There were no decisive developments in the *Lake Nyasa border dispute* with *Malawi*. In January, both sides presented their legal positions to the SADC Forum of Former Heads of State and Government, which had been addressed by both sides for a ruling in December 2012. In April, Malawi withdrew from the process, claiming bias by one of the officials involved, but returned in early May. In June, Malawi complained about Tanzania's plans to start operating passenger ships on the lake. Malawi's President Joyce Banda set a 30 September deadline for the Forum to come up with a resolution, failing which she would take the case to the International Court of Justice. However, at year's end the SADC mediation process was still on-going.

As chairman of the *SADC* Organ on Politics, Defence and Security Cooperation (*SADC Troika*), Kikwete played a crucial role in negotiating a way out of the political crisis in *Madagascar*. During the regular SADC summit on 17 August in Malawi, Kikwete handed over the rotational Troika chair to Namibia's President Pohamba. Kikwete's tenure also witnessed the peaceful but controversial re-election of President Mugabe in Zimbabwe.

Socioeconomic Developments

The overall *macroeconomic performance* again continued to be quite robust and in line with the strong continuous growth trend over more than a decade since the early 2000s. In this period, Tanzania had become one of the fastest growing and most consistently performing economies in Africa, albeit still characterised by a very low absolute level of material wealth. In the 2013 HDI (data for 2012), Tanzania was ranked 152nd (out of 185 countries), in the low human development category. *Per capita income* was estimated to have reached about $ 625 in 2013 ($ 1,615 in PPP terms). In the face of the continuing global economic and financial crisis, Tanzania's economy again proved to be remarkably resilient. The *GDP growth rate* for 2013 was estimated at 7.1%, slightly above the 6.9% in 2012 and on the high side of the growth trend of most preceding years (range of 6%–7%). Climatically, it was a fairly average year with good harvests, which allowed the agricultural sector to grow by about 4.6%. Expectations of a faster and more fundamental transformation of the economy were increasingly linked with the prospect of becoming a significant producer of natural gas, although full commercial exploitation was still a number of years away. In the World Economic Forum's Global Competitiveness Index 2013–14 Tanzania was ranked 125th (out of 148 countries), five places lower than before.

High *inflation* rates in previous years (12.7% in 2011 and 16% in 2012) had been a major cause of growing popular discontent. Inflation was successfully and steadily brought down during the year from 10.9% (January) to 5.6% (December). The year's average inflation rate of 7.9% was largely attributed to a noticeable fall in food prices and the pursuit of a tight monetary policy. This also contributed to the stabilisation of the *exchange rate*; with some minor fluctuations during the year, it was in December (TSh 1,617 : $ 1), just 2% lower than in January. This stability was a clear sign of widely prevailing confidence in the economy's prospects. The *structural trade deficit* grew substantially by almost 20% to $ 5,258 m, principally as a result of unchanged export earnings. While imports grew normally by about 8% to $ 11,159 m (with oil alone accounting for one third), exports practically stagnated at a value of $ 5,901 m. This was partly explained by lower world prices for some commodities, particularly gold, the main export item (accounting for roughly one-third of total exports). On balance, only 53% of Tanzania's import needs were covered by its own export revenues. The (preliminary) *current-account deficit* was thus estimated to have remained at the 2012 level of about 15% of GDP, the highest for several years. Gross *foreign reserves* were further strengthened at $ 4.5 bn (compared with $ 4.0 bn in 2012) by the year's end, sufficient for a comfortable import coverage of over four months. While the *external debt* had previously been substantially reduced to a low of $ 4.2 bn in 2006 as a result of concerted debt cancellations under the HIPC initiative, it had lately been creeping up again rather fast, reaching $ 13.6 bn at year's end (compared with $ 11.6 bn at end-2012). Linked with the many ongoing large investment projects, *FDI* inflows remained very substantial at an estimated $ 1,790 m ($ 1,632 m in 2012). Likewise, *tourism earnings* of $ 1,472 m ($ 1,563 m in 2012) remained Tanzania's most important foreign exchange earner, even topping gold.

On 3 June, the *IMF* completed its sixth and final review under the *Policy Support Instrument (PSI)*, an unfunded IMF instrument designed for countries that do not need balance of payments financial support. The Tanzanian PSI had been operative since June 2010. The IMF commended the Tanzanian authorities "for their commitment to policies aimed at containing demand pressures, strengthening macroeconomic stability, and preserving a sound fiscal position". Simultaneously, a second review was conducted under the 18-month *Standby Credit Facility (SCF)* that had been approved in July 2012 for about $ 228 m as a precautionary measure against the potential downside risks of a global slowdown; in February the government had drawn $ 114 m under this SCF to support the currency. An IMF mission in early November conducted the biennial Article IV discussions, discussed a possible new PSI and assessed the performance under the SCF. Again, the economy was judged to be performing well and the economic outlook was seen as promising, but some concern was expressed about the appearance of fiscal pressures in excess of agreed targets.

On 13 June, Finance Minister William Mgimwa submitted the 2013–14 *budget* to parliament. Contrary to previous practice, the individual ministerial votes had already been discussed since April. A review of the previous financial year's outturn revealed that the overall *fiscal deficit* for *2012–13* had markedly increased to 6.2% of GDP (from 5.0%), mainly the result of the government's overestimation of revenues and underestimation of expenditure. Contrary to ambitious targets, domestic revenues had only increased marginally and foreign aid inflows had also been below initial projections. Significant adjustments to the financing side of the budget had to be made by way of higher than targeted public (domestic and external) borrowing. A seven-year bond for over $ 600 m was issued in March by private placement with banks, but the contemplated issue of a sovereign bond was postponed to 2014 and still needed an official credit rating. The observable finance tendencies seemed to reflect a remarkable recent government policy shift. While the pursuance of a relatively tight monetary policy had successfully controlled the inflation rate, a more relaxed fiscal stance was seen as an appropriate instrument to promote economic growth. An accelerated drive for the development of social and physical infrastructure was clearly intended under the *"Big Results Now"* (BRN) initiative launched by Kikwete on 22 February. This was a copy of a similar successful programme in Malaysia; 300 Malaysians had been invited to coach Tanzanian top civil servants on the approach. BRN was expected to accelerate the transformation of the economy towards the goal of becoming a middle-income country, as envisaged in the Tanzania Development Vision 2025. BRN covered six priority areas, namely energy and gas, agriculture, water, education, transport and resource mobilisation.

The *2013–14 budget* clearly reflected an expansionary intention, with a more than 20% higher volume than the previous budget. Domestic revenue was optimistically expected to increase to a 20.2% share of GDP (compared with 17.6% achieved in 2012–13), and the expected fiscal deficit was set at a reduced 4.4% of GDP. Efforts were to be made to scrap many of the tax exemptions that had in 2011–12 been estimated to have cost 4.3% of GDP. Total expenditure was budgeted at TSh 18,250 bn (about $ 11.4 bn), with 69% foreseen for recurrent expenditure and 31% for development programmes, whereby almost half of the development budget was expected to come from external sources. The breakdown of the total budget funding was as follows: domestic revenue 63%, general budget support (external) 6.4%, foreign loans and grants 14.8%, domestic borrowing 9.3%, non-concessional foreign borrowing 6.9%. In the mid-year budget review, it became evident that revenue was falling short of assumptions and that considerable expenditure arrears had been built up. The IMF expressed concern about the need to attain a fiscal deficit close to the target of 5% of GDP.

In mid-November, new official *poverty* data were released, based on the 2011–12 Household Budget Survey (HBS); 28.2% of the population were assessed to be living below the *absolute income poverty line* of TSh 36,482 ($ 22.7) per month. This seemed to indicate some reduction of poverty from the 33.6% measured in the 2007 HBS, but the methodologies of the surveys had not been strictly comparable. The absolute number of about 12.3 m poor people was, however, roughly the same as in 2001. The incidence of poverty was very unevenly distributed and affected 33.3% of the rural population, but only 4.2% of Dar es Salaam residents and 21.7% of other urban dwellers. Around 10% of the total population did not even reach the *extreme food poverty line* of TSh 26,085 ($ 16.3) per month; this was the case for 11.3% of rural people, but for only 1% in Dar es Salaam. Income inequality was measured as relatively moderate with a Gini coefficient of 0.34 (in Dar es Salaam 0.35, in rural areas 0.29).

Optimistic expectations of a general upturn in the economy centred strongly on increasingly promising prospects for the exploitation of Tanzania's substantial *natural gas* resources, although full commercial benefits were only expected to build up in about seven to ten years. According to some forecasts, the gas sector might then potentially contribute about one-third of GDP. With on-going exploration activities, proven gas reserves had been rapidly updated to around 43 trillion cubic feet, but more seemed very probable. In October, the postponed fourth gas and oil licensing round for seven offshore blocks and the Lake Tanganyika area was launched, to run until May 2014. Production-sharing agreements with 18 international exploration companies were already in existence. The decision of the energy and mining ministry to exclude private Tanzanian business interests from the gas block auctions, with the assertion that capital-intensive exploration activities were beyond their means, provoked strong protests. During the second oil and gas conference in October, the government floated the intention of creating a special "gas revenue fund" to manage all future proceeds. In May, the ministry presented a second draft of a national *natural gas policy*, which outlined a comprehensive framework for the gas sector, but left many concrete specifications open (such as the exact mandate of a regulatory body and the future role of the parastatal Tanzania Petroleum Development Company). The passage of specific legislation to adapt outdated old mining laws was expected in 2014. The gas policy stated clearly that priority should be given to developing the gas sector in order to bring major benefits to the domestic economy, but plans for a liquefied natural gas plant for export were also envisaged. The on-going construction of a Chinese-financed gas pipeline from Mtwara to Dar es Salaam was poised to be completed in late 2014. This would allow a dramatic increase in *electricity* generation and hopefully end the recurring problems of long-endured *power failures*. The heavily loss-making power utility TANESCO continued to be a major financial burden for the government; average tariff increases of about 40% as of January 2014 were deemed to be no more than a partial solution.

Gold production continued to contribute significantly to overall growth and exports, despite some setbacks and gold's relative loss of importance. New *mining* ventures were about to start production of nickel and uranium and were faced with protests from environmentalists. Chinese investors proceeded with an ambitious $ 3 bn project for the exploitation of coal reserves and iron-ore deposits in the south-west. The improvement of the country's physical *infrastructure* (roads, railways, ports, power installations) was a major focus of the government's development strategy, although the implementation of announced projects often remained uncertain. Strenuous efforts to attract more *foreign investors* were somewhat dashed by continued weaknesses in the domestic business climate. In the World Bank's 'Doing Business 2014' report, Tanzania slipped down to 145th place (from 136th). A December announcement raised the prospect of the removal of restrictions on capital flows within the EAC, bringing opportunities for improved integration of regional capital markets. Long-known weaknesses in Tanzania's *education* system were shockingly exposed in February, when two-thirds of students failed the O-level exams. This confirmed a widely-held consensus that the level of education had deteriorated considerably, with drastic consequences for the country's future prospects.

Tanzania in 2014

Throughout the year, most political attention was again absorbed by discussions over the progress of the constitutional review process that had been initiated in 2012. In February, a Constituent Assembly began lengthy deliberations about the detailed formulation of the text of a new constitution that was to be submitted to a general referendum for final approval. The most contentious issue proved to be the delicate question of the future structure of the Union between Zanzibar and the Mainland. While the long-ruling Revolutionary Party (CCM) favoured the continuation of the current system, the suggested draft text of the constitution that had been prepared in 2013 had surprisingly proposed a new three-tier set-up. Fundamental disagreements over the way forward led in April to the exodus of most opposition members from the Constituent Assembly. In October, the CCM majority eventually passed the text of a new constitution and announced a final referendum for April 2015. The acrimony over the constitution strengthened cooperation among the political opposition, while internal power struggles between various CCM factions continued as the party tried to regain some of its lost credibility and was already gearing up towards the next elections in October 2015. A major financial scandal and accusations of high-level corruption severely damaged the government's reputation by the end of the year.

The somewhat strained relations between Tanzania and its EAC partners recovered markedly with improved cooperation on ambitious plans for major infrastructural projects. Bilateral relations with Rwanda, however, continued to be unfriendly and fraught with reciprocal accusations over the handling of Rwandan opposition groups based in the DRC, where a Tanzanian military battalion was engaged with a peacekeeping mandate. Macroeconomic performance remained quite satisfactory and continued to be generally commended by international donors, who were, however, increasingly vocal in their criticism of the lack of government action on the corruption scandal. Substantial parts of promised budget support funds were temporarily withheld, thus seriously complicating the government's fiscal situation. Expectations centred on prospects for Tanzania becoming a major gas producer remained high, but the reaping of tangible benefits was still several years away.

Domestic Politics

The wrangling over the *constitution review process* was strongly aggravated by conflicts between the *long-ruling Revolutionary Party* ('Chama cha Mapinduzi', CCM) and a coalition led by the main opposition parties. The first and second drafts for a new constitution, which had been prepared in 2013 by the *Constitutional Review Commission* (CRC) after an intensive process of public hearings and gathering popular opinion, met long-standing demands from opposition parties and civil society organisations alike, but were strongly rejected by the CCM. The dominant party, however, managed to regain control over the process by using its clear majority in the decisive *Constituent Assembly* (CA), which was mandated to debate and improve the CRC's second revised draft and come up with a final proposal that would be put to all eligible Tanzanians in a referendum.

The *628-member* CA was composed of 346 members of the National Assembly, 81 members of the Zanzibar House of Representatives and 201 delegates from various groups of society; 386 of them were men and 242 women, and 416 came from the Mainland and 212 from Zanzibar. According to the government, about 570 societal groups had proposed more than 5,500 people as suitable candidates for CA membership; it was the prerogative of the president to finally select and appoint the 201 delegates from the names submitted. The list of those chosen was announced on 7 February and was received with mixed feelings. Civil society organisations and the media criticised the fact that several politicians were among those appointed, including many who were affiliated with the CCM. The government, however, explained that it had selected a balanced representation of Tanzanian society with regard to age, gender, religion, regional origin and political affiliation.

The CA was convened on 18 February and in principle given 70 days to complete its task, but the Constitutional Review Bill authorised the president to extend the deadline by 20 days if necessary. The first month of CA sittings was overshadowed by quarrelling about agreements on standing orders and procedures, elections of officials and demands by CA members for an increase in their daily allowances, without any substantial aspects of the draft text being debated. Some NGO and media observers criticised this behaviour as disgraceful and were already calling for the CA to be disbanded as a waste of resources. Minister of East African Cooperation *Samuel Sitta* was elected CA *chairman* on 12 March with an overwhelming majority, after the former attorney-general, Andrew Chenge, had withdrawn his candidacy. As former parliament speaker (until 2010) Sitta had earned some respect from the opposition for his independent stance – which in contrast had made him unpopular among some of CCM's internal factions. It soon became apparent that the CCM was not willing to allow the CA to follow any line that was not in accordance with the party's interests: all but two of the 14 CA committees were chaired by CCM politicians. Furthermore, in his inaugural CA address on 21 March *President Jakaya Kikwete* dropped his previous apparent support for the CRC's draft texts and backed the CCM position on the contested envisaged structure of the Union between Zanzibar and the Mainland. Three days earlier, the CRC *chairman, Joseph Warioba*, had presented the gist of the CRC's draft to the CA and stressed that it represented the opinion of the majority of the population as expressed during the public hearings, but he failed to make an impact on the CCM members of the CA, who enthusiastically applauded Kikwete's speech.

Although the CRC's draft had proposed several important and controversial constitutional changes, such as reduced powers for the president and increased accountability of MPs to an empowered electorate, the debate centred primarily on the recommendations for the *future structure of the Union*. Whereas opposition parties and most delegates from civil society organisations and from Zanzibar favoured the three-tier structure proposed in the CRC's draft (implying the creation of a new government structure for Tanzania Mainland in addition to the already existing Zanzibar government and a drastically reshaped Union government), the CCM strongly rejected this fundamental change in the country's polity, arguing that the operation of three governments would be far too expensive and could also break up the Union. The president's surprisingly open support for his party's position during the crucial CA inauguration was seen by many as a go-ahead for CCM hard-liners, and was therefore strongly criticised by the opposition as a breach of neutrality – and as undermining the CRC's strenuous work.

Apart from antagonism over contentious standing orders and procedures (including a controversy over open or secret voting), even the *basic mandate of the* CA was disputed. Whereas opposition parties and many civil society members were of the opinion that the CA was only tasked to improve and streamline the CRC's draft, the CCM saw the CA as authorised to completely overhaul the draft and reject any of its clauses. These different interpretations of the CA's role, the antagonism about the Union structure, and early position-taking in view of the general elections due in 2015, laid the CA's discussions open to robust party politics and distrust. This quickly led to the formation of *two rival factions* before the end of March. CA members from the main opposition parties, Chama cha Demokrasia na Maendeleo (CHADEMA; Party of Democracy and Progress), the Civic United Front (CUF) and the National Convention for Construction and Reform – Change; NCCR-Mageuzi), and some from the group of 201 civil society representatives, formed the Coalition of the Defenders of the People's Constitution (known by its Swahili acronym UKAWA) to join forces and increase pressure for the adoption of the CRC's draft and the three-tier government structure. With almost 200 members, UKAWA represented around one third of the CA membership. In response, CCM members and some of their allies formed a group called 'Tanzania Kwanza' (Tanzania First).

The confrontation between the two camps escalated when the draft text's most controversial chapters concerning the Union were debated. On 16 April, UKAWA *announced its boycott of the* CA, accusing the CCM of using its majority to protect its party interests. Only ten days later, having reached the original 70-day deadline, the CA *was adjourned* to allow time (and space) for parliament to convene for the regular budget session. With an amendment to the Constitution Review Bill, the CA was given an additional 60 days and reconvened on 5 August. Several fruitless attempts were made by civil society organisations, religious leaders, CA chairman Sitta and even the UNDP to persuade the UKAWA leadership to return to the CA.

UKAWA tried to win support from the general population through public rallies and intensified the *cooperation among its member parties*. On 9 May, Freeman Mbowe (CHADEMA), the official opposition leader in parliament, reshuffled his shadow cabinet and included members of the CUF and NCCR-Mageuzi. CHADEMA's previous claim that it was the only relevant opposition party in parliament had hitherto alienated the other parties. On 26 October, the three parties plus the politically insignificant National League for Democracy signed a *Memorandum of Understanding* for further cooperation after a public rally in Dar es Salaam. The parties agreed to jointly campaign for a 'No' vote in the referendum on the new draft constitution scheduled for 30 April 2015 and to field and support joint candidates in all the 2015 elections, including the presidential election.

On 9 September, UKAWA leaders met Kikwete and seemed to have agreed to *postpone the constitution review process until after the 2015 elections*, and to make some amendments to the electoral laws in order to level the playing field for the elections. Kikwete, however, made it clear that he had no legal mandate to suspend the CA and, since CA chairman Sitta rejected any deviation from the legally prescribed path, the remaining CA *members resumed their work on 5 August* and continued to deliberate the details of the new constitution. There was, however, some anxiety about whether the remaining CA members would meet the *required separate two-thirds majority* from both parts of the Union to approve the final document. After a three-day process of voting chapter by chapter, Sitta announced on 7 October that the text of a new *draft constitution* had been *approved* by the *required quorum* from both parts of the Union. However, there were serious allegations that the quorum had only been met by dint of irregularities in the process. Absent CA members were allowed to vote via SMS, at least one CA member from the Mainland was counted as a Zanzibari (to narrowly meet the separate Zanzibar quorum) and an opposition MP from Zanzibar who had boycotted the CA found his name among those who had approved the proposed constitution. Although including more than two-thirds of the CRC draft's ('Warioba draft') articles, the new draft ('Sitta draft') *differed significantly with respect to most contentious issues*. It retained the current two-tier government structure, rejected clauses that aimed to limit the president's powers and proposed the right for voters to recall their MPs, and excluded the limitation of MPs' terms in office. Nevertheless, the final draft did include provisions that improved the rights of women and children, provided for an independent National Electoral Commission, and allowed independent unaffiliated candidates to compete in elections.

On 19 January, Kikwete *reshuffled his cabinet* for the second time during his second term. This had become necessary after the death of Finance Minister William Mgimwa in January and the dismissal of four ministers in December 2013, following massive human rights violations during the anti-poaching operation 'tokomeza ujangili' (wipe-out poaching). The deputy finance minister, Saada Mkuya Salum (from Zanzibar), was appointed finance minister, while former UN deputy secretary-general Asha-Rose Migiro was appointed minister of justice and constitutional affairs, an important portfolio in view of the ongoing critical constitutional review. In late June, Kikwete established a commission under the chairmanship of retired principal judge and former ambassador Hamisi Msumi to *investigate the anti-poaching operation* of 2013. It was also to investigate allegations that the operation had been sabotaged by high-ranking politicians and business people who were allegedly involved in ivory smuggling, which had increased dramatically.

A financial scandal (Independent Power Tanzania Ltd (IPTL) or *escrow account scandal*) gained significant political prominence in November, although initial revelations had already emerged in March and the underlying case had a history that went back more than a decade. In late November, overcoming legal injunctions to block a public debate, the Parliamentary Accounts Committee (PAC) tabled the findings of a report by the Controller and Auditor General (CAG) about a previous dubious deal in the energy sector and the suspicious transfer of large sums from an escrow account at the Central Bank to private overseas accounts of politicians, civil servants and business people. Subsequent to press reports in March, PAC chairman Zitto Kabwe had pressed for the CAG to investigate the case. In May, Prime Minister Mizengo Pinda announced that the government had also ordered investigations to be undertaken by the CAG and the Preventing and Combating of Corruption Bureau (PCCB). The escrow account had been established at the Central Bank in 2002 in a long-running dispute between the state-owned electricity supplier Tanesco and the privately-owned power company IPTL about charges Tanesco had to pay to IPTL for its services. Tanesco had deposited funds in the escrow account pending the resolution of the dispute. In late 2013, the Kenyan company Pan Africa Power Solutions (PAP) had bought IPTL, which was in provisional liquidation, and the energy ministry had authorised the release of about $122m from the escrow account to PAP. Some of the money had been transferred to a Tanzanian businessman, who in turn distributed it to several senior officials. After the PAC reported its findings to the National Assembly, the *parliament* (inclusive of the ruling CCM) *passed a resolution* on 28 November that called on Kikwete to dismiss Prime Minister Pinda, Energy Minister Sospeter Muhongo, Attorney-General Frederick Werema and other officials for authorising the transfer from the escrow account to PAP. Although declaring that he had not done anything wrong and that his advice had been misunderstood, Werema resigned on 17 December. On 23 December, Kikwete dismissed Minister of Lands Anna Tibaijuka for allegedly accepting a $ 1 m 'bribe' from the aforementioned businessman. Tibaijuka, hitherto regarded as a prominent CCM personality, categorically denied any wrong-doing and explained that she had taken the money in good faith as a donation for a school where she served as a fundraiser. Pinda and Muhongo remained in post, but Kikwete ordered further investigations into the case to be undertaken by the PCCB.

Although the revelation of several scandals had tarnished the ruling party's image in previous years, the CCM *performed well in elections* during the year. In February, the CCM won 23 of 27 wards in municipality by-elections. On 16 March, the son of the deceased finance minister easily won the seat that had been held by his father in by-elections in Kalenga (Iringa Region). Kikwete's eldest son, Ridhiwani, secured an 85% landslide victory on 6 April in by-elections in his father's former constituency, Chalinze (Coast Region). Regular *local government elections* on 14 December – immediately after the 'escrow scandal' had clearly raised the political temperature – also brought a clear 75% victory for the CCM. However, opposition parties improved their results significantly compared with the last local elections in 2009, when the CCM won almost 94% of the seats. As in 2009, the 2014 elections saw numerous shortcomings, such as missing voter lists, incorrect candidates' and voters' names, and a shortage of voting materials, which left numerous voters unable to cast their votes and led to chaotic situations and violent clashes in some polling centres. The problems were due to local authorities' failure to complete preparations in time and more generally to the Ministry of Regional Administration and Local Government's incompetence in handling elections. Calls were therefore made that local government elections should in future be administered by the National Electoral Commission.

The *next general elections in 2015* were already casting their shadow. The CCM appeared somewhat apprehensive, fearing that in-fighting between rival factions could potentially split the party. However, such fears had been expressed in the run-up to all previous elections, but the party had always managed to prevent itself from falling apart. After two terms in office, Kikwete was constitutionally barred from running for the presidency again, so the *selection of his successor* – scheduled for April or May 2015 – was expected to be a very sensitive and contentious issue. In 2008, the forced resignation of the then prime minister, Edward Lowassa, in connection with serious corruption allegations (the 'Richmond saga') had left the party split ever since into an anti-Lowassa and a pro-Lowassa camp. Before his resignation, Lowassa had been seen as a quasi-natural successor to Kikwete, his close ally. Despite his ouster, he remained an important and influential, but highly controversial figure in the CCM. The closer the nomination process drew, the more anxiously were his movements watched by other rival factions. In February, the CCM ethics committee issued a serious but inconsequential warning to Lowassa and five other prominent party members for having started campaigning prematurely for the presidential nomination. No clear pattern of likely candidatures had emerged by year's end, but rumours about a growing number of possible candidates abounded. An opinion poll released by the local NGO 'Twaweza' in November showed a continuing strong, but declining popularity of the ruling party: 51% expressed allegiance to the CCM and 23% to CHADEMA.

Internal rifts in CHADEMA, the main opposition party, continued to weaken its standing. On 2 January, Zitto Kabwe, one of its most articulate and popular politicians, who had been surprisingly stripped of all his party positions in late 2013 for an alleged putsch against the elected leadership, had successfully filed an injunction in the High Court to restrain the party from deliberating, discussing or determining the issue of his membership until his appeal to the party's governing body against his removal had been decided. In view of the unresolved conflict between CHADEMA's leadership and Kabwe, the registration of a *new political party*, the Alliance for Change and Transparency (ACT), in May was noted with interest. Several CHADEMA members defected to ACT, accusing the CHADEMA leadership of having illegally amended the party's constitution and misused party funds for personal interests. These developments led to speculation that Kabwe might also join the ACT if he were expelled from CHADEMA. No final decision was taken before the end of the year, and Kabwe continued to play an influential role in parliament. Mbowe was re-elected as CHADEMA's chairman for a third term during the party's congress in mid-September and its secretary-general, Wilbroad Slaa, was also confirmed in office.

In a worrying continuation from 2013, further *bomb blasts* in Tanzania's most important tourist hubs, Zanzibar and Arusha, caused injuries and death. In *Zanzibar*, two bombs exploded in February, fortunately without causing any casualties: one in front of the Anglican Cathedral in Zanzibar's historical centre and the other in a popular tourist restaurant. On 13 July, another bomb attack in front of a mosque killed one person and injured several others. In *Arusha*, one person was killed and 15 were injured when a bomb exploded in a popular bar on 13 April. On 3 July, two Muslim clerics were injured by a bomb thrown through the window of their house. A week later, eight people were severely injured by a bomb attack on an Indian restaurant. An employee was injured on 5 May by a bomb hidden in a donations box in a Lutheran church hostel in Mwanza. Although the police arrested several people, it remained unclear whether the attacks were linked and who was behind them. Speculation about the perpetrators ranged from linking them to criminal networks to connecting them with the Somali terror group al-Shabaab.

In a ruling on 20 June, the East African Court of Justice banned the Tanzanian government from constructing a paved *road across the northern Serengeti*. The case had been filed in December 2010 by the Kenyan NGO, African Network for Animal Welfare. The government appealed against the ruling, however, and announced that it would instead upgrade the existing dirt track to an all-weather gravel road. The *Maasai land rights* issue attracted international attention in November, when newspapers reported that the government was again pursuing its plans to evict about 40,000 Maasai pastoralists from their traditional land and to sell some 1,500 km^2 of land in Loliondo district, north-east of the Serengeti, to a UAE safari hunting company. After international protests, the government had announced in 2013 that it would stop the project and now confirmed this through separate public statements by Minister for Natural Resources and Tourism Lazaro Nyalandu and President Kikwete.

Reacting to continuing *attacks against people with albinism*, the government launched a new campaign to prevent ritual killings and to persuade communities in the most affected regions to fight against the crime and abandon occult beliefs that threaten the lives of people with albinism.

Foreign Affairs

Generally good relations with the *donor community* were somewhat overshadowed by increasing impatience with corruption and the continuing misuse of donor funds. The fading readiness to tolerate high-level graft was illustrated in October by a decision by the group of main donors (Canada, Denmark, the European Commission, Finland, Germany, Ireland, Japan, Sweden, the UK, the World Bank and the AfDB) to suspend the release of almost $ 500 m in pledged general budget support funds to the 2014/15 budget in response to the escrow account scandal; the suspension was to last until a satisfactory investigation and course of action was undertaken by the government. On 11 December, the US government similarly announced that it would postpone approval of up to $ 700 m under the Millennium Challenge Corporation while awaiting plausible government action. Despite these irritations and increasing pressure to curb corruption, relations with the main donors remained generally good and development cooperation activities and good diplomatic relations remained as amicable as they had been for years.

The traditionally good relations with *China* were strengthened further. The 50th anniversary of the establishment of diplomatic relations between the two countries was celebrated on various occasions throughout the year. China had become Tanzania's largest trading partner and the second largest investor after the UK, with huge investments mainly in infrastructure, the energy sector, the extractive industries and IT-technologies. Tanzanian-Chinese relations also included cultural, academic and medical cooperation activities and a rapidly growing tourism sector. The celebrations were highlighted by Vice-President Li Yuanchao's visit to Tanzania (21–26 June) and Kikwete's six-day state visit to China in October. Nevertheless, several complaints tarnished China's image in Tanzania. Chinese businesspeople were found to be heavily involved in smuggling ivory, rhino horn and tropical hard woods such as ebony, and were found guilty of bribing Tanzanian officials. Counterfeit and poor-quality Chinese products flooded the Tanzanian market and electrical appliances and medical drugs in particular caused serious harm to consumers. Chinese contractors were accused of carrying out cheap but sub-standard work on infrastructure projects. In a newspaper interview, the Chinese ambassador to Tanzania regretted that such "bad Chinese habits" were damaging Chinese-Tanzanian relations.

In a continuation of the antagonism that had arisen in mid-2013, relations with *Rwanda* remained tense. Although any direct contact with Rwandan President Paul Kagame was avoided, Kikwete sent

Minister of State Mark Mwandosya for a week-long visit to Kigali in February to improve diplomatic ties. Remarks by Foreign Minister Bernard Membe, however, extended the war of words when he called the 'Forces Démocratiques de Libération du Rwanda' (FDLR) rebels "freedom fighters" and repeated the accusation that Rwanda had backed the M23 rebels in the DRC and was destabilising the region. Kigali repeatedly accused Tanzania of backing the FDLR, regarded by the Rwandan government as its arch enemies. Despite these political tensions, pragmatic cooperation on joint infrastructure projects in preparation for the central corridor transport system was not interrupted. A Tanzanian *army battalion* continued to be engaged in the eastern DRC as a vital part of the UN's Force Intervention Brigade (FIB) that was mandated to pro-actively contain the threats emanating from the existence of a number of so-called 'negative forces' (rebel groups and militias). Rwanda insisted that the FIB should actively engage against the remaining FDLR rebels, but no such action was undertaken and only a January 2015 ultimatum was set for the FDLR to finally surrender. A new conflict with *Kenya* arose in December, when the Kenyan authorities banned Tanzanian tour operators from picking up tourists from Nairobi airport, allegedly in retaliation for Kenyan tourist vehicles being banned from Tanzanian national parks.

The efforts of the SADC Forum of Former Heads of State and Government mediation team, comprising former presidents Joaquim Chissano, Thabo Mbeki and Festus Mogae, to solve the long-standing *Lake Nyasa border dispute* between *Malawi* and Tanzania again proved futile as both sides maintained their positions. The new Malawi President Peter Mutharika insisted that Malawi's ownership of the entire northern part of the lake was not negotiable. However, he (as well as Kikwete) ruled out all military options and affirmed that an amicable and peaceful resolution of the issue needed to be found through the efforts of the SADC mediation team.

As in previous years, Tanzania played an important role in successfully mediating in a regional conflict. In April, a Tanzanian battalion joined the UN peacekeeping mission in South Sudan and, since the IGAD-led peace process in Addis Ababa had clearly failed to find a mutually acceptable solution to the *civil war* in *South Sudan*, Kikwete offered to conduct complementary talks in Tanzania to mend the conflict between the three warring Sudan People's Liberation Army (SPLA) factions. The talks, organised, facilitated and supervised by the CCM, began with an initial dialogue, held near Arusha in mid-October. The three SPLA groups recognised divisions in the SPLA as the underlying cause of the conflict, as well as their collective responsibility for the war, and finally signed a roadmap agreement to re-unite the party. The process was supported by several other international actors, such as the South African ANC and former Finnish President Martti Ahtisaari's Crisis Management Initiative.

The strains that had in 2013 temporarily threatened to pull the member countries of the EAC apart and to seriously undermine the *integration process* were by and large overcome, but not entirely eliminated. An understanding was reached that member countries were free to pursue joint infrastructural or other development programmes outside of the formal framework of the EAC. This particularly referred to the development of the axes of the so-called 'Northern Corridor' (hinterland of the port of Mombasa) and 'Central Corridor' (hinterland of Dar es Salaam). Tanzania no longer felt excluded, as had been the case in 2013, from the Northern Corridor infrastructure summits and participated as an observer, while pushing its own agenda for a faster development of the Central Corridor. A certain underlying competition between the two concepts was nevertheless inevitable. During a regular EAC summit in November in Nairobi (Kenya), Kikwete was expected to assume the annually rotating EAC chairmanship from Kenya's President Uhuru Kenyatta, but the summit was cancelled at the last minute because Kikwete was still recuperating from an operation he had undergone in the USA and was unable to attend.

Socioeconomic Developments

The overall *macroeconomic performance* continued to be quite robust and in line with the strong continuous growth trend that had persisted since the early 2000s. Tanzania remained in the group of the fastest-growing and most consistently performing economies in Africa, although it was still characterised by a very low level of material wealth for the majority of the population. In the 2014 HDI (data for 2013), Tanzania was ranked 159th (out of 187 countries), in the 'low development' category. A new set of national accounts data nevertheless showed that Tanzania's GDP was significantly higher than had until then been assumed. As in several other African countries, the national accounts base year had been updated from 2001 to 2007 to better capture important changes in the relative weight of different economic activities. The upward revision for the base year 2007 showed GDP to have been *27.8% higher* than previously calculated. On the basis of the new data, average *per capita income* was now estimated to have reached $ 948 in 2013 and about $ 985 in 2014 – fairly close to the government's declared goal of soon reaching the status of 'middle-income country' (defined by the threshold of a $ 1,045 per capita income).

In the face of continuing global economic and financial uncertainties, Tanzania's economy again proved to be remarkably resilient. This was also partly due, however, to the fact that the level of monetisation of the economy and the degree of trade openness with the rest of the world were still considerably lower than the average for SSA, thus shielding the country from negative repercussions. The GDP *growth rate* for 2014 was estimated at 7.1%, very similar to 2013 and quite consistent with the growth trend of most preceding years. Climatically, it was a fairly good year, which allowed the agricultural sector to grow by close to 5%. A bumper harvest of about 2.5 m tonnes of maize led to consideration of possibly exporting up to 1 m tonnes to China in 2015. Since 2011, Tanzania had managed to be more than self-sufficient in basic staple foods. Both the industrial and service sectors grew by about 8%. Expectations of a faster and more fundamental transformation of the economy were increasingly linked with prospects for a significant natural gas production, although full commercial exploitation was still a number of years away. Tanzania's ranking was practically unchanged at 121st (out of 144 countries) in the World Economic Forum's Global Competiveness Index 2014–15, and at 131st (out of 187 countries) in the World Bank's Doing Business 2015 report.

While high *inflation* rates (16% in 2012) had been a major cause of growing popular discontent, inflation was successfully contained in 2014 at an annual average of 6.1% and a low of 4.7% in December. This was largely due to stable food prices as a consequence of favourable weather conditions and to lower domestic fuel prices, resulting from the fall in global oil prices. This also contributed to the relative stabilisation of the *exchange rate*, with only minor fluctuations during the year: the rate in December was TSh 1,735: $ 1, just 10% lower than in January due to the dollar's global appreciation, while the exchange rate with the euro remained stable. The *structural trade deficit* was brought down by about 5% to $ 5,470 m, principally as a result of a slightly (by 1%) reduced import bill of $ 10,918 m, due to cheaper oil prices. Export earnings grew moderately by 3.6% to $ 5,448 m. On balance, just about half of Tanzania's import needs were covered by its own export earnings. The (preliminary) *current-account deficit* was thus estimated to have been somewhat reduced to about 13% of GDP. Gross *foreign reserves* were slightly down at $ 4.4 bn (compared with $ 4.6 bn in 2013) by the year's end, sufficient for a comfortable import coverage of almost five months. While the *external debt* had previously been substantially reduced to a low of $ 4.2 bn in 2006 as a result of concerted debt cancellations under the HIPC initiative, it had lately been increasing again rather fast, reaching $ 14.2 bn at year's end (compared with $ 11.6 bn at end-2012). FDI inflows remained very substantial, while *tourism earnings* (over $ 1.5 bn spent by more than 1 m visitors) were once again Tanzania's most important foreign exchange earner, even topping gold. The idea of raising funds with a Eurobond issue on the international financial markets had been under discussion since 2011, but again did not materialise and was postponed into 2015.

IMF missions visited Tanzania in February and October to review the performance of its current programmes. On 25 April, the IMF simultaneously concluded the regular Article IV discussions and the third and final review of an arrangement under the *Standby Credit Facility* (SCF) that had been approved in July 2012 as a precautionary measure against the potential downside risks of a global slowdown. In February 2013, the government had drawn $ 114 m under the SCF to support the currency, but no further withdrawals were made before the expiry of the SCF on 30 April 2014. The IMF commended the Tanzanian authorities for the broadly satisfactory implementation of their economic programme, underlining that preserving macroeconomic stability was essential for continued strong growth; some concern was expressed about the need to contain public spending within the limits of the budget provisions and about the current-account deficit (about 14% of GDP) remaining among the largest in the region. Tanzania was judged at low risk of debt distress. On 16 July, the IMF approved a new three-year *Policy Support Instrument* (PSI), an unfunded IMF instrument designed for countries that do not need balance of payments financial support, but were helped to implement effective economic programmes. A previous PSI had been operative from 2010 to 2013. A first review under the PSI was undertaken by the IMF's October mission and scheduled to be formally approved in January 2015. Macroeconomic performance was judged to have been satisfactory until mid-year 2014, but to have deteriorated thereafter, with rising risks stemming from delays in disbursements of donor assistance (see above: escrow account scandal) and external non-concessional borrowing, as well as shortfalls in domestic revenues. The PSI programme was broadly on track through the end of 2014, with good progress on the agreed structural reforms, but the targets on domestic revenue were missed. Of particular concern was the accumulation of substantial payment arrears in the public sector.

On 12 June, Finance Minister Saada Mkuya submitted her 2014–15 *budget* to parliament. A review of the previous financial year's outturn showed that the overall *fiscal deficit* for *2013–14* had been considerably brought down to an officially reported 3.4% of GDP (compared with 5% in 2012–13), but analysts considered this somewhat misleading as a rapid accumulation of arrears owed to the private sector and pension funds (roughly estimated as equivalent to about 1% of GDP) had already started to occur, thus bringing the actual deficit closer to about 4.5% of GDP. It was evident that the budget revenue targets had been set over-optimistically and that the government's revenue collection efforts were deficient. This situation led to a general under-execution of the initial 2013–14 budget, ending up with only 84% of the planned financial volume. Particularly hard hit were all development expenditure items, including priority sectors identified under the 'Big Results Now' initiative, of which only 65% were executed. This had a clear delaying effect on the progress of Tanzania's ambitious development goals.

The *2014–15 budget* was again based on rather optimistic assumptions. Total expenditure was budgeted at TSh 19,850 bn (about $ 12 bn), an increase of 8.1% over the 2013–14 budget figures. Again, 68% was foreseen for recurrent expenditure and 32% for development programmes. In the budget speech, an intention to reduce the traditional heavy dependence on external aid funds and to increase domestic revenue generation capacity was emphasised, but the short-term chances of success remained uncertain. The execution of the budget during the first two quarters of the financial year (until December) proved to be exceptionally challenging. Domestic revenue collection still remained slightly below target, while most of the planned general budget support funds (about $ 600 m) were withheld by the group of development partners; only about one-tenth of the total had reached the Treasury by the end of October with no new developments before the end of the year. To simply maintain its regular operations, the government turned to a big increase in domestic borrowing, incurred a further accumulation of arrears and had to slow down the implementation of planned projects. Domestic debt grew by 24% to the equivalent of $ 4.7 bn.

Optimistic expectations of a substantial economic upturn in the near future centred on increasingly promising prospects for the exploitation of Tanzania's substantial *natural gas* resources, although full commercial benefits were only expected to build up from the 2020s onwards. With more ongoing exploration activities, proven gas reserves were updated to 55 trillion ft^3, but more seemed quite probable. The fourth gas and oil licensing round for new offshore blocks and the Lake Tanganyika area came to an end in May. New model production-sharing agreements had been introduced in October 2013, which increased the role of the parastatal Tanzania Petroleum Development Company in the gas sector. Four major international oil companies were involved in planning the future commercial exploitation; no firm decisions were as yet made on the possibility of a liquefied natural gas plant. The significant drop in global oil prices raised fears that developments in Tanzania might take much more time than had been forecast. The political opposition repeatedly complained about the lack of transparency of plans relating to the gas sector. The on-going construction of a Chinese-financed gas pipeline from Mtwara to Dar es Salaam was poised to be completed in mid-2015. This would mean a significant increase in *electricity* generation and hopefully end the long-endured problems of recurring *power failures*. Despite a shock electricity tariff increase of 40% in January, the heavily loss-making power utility TANESCO continued to be a major financial burden on the government.

The improvement of the country's physical *infrastructure* continued to be a major focus of the government's development strategy, although the implementation of announced projects often remained rather uncertain. In September, the World Bank committed $ 565 m for an expansion of the port of Dar es Salaam. The construction of a large entirely new port near Bagamoyo, to be financed and constructed by China, was not yet begun. Various plans for either the rehabilitation of the central railway line or the construction of a new standard-gauge railway were discussed, but remained without any concrete confirmation. Chinese investors began work on an ambitious $ 3 bn project for the exploitation of coal reserves and iron-ore deposits in the south-west, including the construction of a new railway link. *Gold* production continued to contribute significantly to overall growth and exports, although declining in importance because of a slump in global prices. New *mining* ventures were about to start production of nickel and uranium and were faced with protests from environmentalists.

Tanzania in 2015

The political scene was entirely focused on presidential and parliamentary elections in October. In a tight electoral contest with a strengthened opposition coalition, the long-ruling CCM party was able to defend a more than two-thirds majority in parliament and to see John Pombe Magufuli elected as the new president upon the expiry of President Kikwete's two-term mandate. The opposition proved unable to unseat the deeply-entrenched CCM system. Separate elections in semi-autonomous Zanzibar were declared void in dubious circumstances, with no crisis solution in sight before the year's end. A promised referendum on a new constitution was not held. Magufuli introduced an unforeseen new leadership style, stressing discipline, rigorous cost-saving measures and serious ant-corruption efforts in state institutions. This earned him popularity among the general public, but also raised questions about an emerging authoritarian streak. Relations with Western aid donors were slightly strained over dissatisfaction with a lack of reform measures and the Zanzibar election issue. Macroeconomic performance and growth continued to be strong, but managing the budget proved to be difficult.

Domestic Politics

The *October elections* were the first in Tanzanian history that seemed to offer the faint possibility of an opposition victory. Numerous scandals had tarnished the image of the long-ruling CCM ('Chama cha Mapinduzi'/Party of the Revolution). In a reaction to the escrow account scandal in late 2014, President Jakaya Kikwete was forced to execute another *cabinet reshuffle* less than a year before the end of his final term. With the resignation of Energy Minister Sospeter Muhongo on 24 January, all senior officials who were implicated in the scandal had resigned or were dismissed, including two ministers, the attorney-general and some influential MPs and party cadres. This was Kikwete's seventh reshuffle in his ten-year tenure, all caused by alleged gross misbehaviour or underperformance of his ministers.

After an inclusive consultation process, the *Constitutional Review Commission* (CRC) had in 2013 compiled a draft for a new constitution, which had been intended to be discussed and finally adopted by a Constituent Assembly (CA) in October 2014. The CRC's draft had been supported by opposition parties; however, using its majority in the CA, CCM had changed the CRC's draft in some fundamental aspects. This draft was then to be submitted to a *referendum*, scheduled for 20 April. Doubts arose as to whether the referendum date could be met, given the slow pace of the biometric voter registration process, initially planned to start in November 2014, but delayed until February by the government's failure to provide the necessary funds. The National Electoral Commission (NEC) had initially planned to acquire 15,000 registration kits but this was reduced to just 8,000 by financial constraints. However, when registration started on 24 February, the NEC had received only 250 registration kits and it was not until mid-April that 3,000 more kits arrived. Consequently, on 2 April, NEC chairman Damian Lubuva announced that the referendum had to be postponed indefinitely. The voter registration process then continued until early August. The *postponement of the referendum* on the draft of a new constitution was received with satisfaction by opposition parties, the media and civil society organisations; for months they had called for a postponement and had demanded that the issue of the constitution needed to be addressed with consensus and should not be entangled with the election campaigning of competing political parties.

Unlike in many other African countries, there was no attempt to extend Kikwete's two constitutional terms, which were to end with general elections on 25 October. Therefore, CCM's internal selection process for a *presidential candidate* was crucial and turned out to be much more contentious than on any previous occasion. By 3 June, 42 CCM members, the highest-ever number of contestants, had picked up application forms. The unprecedented number of contestants was an indication of the *unpredictability of the selection process*. During recent years, no senior politician had been able to commend her- or himself as an obvious potential successor to Kikwete. Only the former prime minister, *Edward Lowassa*, was regarded by many as a 'natural' candidate. In 2008, he had had to resign following corruption allegations, which he had always denied. He had become the most controversial figure in CCM and among the population – condemned by many as the prototype of a corrupt politician, but celebrated by others as an innocent victim of intrigues and a gifted leader. In the run-up to the elections, the party was clearly split into a Lowassa-camp and an anti-Lowassa-camp. Although he never publicly indicated support for any of the contestants, Kikwete was assumed to favour Foreign Minister Bernard Membe, who came to be regarded as Lowassa's strongest opponent and the favourite of the anti-Lowassa-camp.

The *selection process* followed a well-established procedure. The nine-member party secretariat had to vet all applications using 13 criteria. On 10 July, the CCM National Security and Ethics Committee, led by party chairman Kikwete, scrutinised the applications and gave its recommendations to the 32-member Central Committee, which had to select five candidates from the original 38. The five were: Membe, Minister of Justice and former UN Deputy Secretary-General Asha-Rose Migiro, Minister of Works John Pombe Magufuli, AU Ambassador to the USA Amina Salum Ali and January Makamba, a young, albeit very influential politician, who had served as Kikwete's speech-writer and was the current deputy minster for communication. The *surprise omission of Lowassa* from this shortlist provoked massive protest from his many supporters and accusations of foul play by Kikwete. Despite an apparent split in the party, the large 378-member National Executive Committee continued according to procedures and approved three names to be forwarded to the highest party organ: Magufuli, Amina and Migiro. Although the selection depended mainly on political considerations, it was nevertheless surprising that two of the three recommended candidates were women. The CCM National Congress, consisting of about 2,100 members, met on 11–12 July and approved *Magufuli* as the party's *presidential candidate* with an overwhelming majority of 87% of the votes.

The 55-year old *Magufuli*, who had a PhD in chemistry, had been an MP since 1995 and had held several ministerial portfolios. He had earned public approval as minister of works, when he was seen responsible for successful road construction efforts over the past five years. Nicknamed 'bulldozer' for his record as public works minister, but also for his authoritarian leadership style, he had a reputation for being a hard worker who had never been involved in any scandals and was not well-connected in the innermost party circles. Magufuli named Minister of State for Union Affairs Samia Suluhu Hassan, from Zanzibar, as his running mate. Although the choice of a female candidate was widely welcomed, Hassan was also regarded critically for her hard-line stance as the CA's vice-chairperson. Zanzibar's current president, *Ali Mohamed Shein*, having served only one term, was nominated unopposed as *CCM's presidential candidate for Zanzibar*.

The *opposition alliance*, Coalition of the People's Constitution, (known by its Swahili acronym *UKAWA*), created in the CA context and consisting of CHADEMA ('Chama Cha Demokrasia na Maendeleo'; Party for Democracy and Progress), the CUF (Civic United Front), NCCR-Mageuzi (National Convention for Construction and Reform-Change) and the small NLD (National League for Democracy), had in October 2014 agreed to present a united front in the 2015 elections. Consensual agreement on the nomination of a joint presidential candidate nevertheless proved difficult and no choice had been made by mid-July. The political landscape then changed dramatically, when *Lowassa defected to CHADEMA* on 27 July. UKAWA had agreed to challenge CCM with joint candidates on presidential, parliamentary and council levels. On 4 August, Lowassa was nominated as CHADEMA and UKAWA *presidential candidate*. As expected, UKAWA nominated CUF's Seif Sharif Hamad as joint presidential candidate for Zanzibar. Lowassa's nomination posed several challenges for CHADEMA and UKAWA. The latter was only a somewhat loose coalition of parties with differing political agendas, mainly held together by their common support for the CRC's draft constitution and their criticism of CCM. CHADEMA in particular had over the years gained much of its support for its stance against the 'corrupt system' of the CCM government and had repeatedly named Lowassa as a key player. Before his defection, the new UKAWA presidential candidate had been a prominent figure in the rejection of the CRC draft and an uncompromising supporter of CCM's hard-line stance in the CA, the very factors that had initially led to the formation of UKAWA. No clear public explanation of UKAWA's/Lowassa's position on the crucial constitution issue was given, and it remained unclear how the electorate would respond to the decision to embrace the former foe. The move was also controversial within CHADEMA's leadership, but awareness that Lowassa's unbroken popularity would bring them a strong push in the elections finally convinced party leaders. Nevertheless, a number of opposition politicians expressed their dissatisfaction with the decision and two of the most prominent stepped down in protest against the deal with Lowassa: CHADEMA's secretary-general, Wilbroad Slaa, who had been CHADEMA's relatively successful presidential candidate in 2010 and had been expected to become UKAWA's candidate in 2015, announced his resignation from CHADEMA and from active politics, and the CUF's long-standing chairman, Ibrahim Lipumba, resigned from his leadership post.

Several CCM members also defected from the ruling party and joined the Lowassa camp, among them the former prime minister Frederick Sumaye. Former EAC secretary-general Juma Mwapachu also returned his CCM membership card, but without joining CHADEMA. But what drew most attention was the crossing-over of one of CCM's founders and its former chief ideologist, 85-year old Kingunge Ngombale-Mwiru, to CHADEMA; where he actively supported Lowassa's rallies. Even so, despite several *prominent defections*, CCM managed to retain its unity and to actively rally behind Magufuli.

Of the 22 registered parties, only CCM, CHADEMA and six others nominated presidential candidates. With the exception of ACT-*Wazalendo* (Alliance for Change and Transparency-Patriots), none of the smaller parties was expected to gain any significant support. ACT-Wazalendo, only founded in 2014, was mainly associated with its charismatic leader Zitto Kabwe, a former leading member of CHADEMA and respected chairman of the National Assembly's Public Accounts Committee, who was forced out of CHADEMA in March, after a long leadership wrangle.

The *electoral campaign* started officially on 22 August for the Union and on 7 September for Zanzibar. Apart from some minor incidents, campaign rallies were peaceful, but sporadic clashes between supporters of the two main camps left at least one person dead and several injured. Security forces reportedly used tear gas to disperse CHADEMA members on some occasions, and opposition parties complained about arrests of their candidates in some areas. Both major camps went along with the widely expressed popular *demand for change*. Magufuli centred his campaign around his image as a results-oriented hard worker who would deliver and who had never been involved in any of the many CCM scandals – with the slogan 'Hapa kazi tu' (Here is only work); he deliberately kept a certain distance from the party. In an ironic twist, Magufuli was advocating stricter anti-corruption measures, while Lowassa was at pains to shed his image as a major corruption culprit. Both sides invested *enormous amounts of money* in their campaigns. CCM took full advantage of its incumbency, access to state resources and decade-long control of administrative structures. The state-owned *media* clearly favoured CCM, whereas private media reported in a more balanced way. Election reporting focussed mainly on the two main blocks and hardly covered the smaller parties and their candidates.

The elections were supervised by *two distinct electoral commissions*. The NEC was responsible for the election organisation on the Union level (presidency and parliament) both on the mainland and in Zanzibar and for the local council elections on the mainland. The Zanzibar Electoral Commission (ZEC) organised the elections of the Zanzibar president, the Zanzibar parliament (House of Representatives) and the Zanzibari local councils. The opposition's massive *distrust* of the electoral commissions culminated in its call upon voters to remain close to the polling stations on polling day in order to 'protect their votes' against alleged attempts by the commissions to rig the process.

By and large, *polling day* itself was peaceful, despite some minor incidents of disorder, missing materials and delayed opening of polling stations, but *tensions* increased soon after the polling stations closed. After first results from various polling stations had been released, police entered the CHADEMA tallying centre in Dar es Salaam and arrested more than 150 people for unlawfully posting results in social media. On 29 October, the data centre of the Legal and Human Rights Centre, which hosted the Tanzanian Civil Society Consortium on Election Observation (TACCEO) was raided by police, who temporarily arrested 36 data clerks and confiscated computers and mobile phones under Section 16 of the new Cybercrimes Act. These activities and a generally non-transparent handling of the tallying and tabulation of the results fuelled *allegations of vote rigging*.

In *Zanzibar*, things were even more dramatic. During the ongoing counting process, ZEC chairman Jecha Salim Jecha *declared the election void* on 28 October, citing irregularities in Pemba, the CUF's stronghold, and announced that the exercise would have to be repeated. Two days before, CUF's Seif Hamad had publicly declared himself the winner, referring to accumulated results his party had received from all polling stations. Jecha's unilateral decision was challenged by some other ZEC members, who had not been consulted. It was also doubtful whether the ZEC had the formal competence to void the polls. Despite this dramatic turn, the situation remained calm. *International observer groups* from the EU, the AU, SADC and the Commonwealth and national observer groups protested against the ZEC chairman's decision. The CUF rejected a re-run and urged the ZEC to continue announcing the results. After an initial meeting between Kikwete and Hamad on 7 November, Hamad, Kikwete, Zanzibar's President Shein, former presidents Mwinyi and Mkapa and other high-ranking CCM-politicians were involved in several *closed-door meetings* aimed at overcoming the political impasse. Magufuli, however, remained conspicuously aloof, claiming to have no authority over Zanzibar's internal affairs. Although no solution was in sight by the end of the year, the population remained calm, although affected by drastically rising food prices caused by the prevailing uncertainty.

On 29 October, the NEC declared *Magufuli the winner* with 58.5% of the votes against 40% for Lowassa. It was the worst result for a CCM presidential candidate since the re-introduction of the multi-party system in 1992, and by far the best for an opposition candidate. The opposition was also comparably successful in the *parliamentary elections*. CHADEMA's overall percentage of parliamentary votes increased from 24% in 2010 to 32%, while CCM's fell from 60% to 55%. However, in the winner-takes-all electoral system, this increase in votes did not fully translate into a corresponding increase in seats. CHADEMA managed to win 34 constituencies, compared with 23 in 2010 and the CUF also increased its directly-elected MPS (mostly in Zanzibar) from 24 to 32. ACT-Wazalendo performed badly, winning only Kabwe's constituency, Kigoma-Urban. CCM scooped 196 seats (74% of the constituencies). Despite a united opposition and a widely perceived mood for change, *CCM* thus retained its *overwhelming two-thirds majority* in the National Assembly. The distribution of special seats for women (of which CCM got 66, CHADEMA 37 and CUF 10) was made proportionally to the number of constituencies won. Of the 264 directly-elected MPs, only 25 were women (CCM: 18, CHADEMA: 6, CUF: 1). Voter turnout was about 67%, a significant increase from 43% in 2010. The opposition generally performed well in most urban constituencies, while CCM retained its overwhelming support in rural areas. CCM proved more popular among women and older citizens, whereas UKAWA had most followers among young males and better-educated voters.

The results of the *town and district council elections* presented a similar picture. CCM was able to maintain its control over the vast majority of the councils, winning over 70% of all council seats. However, the opposition managed to win the majority of seats in important town and city councils (such as Dar es Salaam, Arusha, Mbeya and Moshi), while CCM was ahead in Dodoma and Mwanza. UKAWA refused to recognise the official results, claiming that the NEC had manipulated the count in favour of CCM, and boycotted Magufuli's inauguration as Tanzania's fifth president on 5 November. Samia Suluhu Hassan was sworn in as Tanzania's *first female vice-president*.

By several symbolic actions, Magufuli immediately indicated his determination to start a *new era* by implementing his 'Here is only work' slogan and no longer tolerating any 'business as usual' attitudes. A day after his inauguration, he unexpectedly visited the Finance Ministry and demanded information about absent officials. The following Monday, he fired the head of the National Hospital during another surprise visit, after he found patients sleeping on the floor and diagnostic machines out of order. In his crusade against civil servants' idleness, he continued *sacking dozens of officials*, both middle- and high-ranking; others were fired on allegations of corruption and misuse or theft of public property. On 16 December, Magufuli fired the long-serving director of the Prevention and Combating of Corruption Bureau, Edward Hoseah, for ineffectiveness.

A second major theme during his first weeks in office was to the *reduction of unnecessary public expenditure*. Magufuli ordered the suspension of all but essential foreign travel for government officials, and workshops for public servants in expensive hotels with generous allowances were banned. He cancelled the traditionally self-congratulatory Independence Day celebrations on 9 December: Tanzanians should not celebrate Independence, while the country suffered from cholera outbreaks. His call to use the holiday to clean-up the country was widely taken up and he participated personally by cleaning the fish-market area close to State House. In another symbolic move, he ordered a reduction in the cost of the parliament's inauguration party from $ 100,000 to $ 7,000, directing the rest of the money to buy hospital beds.

These measures brought the 'new broom' the expected public support. Magufuli's activities were also followed internationally with great attention, as he seemed to be setting new standards for cleaning-up a notoriously negligent and corrupt system, and was soon seen as a possible *role model for other African leaders.* Critics, however, doubted whether these popular and populist actions would be followed by more systematic approaches and structural reforms. In several cases, the desire of lower-level officials to show commitment to the Magufuli style led to dubious actions against subordinates, who were sanctioned for minor incidents. This new leadership style of directives and short-notice ultimatums given by Magufuli and subsequently by his ministers and other officials, as well as threats to dismiss and even jail subordinates if they failed to meet demands, also raised concerns about an *emerging authoritarian streak.*

On 19 November, Magufuli appointed the virtually unknown *Kassim Majaliwa* as his new *prime minister.* Majaliwa, a teacher by profession, had served in several government positions and been responsible for education as a deputy minister in the prime minister's office. His appointment was seen as an indication that improvements in the dilapidated education sector could become a top priority in Magufuli's first term. The composition of the new cabinet was eagerly awaited for weeks. Magufuli waited until 9 December to announce the names and portfolios of his ministers. In accordance with his cost-cutting policy, he presented a *drastically reduced cabinet* of only 18 ministries, with 34 ministers and deputies (compared with 60 under Kikwete). Initially, the key ministries of finance, education, tourism and public works remained vacant and were only filled on 23 December, since Magufuli took his time to find qualified individuals. Most of the ministers had already served in Kikwete's last cabinet, either as full ministers or as deputies.

Two controversial laws, the Cybercrimes Act and the Statistics Act, provoked national and international protests from opposition parties, civil society groups and academicians, as well as from the EU Delegation and the Development Partners Group. Experts were concerned that some provisions of the *Cybercrimes Act* could be used to restrict freedom of expression by criminalising the dissemination of false, deceptive, misleading or inaccurate information. The *Statistics Act* was criticised because it made it illegal to publish statistics unauthorised by the National Bureau of Statistics. Soon after the Cybercrime Act came into force in September, a student and a businessman were charged in separate cases for disseminating false information through social media networks. The Act was also cited by police to justify the arrest of TACCEO personnel during election observation on 29 October. After meetings with media and civil society stakeholders in June, the government withdrew two other controversial – but long-awaited – media bills, the Media Service Bill and the Right to Information Bill. Fears of a clampdown on *media* arose when the government banned a weekly newspaper, 'The East African', on 21 January for lacking proper registration, although it had been in the market for 20 years.

Foreign Affairs

On 20 February, Kikwete took over the rotating *EAC chairmanship* from Kenya. Since 2013, Tanzania had found itself somewhat isolated in the EAC due to its reluctance to follow Kenya's, Uganda's and Rwanda's fast pace in implementing joint projects, and to strained relations between Kikwete and Rwanda's President Kagame. During the year, relations with EAC partners improved considerably, without Tanzania giving up its somewhat hesitant stance towards an accelerated integration. The change from Kikwete to Magufuli raised hopes that Tanzania could become more active in the block.

Kenya's decision to ban Tanzanian tourist vehicles from accessing Nairobi Airport led to bilateral misgivings early in the year. The *tourism row* was then intensified by Tanzania's Civil Aviation Authority's decision to reduce the frequency of Kenya Airways flights to Tanzania by 67%. During a meeting in Windhoek (Namibia) on 21 March, Kikwete and Kenya's President Kenyatta agreed to lift the ban on Tanzanian vehicles and to allow Kenya's airline to resume its normal flight schedule. Relations between the two countries remained cordial, with Kikwete being only the second foreign leader to address both houses of Kenya's parliament during his farewell state visit in early October. The two presidents agreed to scale up cooperation in the battles against terrorism, drug trafficking and poaching and signed several agreements, including to strengthen *co-operation in defence and security* by combating violent extremism, cross-border crime and human trafficking.

Relations with *Rwanda* improved significantly. In January, a UN report indicated that leaders of the Democratic Forces for the Liberation of Rwanda (FDLR) opposition militia had held several meetings in Tanzania since 2013 and that the Tanzanian government authorities were not investigating activities by and support for FDLR in Tanzania. Kikwete, however, declared his willingness to support a UN military offensive against the rebels. Kikwete and Rwanda's President Kagame met for the first time in two years during the February EAC summit; in March Kikwete attended a Northern Corridor project meeting in Kigali (Rwanda) at Kagame's invitation. Tanzania was not a member of the infrastructure project group, dubbed in 2013 the 'Coalition of the Willing' (Kenya, Uganda and Rwanda), which had explicitly excluded Tanzania and Burundi. On 26 March, Kagame launched the idea of a freight train route linking Dar es Salaam with the border town Rusumo and attended the Central Corridor High-Level Industry and Investor Forum in Dar es Salaam. The leadership change from Kikwete to Magufuli further eased the relationship. In December, Kagame congratulated Magufuli on his crackdown on tax evasion and inefficiency at Dar es Salaam port, which handled over 70% of Rwanda's deep-sea cargo.

Tanzania was regarded as an influential player in the *Burundi crisis*, owing to its good relations and protective role towards that country and its government, although its influence remained limited. During a visit to Bujumbura in March, Kikwete appealed to President Nkurunziza not to seek a third term and to respect the Arusha peace accord, which limited the presidential tenure to two terms. Responding to the escalation of violence that followed Nkurunziza's announcement that he would stand for a third term, Kikwete as EAC chairman sent a team of foreign ministers from Kenya, Uganda, Rwanda and Tanzania on a fact-finding mission to Burundi. The team was to prepare a report for an extraordinary EAC summit on 13 May in Dar es Salaam. At the summit, the presidents condemned the attempted military putsch on the same day in Bujumbura and called upon the authorities to postpone the elections. However, they remained silent on Nkurunziza's third-term ambitions. Tanzania initially opposed the decision of the AU Peace and Security Council to send a peace-keeping force to Burundi, and instead embarked on diplomatic efforts, with Kikwete, and later Magufuli and new Foreign Minister Augustine Mahiga, holding several meetings with Burundian officials. By the year's end, almost 120,000 *Burundian refugees* and more than 64,000 refugees from the DRC were living in overcrowded camps in western Tanzania.

Efforts to mediate in the *conflict in South Sudan* between the warring factions of the Sudan People's Liberation Movement (SPLM) had started in 2014 in Arusha with reconciliation talks between the main SPLM groupings. The talks, hosted by Kikwete and CCM, were concluded with the signing of a unification agreement on 21 January. CCM continued to facilitate the reconciliation process. On 30 November, Kikwete visited the *Comoros* as a special AU envoy in an effort to support the Comorian stabilisation process. He urged all stakeholders to work towards holding free, fair and transparent elections. On 5 May, two Tanzanian peacekeepers with the special *UN Force Intervention Brigade in the DRC* were killed and at least 13 others injured in an ambush, supposedly carried out by the Ugandan rebel group Allied Democratic Forces.

Relations with the *donor community* were ambivalent. The steps taken by the government in reaction to the escrow account scandal were welcomed by the *budget support group*, which in March started to release parts of the pledged general budget support that had been suspended in October 2014 in response to the scandal. Magufuli's determined actions against corruption, fraud and squandering of public resources were also well received by donors. However, concerns were raised about some other significant political developments, especially the nullifying of the elections in Zanzibar and the enforcement of the Cybercrimes Law and the Statistics Act. In a joint statement on 29 October, the election observer groups from the EU, the AU, SADC and the Commonwealth reacted with dismay to the voiding of the Zanzibari elections. On 9 November, the mission heads of 13 European states, the USA, Canada and the EU expressed their concern about arrests under the much-criticised Cybercrimes Act and called upon the government not to infringe fundamental human rights. The US *Millennium Challenge Corporation* (MCC) postponed the approval of Tanzania for a second envisaged compact because of the escrow account scandal. Unlike the budget support group, the MCC was not satisfied by the government's actions and on 17 September expressed continued concern about corruption. In December, the release of the envisaged $ 472 m for electricity projects was again postponed. Although no reasons were officially given, it was assumed that the nullification of the elections in Zanzibar and arrests under the Cybercrimes Law had influenced the decision.

Socioeconomic Developments

The overall *macroeconomic performance* was again quite satisfactory and in line with the strong continuous growth trend that had persisted since the early 2000s. Tanzania remained in the group of the fastest-growing and most consistently performing economies in Africa, although it was still characterised by a very low level of material wealth for the vast majority of the population. In the 2015 HDI (data for 2014), Tanzania was ranked 151st (out of 188 countries), in the 'low human development' category, whereas a year earlier it had been ranked 159th. On the basis of new national accounts data (revised in 2014), average *per capita income* (in nominal terms) was now estimated to have just passed the threshold of $ 1,000 per year – thus practically attaining the government's declared goal of reaching the status of a 'middle-income country' (defined by the threshold of a $ 1,045 per capita income). According to the 2015 HDI, the per capita income (in PPP terms) had been $ 2,411 in 2014 and a *Gini coefficient* of 38 showed a relatively modest level of unevenness of income distribution.

In the face of persistent global economic and financial uncertainties, Tanzania's economy continued to remain remarkably resilient. This was also partly due to the fact that the level of monetisation of the economy and the degree of trade openness with the rest of the world were still considerably lower than the average for SSA, thus shielding the country from negative repercussions. The *GDP growth rate* for 2015 was estimated at 7.1%, very similar to 2013 and 2014 (7.0%) and consistent with the growth trend of the last decade. Climatically, it was a difficult, but not disastrous year, with unfavourable weather conditions. The agricultural sector thus only expanded by 2.6% and the food stock of the National Food Reserve had to be run down to 180,000 tonnes by the year's end, compared with 460,000 tonnes in January. The main drivers of growth were the communications, mining and financial services sectors. Expectations of a faster and more fundamental transformation of the economy were increasingly linked with prospects for significant natural gas production, but with the depressed global oil markets it remained uncertain when the start of full commercial exploitation would finally get underway. Tanzania's ranking was practically unchanged at 120th (out of 140 countries) in the World Economic Forum's Global Competitiveness Index 2014–16, and at 139th (out of 189 countries) in the World Bank's Doing Business 2016 report.

Inflation had been successfully contained in 2014, thus opening the year with a 4.0% rate in January. Consumer price inflation then gradually rose to a high of 6.8% in December (average for 2015: 5.6%), largely driven by higher food prices resulting from poor weather conditions and by the effects of the *exchange rate depreciation*, which raised the domestic cost of imported goods. The shilling depreciated continuously throughout the year by about 24% against the dollar, attaining a rate of TSh 2,149: $ 1 by the end of December. This was the combined effect of the global strength of the dollar, high liquidity in the domestic banking system, seasonally low export earnings, high repatriation of corporate dividends and delays in the mobilisation of expected external programme financing. The *structural trade deficit* was remarkably brought down by almost 30% from $ 5.6 bn (2014) to $ 4 bn, principally as a result of a significantly reduced (by 10.8%) import bill of $ 9,743 m, largely due to lower oil prices. Export earnings grew strongly by 7.6% to $ 5,725 m, mainly on account of manufactured goods, while traditional agricultural exports declined in value. On balance, and for the first time, almost 60% of Tanzania's import needs were covered by its own export earnings. The (preliminary) *current-account deficit* was thus estimated to have been considerably reduced from about $ 5 bn in 2014 to $ 3.1 bn, equivalent to an exceptionally low 7% of GDP. Gross *foreign reserves* remained more or less unchanged; at the end of June they amounted to $ 4.3 bn, sufficient to cover four months of imports of goods and services. While the *external debt* had previously been substantially reduced to a low of $ 4.2 bn in 2006 as a result of concerted debt cancellations under the HIPC initiative, it had in recent years been increasing again rather fast. The external debt stock reached a new high of $ 15.4 bn at year's end (compared with $ 14.2 bn at the end of 2014). The central government was accountable for around 80% of this debt. Almost half of the debt was owed to multilateral agencies and about 10% to bilateral donors, with the remainder composed of commercial debts and export credits. *FDI* inflows remained quite substantial, while *foreign exchange earnings* increased by 10.3% to $ 3.7 bn, mainly from travel and transportation services. *Tourism* earnings alone ($ 2.2 bn) from over 1.2 m visitors remained Tanzania's most important foreign exchange earner, even topping gold. The idea of raising funds with a Eurobond issue had been under discussion for years, but was again postponed because of unfavourable conditions on the international financial markets.

IMF missions visited Tanzania in March and September to conduct the second and third reviews of the country's performance under the current three-year *Policy Support Instrument (PSI)*. Macroeconomic performance was judged to have remained strong and medium-term prospects were seen as favourable. Most assessment criteria under the PSI for June were met, but implementation was seen as having slowed ahead of the elections. Revenue and financing shortfalls, together with weak commitment controls, were identified to have led to the accumulation of further domestic arrears in the financial year 2014/15. While some progress on the achievement of structural reforms was noted, a number of benchmarks were detected as having been missed. Tanzania was seen as having a low risk of debt distress and to be eligible for more flexible debt conditionality. Tanzania's total national debt (external and domestic) of $ 19.4 bn by year's end was estimated to grow to around 43% of GDP in 2015–16.

On 11 June, Finance Minister Saada Mkuya submitted her *2015/16 budget* to parliament. Total expenditure was optimistically budgeted at TSh 22,495 bn (about $ 10 bn), a remarkable increase of 13% over the 2014/15 budget figures in view of clearly existing public finance problems. A high 74% share was foreseen for recurrent expenditure and only 26% for development programmes. The revenue forecast was composed of domestic tax and non-tax revenue (55% and 7%, respectively), domestic borrowing (27%) and external general budget support (GBS) and loans (10%). The GBS assumptions were drastically reduced compared with 2014/15 (24%) in reaction to the 2014 experience, when the group of development partners had withheld most of the budgeted GBS support as sign of disapproval over the lack of government action about a major corruption scandal. With increased efforts on domestic revenue generation, the tax share of GDP was expected to rise to 13%, still low by comparable SSA standards, and a target budget deficit of 4.2% of GDP was set. Budget priorities were given as financing the elections, completion of ongoing capital projects and special emphasis on rural electrification, water supply and human capital development. Towards the year's end, the new Magufuli government adopted a revised budget framework with a focus on curtailing non-priority current expenditures and postponing a number of not yet started investment projects, with the adjustments amounting to about 1% of GDP and aiming to maintain the deficit target.

The *2014/15 budget* had ended with an overall deficit that exceeded the target (3.8% of GDP) once the significant accumulation of expenditure arrears that had been building up in 2014 was taken into account. It also reflected shortfalls in revenue generation and financing, combined with weak expenditure controls. Even with the relaxation of the 2014 GBS freeze and the disbursement of delayed GBS funds in March, overall donor support fell somewhat short of expectations. The main shortfall, however, was due to $ 300 m less than planned external non-concessional borrowing, reflecting unfavourable conditions on international financial markets. The overall fiscal deficit was thus estimated to have attained around 4.5%, while the accumulated payment arrears had risen to about 1.1% of GDP.

The new incoming government was tasked with settlement of existing verified arrears, mostly to suppliers and pension funds.

Optimistic expectations of a quick economic upturn in the near future, centred on the exploitation of Tanzania's substantial *natural gas resources*, were somewhat dampened with the realisation that a much longer time horizon was likely before full commercial benefits could be expected. This was due to the significant drop in global oil prices and the reluctance of international oil companies to commit substantial new investments. More exploration activities nevertheless continued and the volume of proven gas reserves was updated to 57 trn ft^2 (82% of which offshore), with more strikes being very probable. In August, the first gas from Mnazi Bay (near Mtwara) was transported to Dar es Salaam through the new Chinese-financed-and-built pipeline; this was a major step towards easing the long-endured problems of insufficient electricity generation and recurring *power failures*. After long delays, a new *Petroleum Act* guiding legislation on all aspects of the oil and gas industry was finally discussed in parliament and passed in July. The parastatal Tanzania Petroleum Development Company was to lose all regulatory functions and to become a commercial company, while separate state agencies were to regulate all upstream and downstream activities in the industry. The legislation built on experiences from Algeria and Norway, provided more transparency than hitherto and had no nationalistic bias (as had been feared by some observers). TANESCO, the heavily loss-making parastatal *power utility* continued to be a major financial burden on the government: by mid-year, TANESCO had accumulated arrears to its suppliers (mostly private energy producers) of TSh 700 bn, while the government had in turn run up substantial arrears to TANESCO. The IMF viewed a solution to TANESCO's financial misery as an upmost priority for the incoming government.

The improvement of the country's physical *infrastructure* continued to be a major focus of the government's development strategy, although the implementation of announced projects often remained rather uncertain. In October, preliminary works began for the construction of a large entirely new port near Bagamoyo, to be financed and constructed by China. New *mining* ventures were about to start production of nickel and uranium and were faced with protests from environmentalists. Gold production continued to contribute significantly to overall growth and exports, although declining in importance.

Tanzania in 2016

President Magufuli, in his first full year in office, stringently pursued a hitherto unaccustomed leadership style, stressing discipline, rigorous cost-saving and anti-corruption measures in state institutions, pushing for higher revenue generation and exercising power by continuous single-handed directives (including dismissals of top functionaries), often without regard for formal procedures. This earned him popularity among large sections of the general public, but also raised fears about authoritarian tendencies and a loss of space for dissenting voices (including the media). Public activities of opposition parties were curtailed and some of their leaders were repeatedly interrogated by police. A repeat of the allegedly fraudulent 2015 elections in semi-autonomous Zanzibar was boycotted by the opposition and led to a single-party situation in parliament. Magufuli took control of the dominant long-ruling CCM party and introduced sweeping changes to its structures in an attempt to consolidate his (not entirely undisputed) position. Relations with Western aid donors were slightly strained over the Zanzibar election issue and dissatisfaction with a lack of economic reform measures, while relations with key neighbours and EAC partners improved. Indicators of macroeconomic performance and growth continued to be strong, but uncertainty over the government's future course and prevalent liquidity problems throughout the economy somewhat stifled the private sector and led to fears about an economic slowdown.

Domestic Politics

Throughout the year, President John Pombe Magufuli showed that he had no intention to slow down the pace of *implementing his agenda* of 'Hapa Kazi Tu' ('here only work'), the slogan of his 2015 electoral campaign. In his *fight against corruption, inefficiency and embezzlement of public funds*, he and his subordinates sacked or transferred more than 300 civil servants, among them the heads of the Tanzania Revenue Authority, Tanzania Investment Centre and several other institutions. Ministers and other senior leaders followed Magufuli's example of dismissals for alleged non-performance. Misappropriation and theft of public funds, fraud, violation of regulations and other illegal practices were revealed, ultimatums were set and even senior civil servants were fired in numerous state agencies and authorities. Some of those who lost their jobs over accusations of fraud, theft, corruption and the like, found their bank accounts frozen and were brought before the courts.

In the *fight against misappropriation of public funds* and to *reduce government expenditure*, the government also addressed the problem of so-called *ghost workers*, i.e. 'employees' of public sector institutions who did not exist (or had died) but whose names nevertheless appeared on the payrolls. In a nationwide audit between March and September, more than 16,000 ghost workers were detected and removed from the public sector payroll. All civil servants were required to prove their identity and their qualifications.

Various measures were introduced to *reduce government expenditures* and to *increase revenues*. This included a consistently restrictive approach towards foreign travel for state functionaries and government workshops in luxury resorts, as well as salary cuts for senior civil servants. Although welcomed by the general public, the *austerity policy* had some negative consequences for the economy and on the social situation of the poorer segments of the population (such as budget reductions in the Health Ministry leading to medication shortages in government hospitals). Strict controls were introduced to *increase tax discipline* and to *reduce tax evasion*. In addition, *new taxes* were introduced, including on mobile phone transactions, in the already highly-taxed tourism sector, and on transactions on the Dar es Salaam Stock Exchange. There were, however, fears that some of the new taxes would hit small businesses and the general population too hard. Local governments were urged to increase their own revenues, prompting some authorities to introduce several questionable taxes on small businesses. In response to complaints, Magufuli decreed that these local taxes should only be collected from larger businesses.

As promised during the election campaign, *school fees were abolished* up to lower secondary school level. The government also abolished additional charges that had been demanded in primary schools (such as parents' contributions to security, cleaning, construction of classrooms, etc.). This led to a dramatic increase in enrolment, especially in primary schools. Although extra operational funds were provided by government, it became obvious that schools were not prepared to accommodate such large numbers of students. A severe lack of classrooms, furniture, textbooks and teachers was reported. Audits and investigations revealed that fraud, theft, corruption and related vices were rampant in the education system. Nearly 7,500 students attending a special diploma course in education at the University of Dodoma were suspended after an investigation by the Ministry of Education showed that they lacked the required qualifications. Almost 500 students at a private university were suspended by the ministry for similar reasons.

Following established party tradition, the chairman and former president of CCM ('Chama cha Mapinduzi' / Revolutionary Party), Jakaya Kikwete, handed over the *CCM party chairmanship to Magufuli* at an extraordinary CCM congress on 22 July. Rumours that the party would break with this tradition and continue with Kikwete until regular party elections in 2017 indicated that some CCM sections were not happy with Magufuli's fight against corruption, since it posed a threat to their own personal interests, but he was unanimously elected by the nearly 2,400 delegates. In mid-December, the CCM National Executive Committee (NEC) proposed *several wide-ranging changes to the CCM constitution*, which remained to be approved by an extraordinary congress in February 2017. The changes focussed on reducing the membership of key decision-making organs. The NEC was to be reduced from 388 to 158 members and the

Central Committee from 34 to 24. Under the new composition, MPs were no longer allowed to be members of both bodies. While the size reduction of the two organs was widely welcomed, the exclusion of MPs was received more negatively as a measure to restrict democracy and participation within the party. There were proposals for several party posts to be abolished and the frequency of party meetings to be reduced.

The government's stern measures found wide *approval from the general public*, as they tackled crucial weaknesses in Tanzania's political and administrative system, such as negligence, theft, embezzlement, corruption, wastefulness – and impunity. Furthermore, they were directed against members of the state apparatus, who were widely perceived as selfish profiteers of Tanzania's economic growth (which had failed to benefit the majority of poor people) and seen as responsible for the poor results of development achievements. A representative opinion poll, conducted in June by the civic-empowerment NGO Twaweza, showed that 96% of Tanzanians approved Magufuli's activities and 70% stated that services of government institutions had improved under his presidency. Although several of his austerity measures had (short-term) negative effects on many people, Magufuli maintained the image of a *man of the small people*, who was targeting the allegedly greedy and corrupt big fish in order to help the poor and provide better services for them.

Many observers, however, expressed some *scepticism* as to whether these measures would in the longer run bring the desired results. The new political style was characterised by surprise visits by the president, ministers or other office holders to government institutions. Whenever they discovered any deficiencies, they either fired the officers responsible or gave them a specified short time to fix the problems. This *authoritarian leadership style* tended to instil a culture of fear rather than one of dedicated work. There was criticism that government employees were punished without correct procedures being followed and in some cases even by violating human or civil rights. There were also questions as to whether the frequent ultimatums and dismissals undermined established mechanisms of the democratic political process and would in the longer run weaken state institutions. Another point of criticism was that the shortcomings that led to the punishment of individual civil servants had often been caused by structural problems such as underfunding.

Having been elected as CCM chairman, Magufuli informed the party congress that he was determined to accomplish the *shift of the seat of government* from Dar es Salaam to *Dodoma* by 2020. Dodoma had officially been declared Tanzania's capital city in 1973, but plans to move the government had never been implemented. Questions immediately arose concerning the high costs and logistical challenges of such a move. An estimated 120,000 government employees and their families would have to be transferred, with virtually no preparations made so far. On 30 September, the office of Prime Minister Kassim Majaliwa moved to the new capital.

There was no development in the stalled *constitution review process*. Although it had been among CCM's pledges in its 2015 election manifesto, Magufuli made clear that it was not among his government's priorities. However, civil society organisations such as the Tanzania Constitutional Forum called on the government to continue the process, which had been controversially aborted in April 2015, and made suggestions on how to restart it.

Magufuli translated his *'here only work' slogan* not only into tackling corruption and wastefulness, but also into actions *against criticism, democracy and activities of the political opposition*. It emerged that he was much less open to criticism and media freedom than his predecessor Jakaya Kikwete had been. He also seemed to have little sense of the role of a political opposition, as he expected it to remain silent and not to interrupt government in its work. Several *opposition politicians were temporarily arrested* during the year, and two *radio stations and one newspaper were banned* for allegedly inciting violence and publishing seditious material.

The government charged several people under the restrictive *Cybercrimes Act* of 2015 and other laws. In June, one man was sentenced to three years in prison or a fine of TSh (shilling) 7 m for allegedly insulting the president on social media and another separately faced the same charge. In September, five people appeared before the court and a university lecturer was also arrested, again on the same charge. On 13 December, Maxence Melo, co-founder of the popular whistle-blowing and discussion site 'Jamii Forums', was arrested under the Cybercrimes Act for refusing police demands for forum members' personal data; subsequently, the police raided the 'Jamii Forum' offices. In mid-December, parliament finally, after years of controversial discussions, endorsed the *Media Services Act*, which called for increased professionalism in the media sector. It required every journalist to seek accreditation from a newly created government-appointed board, which could also revoke the accreditation. Media organisations were strongly critical that the new regulations imposed government control on journalists' work and heavily curtailed press freedom.

In January, Information Minister Nape Nnauye announced that the government would *stop the popular live broadcasting of parliamentary sessions* by the public Tanzania Broadcasting Corporation (TBC) to reduce the allegedly high costs. This brought objections from media and human rights organisations and from opposition parties, who accused the government of censorship – since the live broadcasts were among the rare opportunities the opposition had to publicise its positions to the electorate. A Twaweza opinion poll showed that 79% of citizens rejected the government's decision and 92% regarded the live broadcasts as important. Although the major opposition party, CHADEMA (Party for Democracy and Progress), offered to pay for the service, live broadcasts ended on 19 April. TBC subsequently distributed selected debate highlights to private TV stations.

In June, CHADEMA announced that it was to stage *nationwide protests* against the ban of live broadcasts of parliamentary sessions and against Magufuli's leadership style, which they described as dictatorial. After CCM stated that they would counter CHADEMA's protests with their own public rallies, the *police banned all political rallies* for security reasons until further notice. On 23 June, Magufuli banned all political rallies and public demonstrations until the next elections in 2020, arguing that it was now time for work and not for politicking. CHADEMA launched a *campaign against dictatorship* (Ukuta) and called for demonstrations in a '*Day of Defiance*', to take place on 1 September. However, the police reminded CHADEMA of the existing ban and went even further, *banning internal party meetings* on the grounds that they served to create chaos. Several CHADEMA leaders and party members were temporarily arrested for incitement. In an atmosphere of rising tensions, religious leaders, political analysts and human rights activists called for dialogue and CHADEMA finally called off the demonstrations. Magufuli's popularity and his fight against corruption and public sector slackness, which the opposition had always demanded, made it difficult for the opposition to attract much attention. They therefore increasingly concentrated on his controversial leadership style and growing authoritarian trends.

Although still unsolved, the *Zanzibar crisis* faded from the political limelight after the nullified 2015 elections were repeated on 20 March. After the nullification, Seif Sharif Hamad, the secretary general of Zanzibar's main opposition party, the CUF (Civic United Front), had *called for dialogue* to resolve the crisis instead of conducting a re-run. Nine rounds of closed-door meetings between Hamad and high-ranking CCM officials, including Zanzibar's President Ali Mohamed Shein, were held, but without arriving at a solution. After two months of negotiations, Hamad told a press conference on 11 January that the talks had failed to reach a consensus and called upon Magufuli to help finding a solution acceptable to all. Magufuli remained reluctant to intervene, saying the matter rested with the Zanzibar Electoral Commission (ZEC). In early February, he eventually declared that he saw a repeat election as the best solution to the political deadlock and called on the CUF to take part. On 22 January, ZEC Chairman Jecha Salim Jecha announced *20 March* as the date of the *election re-run*, which was to be conducted with the same candidates as in the 2015 polls – even if parties refused to take part in the repeat exercise. The CUF governing council formally decided on 28 February not to participate and most other small and politically insignificant parties followed suit. The *elections* were conducted with a heavy *police and military presence*. *Shein*, the incumbent president, *received 91.4%* of the votes, while second-placed Hamad Rashid Mohamed (Alliance for Democratic Change) took just 3%. CCM candidates won all the seats in the House of Representatives, the parliament of semi-autonomous Zanzibar. According to the ZEC, voter turnout was 67.9% (341,865 voters), but the CUF challenged the figure, claiming it had counted only 100,726 voters (20%).

Western donors reacted with strong disapproval to this electoral process. On 22 March, the embassies and high commissions of 16 Western donors, including the US and the EU, issued a joint statement regretting the ZEC's decision to hold the re-run without a negotiated and mutually accepted agreement. They also made clear that they expected the Tanzanian government to find a solution to the impasse. In reaction, the US *Millennium Challenge Corporation* (MCC) cancelled a grant worth $ 472 m (designated for rural electrification). The MCC had already twice postponed the approval of the grant due to concerns about corruption and bad governance and said this final cancellation was based on the MCC's dissatisfaction with the government's non-adherence to democratic principles.

Zanzibar's 2010 constitution required the president to form a *Government of National Unity* (GNU) from all parties elected to the House of Representatives and to appoint the first vice president from the strongest opposition party, which had to have secured at least 10% of the votes. These regulations had been introduced before the 2010 elections to allow the CUF a share in the government and to calm the ever-growing tensions between the two rival camps, which had resulted in deep divisions in Zanzibar's society. But with no opposition MPs in parliament, Shein could neither form a GNU nor appoint a first vice president. Instead, he appointed to the

House of Representatives three members of small parties that had not boycotted the election re-run and also made them ministers in his new 15-member cabinet.

After five years of relative harmony under the power-sharing arrangement of the GNU, Zanzibar had in practice returned to a *one-party situation and the politics of exclusion.* Despite continuing problems and distrust between the two camps, the GNU had been the precondition for reducing political tensions and reconciling Zanzibari society, which was also split along party lines. By terminating the CUF's participation in the GNU, the CCM had excluded about half of Zanzibar's population from political participation and also put societal peace and cohesion at risk. However, it appeared that Zanzibaris preferred political acquiescence and agony to open protest – probably a consequence of bad experience from the pre-GNU period. After the repeat election, the CCM simply continued with business as usual and showed no inclination to make conciliatory moves towards the CUF.

The *CUF tried to win international support*: Hamad travelled to the US, Canada, the EU and several European countries in July, where he met with representatives from political parties, democratic institutions and the ICC, accusing the CCM of violating democratic principles and human rights. He also presented a six-point plan to resolve the crisis, which included the formation of an interim GNU headed by a Zanzibari personality not affiliated to any party. That interim GNU was to prepare elections within six months, to be held under the supervision of a neutral international body. Hopes that Magufuli could try to reconcile the two parties were dashed during his first visit to the isles after his election. In a speech in Pemba in early September, Magufuli strongly criticised Hamad and the CUF, telling them that the elections were over and they had to wait until the next round in 2020.

The *CUF's exclusion from the formal political process* also had consequences for the party itself. It owed much of its support to Hamad's popularity and he had for years managed to hold different factions together and avoid a radicalisation of party members and supporters who were sceptical about his conciliatory approach towards the CCM. Although some within the CUF (like some within the CCM) found this hard to accept, the establishment of the GNU as a means for the CUF to participate in government had strengthened his position against more radical tendencies. Now that his dialogue-oriented approach had failed, it remained unclear whether the 72-year-old Hamad could maintain his authority. But even the future of the party remained uncertain. A severe *leadership wrangle* posed a first challenge, when its former chairman, Ibrahim Lipumba, reclaimed his previous position in June. He had stepped down in August 2015 in protest against Edward Lowassa's nomination as the opposition coalition's presidential candidate and was due to be replaced at the CUF's national congress. Lipumba's intention to return was strongly rejected, mainly by the Zanzibar wing and Hamad. The eruption of chaos at the congress on 21 August revealed a deep rift between the primarily Zanzibar-based Hamad wing and the Lipumba wing, which got most of its support from the Mainland. Although a large majority seemed to support Hamad's faction, the congress failed to resolve the leadership question and the CUF remained split and weakened until the year's end.

Foreign Affairs

Magufuli paid much *less attention to foreign policy* and diplomacy than his predecessor, focussing energetically on domestic issues. But he placed some new emphasis on *regional cooperation in the EAC*, where Tanzania had been somewhat side-lined in recent years. Mainly to reduce costs and to demonstrate his concentration on urgent domestic reforms, Magufuli skipped several international meetings, where Tanzania was represented by Vice President Samia Suluhu Hassan or ministers. Magufuli made only three foreign visits: to Rwanda (April), Uganda (May) and Kenya (November). During the EAC summit on 2 March in Arusha, *Tanzania's tenure as chair* was extended for another year. Magufuli declared his intention to extend his anti-graft and austerity approach to the EAC, demanding, amongst other measures, reductions in costs for travel and extravagant conferences. Relations with the EAC's neighbours improved noticeably, since Magufuli's administration displayed a much more active approach towards the EAC integration process and focussed more on business cooperation and joint infrastructure projects than on political issues. This was, however, somewhat contradicted by the imposition of stricter rules for Tanzanian work permits for foreigners, including those from EAC countries.

Under Magufuli's presidency, *relations with Kenya* had somewhat cooled, partly due to suspicions about his personal friendship with Kenya's opposition leader Raila Odinga and to complaints about difficulties faced by Kenyans working or running businesses in Tanzania. Ugandan and Rwandan decisions to construct important infrastructure projects (oil pipeline and railway line) across Tanzania and not through Kenya – as earlier agreed – and Tanzania's rejection of the EPA between the EU and the EAC, which Kenya had already signed, further exacerbated the long-existing rivalry. During Magufuli's state visit to Kenya in early November, he and President Uhuru Kenyatta nevertheless reaffirmed their commitment to strengthening ties.

The government displayed only a modest commitment to attempts to resolve the two major current *crises in the East African region*. Tanzania's former president Benjamin Mkapa was appointed as facilitator of the *Inter-Burundi Dialogue* at the EAC summit in March. In several consultative meetings, a roadmap for the dialogue was developed and presented to EAC heads of state on 8 September. The future of this roadmap remained uncertain, however, since Burundi's opposition alliance accused Mkapa of having sided with Burundi's President Pierre Nkurunziza, who had refused the alliance's participation in the talks.

According to UNHCR, Tanzania was hosting more than 235,000 *Burundian refugees* in camps in western Tanzania. After the CCM had played a positive role in 2015 in reconciling warring factions in *South Sudan*, no further Tanzanian activities to mediate in the continuing civil war were reported.

Magufuli's efforts to curb corruption and waste earned Tanzania *worldwide approval*, but relations with *Western donor countries* remained somewhat ambivalent. On the one hand, they welcomed the government's reform efforts, which they had been calling for for years. Tanzania was one of only two African countries invited to the UK's Anti-Corruption Summit in London in May. On the other, they were critical about the evident erosion of democratic governance, including through harassment of opposition parties and restrictions on press freedom, freedom of expression and freedom of assembly. The handling of the Zanzibar election crisis was another major point of criticism. Some Western countries and institutions still continued to provide substantial aid, but were reluctant to provide unspecified budget support. Asian countries, specifically *China* and *India*, remained equally important as investors and providers of credit for Tanzania's economic and infrastructure development.

Socioeconomic Developments

According to most standard indicators, the overall *macroeconomic performance* was again quite satisfactory, in line with the strong continuous growth trend that had persisted since the early 2000s. Tanzania remained in the top group of the fastest-growing and most consistently performing economies in Africa, although it was still characterised by a very low level of material wealth for the vast majority of the population (about one-third were living below the poverty line). In the 2016 *HDI* (data for 2015), Tanzania was again ranked 151st (out of 188 countries) in the 'low human development' category. The average *per capita income* (in nominal terms) was estimated to be around $ 1,000 per year – thus practically attaining the government's declared goal of reaching the status of a 'lower middle-income country'. The per capita income (in PPP terms) was calculated at $ 2,467 in 2015.

Tanzania's economy continued to remain remarkably resilient in a difficult global setting of continued financial uncertainties and weak growth in SSA. This was partly due to the fact that the level of monetisation of the economy and the degree of outward trade openness were still considerably lower than the SSA average, thus shielding the country from negative repercussions. The *GDP growth rate* was estimated at 7.0%, slightly lower than planned (7.2%), but similar to preceding years and consistent with the growth trend over more than a decade. Climatically, it was by and large a fairly regular year, but the normal year-end rains failed in many parts of the country, raising fears of serious food shortages (which were denied by government). The *agricultural sector* again performed poorly, with a growth rate of just above 2%, and the food stock of the National Food Reserve had to be run down to 90,000 tonnes by the year's end, compared with 180,000 in 2015 and 466,000 in 2014. The main *drivers of growth* continued to be the communications, mining and services sectors, while manufacturing industries (after remarkable expansion in recent years) were hampered by difficulties in obtaining credit and a slowdown of demand due to a general shortage of liquidity throughout the economy. For some years, expectations of a faster and more fundamental transformation of the economy had been linked with prospects for substantial natural gas production (based on significant proven reserves), but, with depressed global oil markets, full commercial exploitation (including liquid natural gas [LNG] for export) did not appear realistic before sometime in the 2020s. Tanzania's ranking was just slightly improved at 116th (out of 138 countries) in the World Economic Forum's Global Competitiveness Index, and at 132nd (out of 190 countries) in the World Bank's Doing Business report. In the World Bank's 2015 Country Policy and Institutional Assessment, Tanzania scored 3.6

(out of 6); despite a slight deterioration compared with 2008, it remained well above the SSA average, ranking joint sixth of 38 countries assessed. This appraisal reflected the government's relatively prudent management of the economy.

Headline *inflation* was successfully contained close to the medium-term target of 5%, at an average rate of 5.2% for the year. For a fourth consecutive year, a prudent monetary policy thus met its desired target. Contrary to a substantial depreciation of 24% against the dollar in 2015, the *exchange rate* of the shilling remained unusually stable throughout the year, reaching TSh 2,173: $ 1 at year's end. This was largely the result of a tight liquidity situation in the domestic banking system and above all of a significantly improved balance of payments situation. For a second year running, the *structural trade deficit* was brought down by a further 33% from $ 5.6 bn (2014) and $ 4.4 bn (2015) to $ 3.0 bn, principally as a result of a much reduced (by 12%) import bill of $ 8,661 bn. This fall was largely due to a sharp decline in the import of capital goods (as a result of reduced large investments) and consumer goods. Export earnings grew by 5.3% to $ 5,689 bn, mainly from minerals and a recovery of traditional agricultural exports (by 12%). Manufactured goods fell in value by 20%. On balance, two-thirds of Tanzania's import needs were covered by its own export earnings – the highest ratio ever achieved. Coupled with a strongly improved surplus (by 83%) in the service sector account (largely from tourism, the main foreign exchange source), this led to the *current-account deficit* being almost halved (from $ 4 bn in 2015 to $ 2 bn), equivalent to an estimated 4.4% of GDP (exceptionally low compared with around 10% in previous years). *Gross foreign exchange reserves* remained practically unchanged; by the end of December they amounted to $ 4.3 bn, sufficient to cover 4.2 months of imports of goods and services. While the *external debt* had been substantially reduced in the early 2000s to a low of $ 4.2 bn in 2006 as a result of debt cancellations under the HIPC initiative, it had recently been increasing again rather fast. External debt reached a new high of $ 17 bn at year's end (compared with $ 16.5 bn in 2015). Almost 80% of the debt was owed by central government and 20% by the private sector; 47% of the debt was owed to multilateral agencies and 11% to bilateral donors, with the remainder composed of commercial debts and export credits. A debt sustainability analysis indicated that the value of the external debt was equivalent to 19.9% of GDP, well below the critical international threshold of 40%, implying that Tanzania's debt was quite sustainable.

IMF missions visited Tanzania in March and October to conduct the fourth and fifth reviews of the country's performance under the current three-year *Policy Support Instrument* (PSI). Macroeconomic performance was judged to have remained strong and the medium-term outlook was seen as favourable. Most assessment criteria under the PSI and all indicative targets were met. The IMF welcomed the authorities' ambitious reform and development agenda, but also pointed to downside risks to economic growth in the short term, stemming from the current tight stance of fiscal and monetary policies, the slow pace of credit growth, the laggard implementation of public investment programmes and private sector uncertainty about the government's new economic strategies. The pace of structural reforms was also seen as in need of acceleration.

On 8 June, Finance Minister Philip Mpango submitted the current government's maiden *budget for fiscal year 2016/17* to parliament. It was premised on a fairly optimistic economic outlook and foresaw *highly ambitious targets*, assuming significant progress in improving public-sector efficiency and revenue generation. Total expenditure was budgeted at TSh 29,540 bn (about $ 13.5 bn), a staggering increase of 31% over the 2015/16 budget figures. An unprecedented 40% of the total budget was earmarked for development expenditure, while previously well over 70% had always been allocated for recurrent expenditure (mainly salaries for about 550,000 civil servants). The revenue forecast was composed of domestic tax and non-tax revenue (51% and 9%, respectively), domestic and external borrowing (25%) and external financing from development partners (12%). There was a cautious estimate that only 1.6% was expected to come in the form of external general budget support (GBS), based on recent experience of donor countries withholding promised GBS as a sign of disapproval of certain government actions. With stricter enforcement of existing tax regulations and a widening of the tax base (for example, by introducing VAT for tourism-related services despite sharp protests from the tourism industry), the tax share of GDP was expected to rise to 13.8% (still low by comparable SSA standards), and a slightly rising fiscal deficit of 4.5% of GDP was foreseen.

The *2015/16 budgetary outcome* was marked by the satisfactory achievement of most domestic revenue targets (except for local government authorities), but by external financial shortfalls and a continuing decline in grants. Recurrent expenditure was somewhat higher than budgeted, while only 87% of budgeted development expenditure was in fact used. The fiscal deficit turned out at around the targeted 3.5% of GDP. In March, Magufuli stopped the ongoing settlement of considerable payment arrears that had accumulated over the years (e.g. to contractors, suppliers, pension funds), totalling about 1.9% of GDP by mid-2016, pending a general review of genuine verified arrears. *Budget execution* during the first half of 2016/17 was slower than expected, largely on account of ongoing external financial shortfalls. Tax revenue was broadly in line with the ambitious targets, due to rigorous collection efforts by the tax authorities. Spending (particularly development expenditure) was, however, considerably lower than budgeted, due both to slow disbursements of aid funds and to delays in spending authorisations stemming from insufficient planning capacities.

The new *2nd Five-Year Plan 2016/17–2020/21* provided the medium-term framework for the government's ambitious goal of transforming Tanzania into a semi-industrialised *middle-income country by 2025*. However, uncertainties about the government's concrete intentions and about Magufuli's often spontaneous directives led to a widely-felt atmosphere of insecurity, particularly with respect to private sector activities. Some critical observers even sensed a partial return to authoritarian state-led economic strategies, reminiscent of Tanzania's socialist past under Julius Nyerere, although the government officially stressed its unequivocal support for private-sector activities. The anti-corruption and revenue-generation drives, coupled with problems in the banking sector (a sharp increase of non-performing loans and a shift of all public-sector accounts from commercial banks to the Bank of Tanzania [BoT] in response to a Magufuli directive), contributed to a widely-felt liquidity squeeze and a slowdown of private-sector activities. In line with advice from the IMF, the BoT eventually began to ease the liquidity situation for the private sector. Magufuli's reformist steps thus proved to be somewhat disruptive in the short run, but were expected to be beneficial in the longer term.

The improvement of Tanzania's physical *infrastructure* as a precondition for faster industrialisation continued to be a major focus of the government's development strategy, but the pace of implementation often remained somewhat uncertain. The long-endured situation of insufficient electricity generation and frequent *power failures* saw a noticeable improvement, with 45% of available generated power already coming from natural gas and with further expansion underway. With more exploration activities, the volume of *proven gas reserves* was updated to 75 trn cubic feet, but no decision for the construction of an LNG plant for gas export was in sight. TANESCO, the heavily loss-making parastatal *power utility*, continued to be a major financial burden on the government; it had accumulated large arrears with its suppliers (mostly private energy producers) and had simultaneously been unable to recover huge arrears from its customers (including government departments, specifically Zanzibar). An 8.5% electricity tariff increase, approved for January 2017, was abruptly stopped by Magufuli for fear of social protests while looking for a more sustainable solution.

In February, Uganda agreed to the construction of a 1,120 km *oil pipeline* from its oil fields (Hoima) across northern Tanzania to the export port of Tanga; this decision overturned earlier plans to build the pipeline across Kenya and was viewed as a victory in the perennial competition between Kenya and Tanzania. China offered a credit of $ 7.6 bn for the construction of a new *standard-gauge railway* to replace the existing dilapidated central railway line, but plans remained to be finalised in 2017. The start of Chinese-financed projects to develop large *coal and iron ore deposits* in south-western Tanzania was further delayed, awaiting the conclusion of protracted discussions over government subsidies. In August, the government *banned the import of coal* to strengthen the local coal industry, but this met with strong protests from local consumers (specifically the cement industry) due to the low quality of local coal. This led to a major conflict over a cement factory in Mtwara, opened in 2015 by Nigerian billionaire Dangote with a $ 500 m investment; it had created 10,000 jobs and supplied a third of the local market. Dangote threatened to close the factory because promises by the previous government had not been met. Only upon Magufuli's intervention was a solution found that allowed the factory to obtain gas at an acceptable price.

In July, the government backed away from the expected ratification of the long disputed EPA between the EAC and the EU, citing newly arising uncertainties over Brexit and fears over its negative consequences for Tanzania's future industrialisation. With diverging positions of Kenya and Rwanda, no common EAC position had been found by year's end. In November, parliament unanimously rejected the EPA and supported the government's stance. The EPA question clearly underpinned the government's latent protectionist and nationalistic economic tendencies, which were also visible in a number of other domains.

Tanzania in 2017

President Magufuli, in his second year in office, ever more vigorously pursued an authoritarian leadership style that significantly narrowed the previously existing democratic space and curtailed critical public debate. The freedoms of assembly and of expression of opposition voices were frequently restricted by state authorities, political rallies were banned outside of election periods, many opposition politicians were repeatedly arrested, interrogated and intimidated, critical media were closely scrutinised and the state organs showed an increasing intolerance of any dissenting opinion. Despite a noticeable deterioration in the general political climate, the stability of the political system was not under threat and the dominant long-ruling CCM ('Chama cha Mapinduzi' / Revolutionary Party) was able to control all spheres of public life and still enjoyed the unwavering support of the majority of the population. Magufuli further consolidated his grip on the CCM, despite continued discontent within party ranks. On the surface, the situation in semi-autonomous Zanzibar remained relatively calm, but the long-standing confrontation between the CCM and the opposition CUF did not vanish. Neighbourly relations with Rwanda and Uganda were strengthened, amid minor disputes with Kenya over trade issues. Relations with Western aid donors became more strained over dissatisfaction with Magufuli's erratic governance style, while cooperation with China was further intensified. Indicators of macroeconomic performance continued to be good, with a solid 7.1% GDP growth rate, but uncertainty over the government's strategic orientation of stressing economic nationalism and continuing severe liquidity problems weakened private sector initiatives, raising worries about a looming economic slowdown.

Domestic Politics

The Magufuli administration continued to drastically change the country. The *fight against corruption and fraud*, negligence and indiscipline in the public sector, and embezzlement and waste of public funds remained high on the government's agenda. The government demonstrated its willingness to *stop the culture of impunity* and to take strong action, even against prominent people. As in 2016, numerous public servants were sacked on allegations of corruption, fraud, misuse of funds or alleged underperformance in office, among them Minister of Energy and Minerals Sospeter Muhongo, who was forced to resign in late May for failing to supervise the mining sector, after Magufuli had received the first of two investigation reports that had concluded that mining companies had understated the value of their exports (see Socioeconomic Developments). In mid-June, two key suspects in the *Tegeta Escrow case* were arrested and charged with economic sabotage. In mid-September, Air Tanzania's former managing director and former chief finance officer were sentenced to six years in jail or a fine of TSh (shilling) 35 m for causing the national airline a loss of almost $ 1 m through fraudulent deals in 2007. Two officials from the Ministry of Energy and Minerals were brought before court in mid-September and accused of causing a $ 1.1 m loss in tax revenue by undervaluing an export-bound consignment of diamonds that had been seized at Dar es Salaam airport.

After detecting more than 16,000 so-called ghost workers and removing them from the public sector payroll in 2016, the president fired almost 10,000 civil servants in May after a verification process found that they had forged academic certificates. However, several of those affected insisted that they held authentic certificates and appealed against their dismissals. Given the shortage of civil servants in some crucial sectors such as justice, health and education, the decision to fire 10,000 people was received with some reserve. In February, the Tanzania Commission for Universities threatened to expel more than 7,000 students on the grounds that they lacked the required qualifications. They were given one week to prove their academic credentials.

In its *drive to put the country in order*, the Magufuli administration went against anything it perceived as "wrong, immoral, inappropriate, dangerous or obstructive" to the government's efforts to develop and industrialise the country. However, most measures aimed at punishing individual misbehaviour and not at bringing about structural or procedural reforms. The efforts to promote *better work ethics, discipline* and a *result-oriented civil service* were not always successful, with some of the measures even being counterproductive. The president's spontaneous and frequently erratic decisions led to an *atmosphere of fear* in some parts of the civil service, where decision-makers were reluctant to decide anything because of a constant threat that any 'wrong' decision could immediately cost them their job. On the other hand, some politicians and civil servants acted over-zealously. Several office-holders overstepped their constitutional competences by issuing directives or ordering arrests, which they were not legally entitled to do, and with complete disregard for legal procedures.

The government's efforts to *contain smuggling and abuse of illicit drugs* took a strange twist in mid-February, when Dar es Salaam Regional Commissioner Paul Makonda presented a list of 97 names of people allegedly involved in the use of and trade in illegal drugs. The list included prominent politicians, among them the leader of the strongest opposition party CHADEMA (Party for Democracy and Progress), Freeman Mbowe, well-known artists, leading business people and religious leaders. In a series of televised press conferences, Makonda named suspects and summoned them to police stations, where they were interrogated and had to undergo a drugs test. Some of those on Makonda's list rejected the accusations and threatened to sue him for defamation. Makonda's actions aroused strong criticism from members of parliament and Information Minister Nape Nnauye, who considered the public naming of suspects unlawful. In mid-March, Makonda, accompanied by armed police, stormed a TV and radio station late at night and (unsuccessfully) demanded that they broadcast a video-clip in which one of his critics was accused of illegitimate and immoral behaviour. Following a public outcry, Nnauye set up a team to investigate the issue, which in its report harshly condemned Makonda's action as an attack on media freedom. The following day, Magufuli, who had backed Makonda throughout the entire affair, sacked Nnauye and replaced him with former justice minister Harrison Mwakyembe.

The government's quest to clean up the country also saw a further crackdown on people accused of *practising or promoting homosexuality*, which was illegal in Tanzania but never aggressively persecuted. In February, Health Minister Ummy Mwalimu announced that 40 privately-run health centres would be stopped from providing HIV/AIDS related services, accusing them of promoting homosexuality. In mid-September, 20 people undergoing training in HIV/AIDS education programmes were arrested in Zanzibar on allegations of being implicated in homosexuality. One month later, 13 people were arrested in a Dar es Salaam hotel for allegedly promoting homosexuality. This arrest seemed to be politically motivated rather than being part of the government's campaign against homosexuality. The group, including an acclaimed human rights lawyer from South Africa, had convened for a legal consultation on the possibility of mounting a court case against the government's HIV/AIDS policies. Dozens of men suspected of being gay were reportedly detained and taken to hospitals to undergo forced anal examinations.

In yet another arena of his campaign against 'immorality', Magufuli told a public rally on 22 June that he would never allow *pregnant school girls* to return to government schools after giving birth. Magufuli's statement contradicted his party's 2015 election manifesto and the Education Ministry's long-standing efforts. During the parliamentary budget debate in mid-May, the Parliamentary Social Services Committee, together with the opposition, had urged the education minister to accelerate preparations for the already signalled guidelines for the re-entry policy. Magufuli's statement caused an outcry within and outside Tanzania. Although the president and Home Affairs Minister Mwigulu Nchemba threatened to deregister NGOs that campaigned for allowing teenage mothers to return to school, and to fire all head teachers who failed to comply with the orders, on 29 June, a group of 26 Tanzanian NGOs jointly called on the government to reconsider its decision. The pan-African women's organisation Femnet set up an online petition and numerous people used social media platforms to criticise the president's statement. On 6 July, at least 22 global and African human rights organisations jointly stated their support for the 26 Tanzanian NGO's concerns and demands. On 3 August, the African Commission on Human and People's Rights, together with other AU human rights institutions, criticised Magufuli's statement and urged the government not to undermine the girls' right to education and equality. Obviously unimpressed by the criticism, the government pursued its fight against teenage mothers. On 11 December, Mwanza Regional Commissioner John Mongella directed that all pregnant school-girls be arrested and taken to court in order to prevent other school-girls from having love affairs and to force them to reveal the names of those who had impregnated them.

The *human rights situation deteriorated significantly.* The opposition's opportunities to exercise their legal rights were severely limited by the prolonged presidential directive to ban politicians from political activities outside of their respective constituencies until the next elections in 2020. Provisions of the proposed *new Political Parties Act* sought to permanently institutionalise the presidential directive. The Magufuli administration intensified its drive to *clamp down on the opposition* with a strategy of demoralisation through constant harassment and frequent short-term arbitrary arrests, interrogations and court charges. About 400 members of the leading opposition party CHADEMA, but also from the small ACT (Alliance for Change and Transparency)-Wazalendo party, including MPs and the party leadership, were temporarily arrested and interrogated by security forces for conducting political activities outside their constituencies, criticising the president or talking for longer than their allotted time during a rally or disputing government data on economic growth, and other charges. One of the most outspoken opposition politicians, CHADEMA's chief whip in parliament Tundu Lissu, was arrested six times and his residence invaded and searched several times by the police. In February, Lissu announced that he would stand for election as president of the Tanganyika Law Society, the country's bar association. Justice Minister Mwakyembe thereupon threatened to deregister the association, but Lissu was nevertheless elected on 18 March. On 7 September, Lissu sustained life-threatening injuries in an attempt on his life, when unknown assailants fired about 30 bullets at his car. He was rushed to Dodoma General Hospital and later flown to a hospital in Nairobi (Kenya), where he slowly recovered. Nobody was arrested, and the government turned down demands from CHADEMA to request the US for assistance with the investigation.

Assaults and abductions by 'unknown assailants' became a new but increasing phenomenon. In April, three local singers were reportedly abducted and tortured by unknown individuals, before being released. Journalist Azory Gwanda disappeared on 21 November in unclear circumstances and continued to be missing. Journalists and media associations started campaigns to urge the authorities to intensify their investigations and bring the journalist back.

In August, the police claimed victory in the so-called *Kibiti killing case*. Since 2014, more than 40 people, mainly police officers and local political leaders (mainly from CCM) but also ordinary citizens, had been mysteriously killed in Kibiti, Mkuranga and Rufiji Districts of Coast Region. The reasons behind the killings remained unclear, but the security forces assumed a criminal background. The police finally raided a forest camp and killed 13 suspects in early August. In September, a person suspected of being the mastermind behind the killings was caught and shot by police in Dar es Salaam. However, the abduction in November of journalist Azory Gwanda, who was researching the Kibiti killings, indicated that the case was not yet solved.

The government and administration imposed *extreme restrictions on suspected dissidents* and intimidated or arrested politicians, civil society activists, journalists, lawyers, musicians and ordinary people, thus creating a widely-felt atmosphere of fear. The space for NGOs shrank significantly. They were threatened with deregistration by the administration, the president and ministers; their staff and supporters were intimidated and temporarily arrested, and their activities were blocked by police or civil servants. A popular local rapper was arrested in March for mocking the president, but – on Magufuli's personal order – was released the following day. *Media freedom and freedom of expression* were severely curtailed. Four newspapers were temporarily banned, for "sedition", "threatening national security" or publishing "false information". Leading politicians, including the president, warned the media not to "overextend their freedom". Several journalists were temporarily arrested or intimidated by the authorities. Maxence Melo, managing director and co-founder of the popular online forum and whistle-blower website JamiiForums, faced juridical harassment throughout the year. He had been arrested but granted bail in December 2016 under the Cybercrimes Act of 2015 for refusing to reveal the identities of anonymous whistle-blowers. In January, Mike William Mushi, another JamiiForums founder, was also charged in court. But some ordinary citizens were also charged, or remanded for several hours or days without charge, after posting messages critical of the government on social media or WhatsApp groups.

In September, the government tightened *control on social media* and introduced the *Electronic and Postal Communications (Online Content) Regulations*. Some of its provisions posed a further threat to the freedom of expression. It was aimed at controlling content on social media and imposed enormous fines on individual users and online providers. All digital media platforms, including online forums and blogs, were required to be registered with the Tanzania

Communications Regulatory Authority, which had the right to deny registration or to deregister a website, forum or blog. Bloggers and forum providers were to be held responsible for any content posted on their sites and had to block anonymous users, identify sources of contents and cooperate with law enforcement officers. Tanzania fell ten places in the World Press Freedom Index of Reporters without Borders – making a total drop of 22 places since 2015.

The growing intolerance of criticism, political opposition, public debate, expressions of dissent, media freedom, violations of the rule of law and of the separation of powers, disrespect for due procedures, and the dramatic narrowing of the democratic space provoked *increasing criticism* from various angles. The new communication regulations were widely criticised in the media and by civil society organisations. In mid-January, three local human rights and media organisations lodged a petition in the East African Court of Justice to challenge the *Media Services Act of 2016*. Somewhat surprisingly, bishops of several churches also criticised the authoritarian streak, but were immediately threatened with deregistration of their churches by the home affairs minister. In a speech delivered in late August to the African Leadership Forum in South Africa, Magufuli's immediate presidential predecessor *Jakaya Kikwete* called upon African ruling parties to view opposition parties not as enemies, but as partners in fostering democratic principles based on the rule of law. In Tanzania, Kikwete's words were widely understood as advice to Magufuli to reconsider his clampdown on the opposition. Several NGOs continued to demand the resumption of the *constitutional reform process*, while the government clarified that this was not on its list of priorities.

Notwithstanding the accusations that democracy and the rule of law were being undermined, opinion polls indicated that *Magufuli still enjoyed wide popular support*. In mid-June, the NGO Twaweza published the results of an opinion poll, which indicated a 71% approval rate for Magufuli from the 1,805 respondents. Although this rate was significantly higher than Magufuli's election result of 58%, it was a sharp decline of his popularity compared with the 96% he had polled in a similar Twaweza survey in June 2016. Respondents approved his fight against corruption and improvements in public service delivery.

The opposition was further weakened by prominent *defections to the ruling* CCM, after politicians received offers from the party or the government, among them the ACT-Wazalendo former chief advisor and its chairperson and 2015 presidential candidate. In October, ten senior ACT leaders announced their collective defection. In late November, Magufuli appointed one of the formerly fiercest critics of CCM, former CHADEMA presidential candidate Wilibrod Slaa, as ambassador to Sweden. At parliamentary and lower levels, too, numerous politicians quit the opposition and joined CCM, where they were rewarded with government or party posts.

By-elections for local councils on 26 November in 43 wards across the country were marred by irregularities and *unprecedented violence*, which left dozens of people injured, some seriously. Observers from the Legal and Human Rights Centre (LHRC) reported excessive use of force by the security forces, arrests and abductions of party leaders, representatives and voters and attacks with machetes, beatings and torture. The violence indicated the dramatically increased level of intolerance and hatred between the two main political parties. Later, the authorities imposed a TSh 60 m ($ 27,000) fine for airing "seditious information" on five TV stations that had broadcast the LHRC report. CCM won all but one of the contested seats.

The leadership wrangle in Zanzibar's main opposition party, the *Civic United Front* (CUF) escalated further. Since 2016, the party had been split into two factions, one led by the former chairman Ibrahim Lipumba, the other by the former secretary-general Seif Shariff Hamad. In July, Lipumba stripped eight MPs affiliated with the Hamad faction of their party membership, so that they automatically lost their seats in parliament. They were replaced by eight other legislators, sworn in in September. In November, the eight ousted

MPs demanded their reinstatement, after the High Court ruled that their expulsion from the party was unlawful.

Magufuli's leadership was widely supported by his *ruling CCM* and the dissent that existed was hardly expressed openly. He further strengthened his control over the party when on 11 March the CCM's National Executive Committee (NEC) *expelled 18 senior party members* and issued strong warnings to four others for "unethical conduct". This was widely understood as a measure to purge the party of supporters of the influential former prime minister, Edward Lowassa, who had defected to the opposition in the run-up to the 2015 elections. The *party structures were radically streamlined* at an extraordinary National Congress on 12 March, attended by more than 2,300 delegates. The NEC was reduced from 388 to 163 members and the Central Committee from 34 to 24. Various party organs were reduced in size and the frequency of their meetings was minimised. Several party positions were removed and multi-leadership posts were prohibited. According to CCM chairman Magufuli, the reforms were aimed at strengthening party efficiency, reducing costs and dependency on rich business people, and bringing "the party back to the people".

Foreign Affairs

Magufuli pursued his *low-profile and business-oriented foreign policy*. As in 2015 and 2016, he skipped several high profile international meetings, where Tanzania was represented by the vice president or ministers. As a reflection of the intensifying alliance with *Uganda*'s President Yoweri Museveni, several joint infrastructure and trade projects were launched and agreements on cooperation in trade, electrification and health care signed. The most significant infrastructure project was the construction of a crude oil pipeline from western Uganda to the port of Tanga, which had originally been planned to be built through Kenya. The opening of a one-stop border post was intended to partly divert Uganda's imports and exports from Kenya to Tanzania.

Relations with *Kenya* remained difficult due to ongoing trade disputes. Both countries blocked several products from the other country or imposed duties. In October and November, the Tanzanian government seized and auctioned 4,000 cows belonging to Kenyan Masai herders. The authorities blamed the influx of 18,000 cows from neighbouring countries for environmental destruction. In early November, Tanzanian authorities seized 6,400 one-day-old chickens, allegedly smuggled from Kenya, and burnt them to death on suspicion that they could spread bird flu.

During his tenure as EAC *chairman*, which ended on 20 May, Magufuli introduced his cost-cutting measures to the regional body. According to him, the secretariat alone had reduced its expenditure by more than 25%. But no solution was found to the conflict over EPA trade deals with the EU. Kenya and Rwanda wanted the EPAs to be signed whereas Tanzania rejected them.

Magufuli condemned the ICC decision to investigate alleged human rights abuses in *Burundi*, saying it would interfere with the EAC's efforts to restore peace, which, however, did not progress. The Burundi peace dialogue mediator, former Tanzanian president Benjamin Mkapa, was accused of taking sides with Burundi's President Nkurunziza. According to UNHCR, Tanzania was hosting about 360,000 Burundian refugees by the end of October.

Holding the SADC Troika chair until August, Tanzania was involved in trying to find a solution to the conflicts in the *DRC*. In April, Foreign Minister Mahiga led a SADC mission to the DRC to assess the political and security situation. The mission stressed the need for peaceful and transparent elections and called for the establishment of a government of national unity in the DRC. On 7 December, at least 14 Tanzanian UN *peacekeeping soldiers were killed* and more than 40 injured in a rebel attack in North Kivu.

After eight Tanzanians were arrested and charged with espionage in *Malawi* in January, Foreign Minister Augustine Mahiga and

Malawi's President Peter Mutharika agreed to revive talks to resolve the long-standing misunderstandings between the countries, resulting from the simmering *Lake Nyasa/Lake Malawi border conflict.*

During a two-day official visit on 22–23 January, *Turkish President Erdoğan* signed nine agreements with Magufuli on cooperation in defence, economic development and health. Magufuli asked for a loan to help finance a stretch of the proposed new standard-gauge central railway line. Erdoğan urged Tanzania to shut a number of schools allegedly linked to the Gülen movement, but the targeted schools denied any link to the movement. Only one week after Erdoğan's visit, a Turkish-Portuguese consortium was awarded the tender for the construction of 205 km of the new railway line. The tender had previously been awarded to Chinese companies, and the Chinese government had agreed a $ 7.6 bn loan but Magufuli had suspended the contract over irregularities shortly after assuming office, and fresh bids were invited.

Despite the dispute over the railway project, *cooperation with China* intensified. China had become Tanzania's largest trading partner and second biggest investor after the UK. During the CCM national congress, the ruling party stressed its close traditional links with the Communist Party of China. Chinese Foreign Affairs Minister Wang Yi visited Tanzania on 9–10 January and promised support for Tanzania's industrialisation drive and to upgrade the TAZARA railway. On a return invitation, Mahiga travelled to China on a four-day official visit in December and met several potential investors.

India remained an important partner for investment and trade, with Tanzania being among India's five top investment destinations.

Tanzania was among the several countries accused of violating the *UN sanctions against North Korea*, allegedly having entered into a military-related contract with a North Korean firm. Mahiga, however, denied the accusations, explaining that Tanzania had ceased military cooperation with North Korea in 2014.

On 25 April, Tanzania expelled the *head of the UNDP mission* in the country for the allegedly deteriorating performance of her office. The media, however, linked the dismissal to her criticism of the controversial Zanzibar elections.

Although *Western donors* were increasingly concerned about the authoritarian drive, they lauded the government for improvements in education, public service delivery and the fight against corruption, waste of public funds and mismanagement, and continued to fund development projects.

Socioeconomic Developments

According to most standard indicators, *macroeconomic performance* was again quite satisfactory, generally in line with the strong continuous growth trend since the early 2000s. Tanzania remained in the top group of the fastest-growing and most consistently performing economies in Africa, although it was still characterised by a very low level of material wealth for the vast majority of the population (almost half living below the international poverty line). In the latest HDI (March 2017, data for 2015), Tanzania was ranked 151st (out of 188 countries) in the 'low human development' category. The (nominal) *average per capita income* was estimated to be around $ 1,000 per year – thus close to attaining the government's declared goal of achieving the status of a 'lower middle-income country'. The *average per capita income* (in PPP terms) was calculated at about $ 2,500. In the World Economic Forum's new 2018 Inclusive Development Index, Tanzania was rated 48th of 74 listed emerging economies and in top position among SSA countries.

Tanzania's economy continued to show remarkable resilience in a difficult global setting, its low level of outward trade openness somewhat shielding it from negative external repercussions. The *GDP growth rate* was estimated at 7.1%, better than foreseen throughout the year, but close to the government's original target and consistent with the growth trend over more than a decade.

Climatically, it was a rather mixed year. Due to prolonged *drought* conditions early in the year, the government had to admit problems of food security for sections of the population, causing steep increases of food prices. Subsequent favourable rainfall then eased the situation for the rest of the year.

The *agricultural sector* again performed poorly, with a growth rate of just above 2%. The main *drivers of growth* were communications, tourism and other services sectors, while mining activities encountered unforeseen problems and manufacturing industries continued to be hampered by difficulties in obtaining credit and a slowdown of demand due to a general shortage of liquidity throughout the economy. Existing expectations of a faster and more fundamental transformation of the economy, linked with prospects for substantial natural gas production and export of liquefied natural gas, remained somewhat elusive, since full commercial exploitation did not appear realistic before sometime in the 2020s.

Headline *inflation* was again successfully contained at close to the 5% target, at an average rate of 5.3% for the year and a low of 4.0% in December. A prudent monetary policy thus again met its desired target. For a second consecutive year, the *exchange rate* of the shilling to the dollar remained unusually stable throughout the year, reaching TSh 2,230: $ 1) at year's end. This was largely the result of a tight liquidity situation in the domestic banking system and above all of a further strongly improved balance of payments situation. The *structural trade deficit*, which had been significantly lowered in 2016 to $ 2.8 bn, was contained at that level (provisionally estimated $ 2.9 bn), principally as a result of a further reduced import bill of an expected $ 7.9 bn. This fall was mainly due to a decline in the import of capital goods (resulting from reduced investments) and a lower oil bill. Export earnings also declined to about $ 5.0 bn, mainly due to reduced mineral exports. On balance, two-thirds of Tanzania's import needs were thus covered by its own export earnings. The *services account* again improved significantly (by 39%) to a new record surplus of $ 1.9 bn, largely resulting from tourism as the main foreign exchange source. These achievements contributed to another reduction of the *current-account deficit* to about 3%, the lowest level in recent history. Gross *foreign exchange reserves* grew strongly to $ 5.9 bn by the end of December, sufficient to cover 5.4 months of imports of goods and services. Since the debt reductions in the early 2000s, the *external debt* had again been increasing rapidly in recent years, reaching a new high of $ 19.2 bn at year's end (from $ 17.2 bn in 2016). The composition of external debt remained practically unchanged (around 80% owed by the state, 20% by the private sector); 47% of the debt was owed to multilateral agencies and under 10% to bilateral donors, while the remainder was composed of commercial debts and export credits. Several observers warned of the trend towards more borrowing, but a debt sustainability analysis by the IMF concluded that Tanzania remained at low risk of external debt distress. Under somewhat mysterious conditions, the government obtained a $ 500 m syndicated loan from Crédit Suisse in August, but the long-envisaged issue of a eurobond again did not materialise.

IMF missions visited Tanzania in April and December to conduct the sixth and seventh reviews of the programmes under the extended current *Policy Support Instrument* (PSI). Macroeconomic performance was judged to have been satisfactory and most quantitative targets under the PSI were met, though implementation of structural measures and budget implementation (particularly in development spending) were considered lagging. Identifying a mixed economic performance, the IMF viewed the outlook as subject to emerging risks and warned that various indicators, particularly private sector concerns about the authorities' enforcement of rules, suggested a weakening of economic activity.

On 8 June, Finance Minister Philip Mpango submitted the *budget for the fiscal year 2017–18* to parliament. Total expenditure was budgeted at TSh 31,712 bn (about $ 14.2 bn), a seemingly realistic increase of only 7.3% over the 2016–17 budget, whose ambitious goals had proved very difficult to implement. 38% of the total budget was earmarked for development expenditure, while, under previous governments, well over 70 % had always been allocated for recurrent expenditure. The focus was clearly on infrastructure projects and on laying the foundations for industrialisation. The revenue forecast was composed of tax and non-tax revenue (63%), domestic and external non-concessional borrowing (24%) and external financing from development partners (13%). Only 3% was cautiously expected to come in the form of general budget support, since donor countries showed increasing reluctance to provide such generous untied aid. The fiscal deficit was expected to be reduced to 3.8% of GDP.

The *2016–17 budgetary outcome* was marked by the achievement of most domestic revenue targets, but by continued external financial shortfalls. The government strongly emphasised efforts to widen the tax base and curb tax evasion, restrict leakages and wastage of government resources and control public expenditure. Domestic revenue collection thus increased to 15.3% of GDP. The fiscal deficit turned out at 1.7% of GDP, the lowest level in seven years and less than planned. This was primarily the result of serious under-execution of budgeted development expenditure (62% execution rate), a rigorous slashing of recurrent expenditure and a further build-up of government arrears (around 6% of GDP) to contractors, suppliers and public servants. A verification exercise to determine the genuineness of all pending claims took much longer than expected and the unresolved arrears issue remained a serious economic problem throughout the year, since it negatively affected many businesses and sharply reduced liquidity. *Budget execution* during the first half of 2016–17 was again problematic and remained behind set targets: while somewhat lagging tax collection was still expected to catch up, an execution rate of 59% for development expenditures demonstrated clearly the government's inability to achieve its ambitious development goals and left the credibility of the budget exercise in doubt.

The *2nd Five-Year Development Plan 2016/17–2020/21* provided the medium-term framework for the government's goal of transforming Tanzania into a semi-industrialised middle-income country by 2025. Magufuli consistently emphasised the build-up of modern *infrastructure* and faster *industrialisation* as his overarching developmental orientation. Recurring uncertainties about the government's concrete intentions and Magufuli's often erratic directives (regarding both projects and personnel) led, however, to a widely-felt atmosphere of insecurity, particularly with respect to private-sector business activities. A growing negative business sentiment was observed not only by the IMF and the World Bank, but also by all domestic business institutions and spokespersons, although the government repeatedly stressed its unequivocal support for private-sector activities. Magufuli expressed the view that the 1990s privatisation of former parastatal enterprises had been a mistake and declared the intention to repossess the firms (about 200) that had remained dormant in private hands. A new form of *economic resource nationalism* thus clearly gained ground in Magufuli's pronouncements. Some activities seemed strangely reminiscent of the authoritarian state-led economic strategies during Tanzania's socialist past under Julius Nyerere. The anti-corruption and harsh revenue-generation drives, coupled with problems in the banking sector (sharp increase of non-performing loans), contributed significantly to a widely-felt credit and liquidity squeeze and a slow-down of private sector activities. All this culminated in a strange mismatch between continued good macroeconomic indicators and low-key business sentiment. In the Global Competitiveness Index 2017–18, Tanzania nevertheless obtained a slightly higher score, ranking 113th (up from 116th) out of 137 countries; the World Bank's Doing Business Report 2018 showed a score at 137th (down from 132nd).

Unforeseen attention turned on the *mining sector* throughout the year. On 3 March, the government, suspicious of having long been deceived about true values and desiring to force mining companies to introduce a higher level of in-country beneficiation, announced an immediate *ban on the export of all unprocessed minerals*. The main addressee was Acacia Mining, the largest operator (three *gold mines*). Two commissions of enquiry were subsequently tasked to investigate this complex issue and to recommend fundamental changes to mining legislation. In July, three mining laws were passed that drastically changed the relationship between the government and foreign mining companies. The dispute with Acacia escalated when an outrageous tax bill for $ 190 bn was slapped on the company in July. After acrimonious discussions, an agreement was reached in October with Acacia's Canadian parent company Barrick Gold, which included a $ 300 m compensation payment to the government, a 16% government equity stake in Acacia and an equal share in all future profits. In September, *raw diamonds* from the Williamson mine were confiscated, and Magufuli ordered the construction of a wall around the area of artisanal *Tanzanite mines* near Arusha. Magufuli was exuberantly praised in parliament for his strong defence of the national interest against international mining giants, but no nationalisation was planned.

Several major *infrastructure projects* were either launched or approved for future execution. In August, Magufuli and President Museveni of Uganda laid the foundation stone for the construction of a $ 3.6 bn *pipeline* for the export of Ugandan oil via Tanga port. The construction of the first section (Dar es Salaam-Morogoro) of a new *electrified standard-gauge railway*, paid for from Tanzania's own resources, started in April; an agreement for the second section up to Dodoma was subsequently concluded. In December, the government, after a period of uncertainty, finally approved a joint venture between Oman and China for a $ 10 bn project to build a major new port and a special economic zone near Bagamoyo; the government withdrew its own envisaged participation due to non-availability of funds. Nevertheless, important expansion works were taking place at Dar es Salaam's port. A government decision to pursue the long-discussed Stiegler's Gorge mega-project (2,100 MW *hydropower* in Rufiji Basin) met strong resistance from environmentalists, with finalisation being many years away. Two new *natural gas power plants* in Dar es Salaam, built and financed by Japan, greatly relieved the hitherto often precarious electricity availability. Over 50% of Tanzania's installed grid capacity of 1,400 MW now already came from natural gas. After long delays, an agreement was finally concluded between the National Development Corporation and a Chinese company for the exploitation of substantial coal (Mchuchuma) and iron ore (Liganga) deposits in the south-west.